DATE DUE

BRITISH BAPTISTS

This is a volume in the
Arno Press collection

THE BAPTIST TRADITION

Advisory Editor
Edwin S. Gaustad

See last pages of this volume
for a complete list of titles.

BRITISH BAPTISTS

ARNO PRESS

A New York Times Company
New York • 1980

Editorial Supervision: Steven Bedney

Reprint Edition 1980 by Arno Press Inc.

The Life and Faith of the Baptists and *The Fellowship of Believers* have been reprinted by permission of The Baptist Union of Great Britain and Ireland.

THE BAPTIST TRADITION

ISBN for complete set: 0-405-12437-6
See last pages of this volume for titles.

Manufactured in the United States of America

Library of Congress Cataloging in Publication Data

Main entry under title:

British Baptists.

   (The Baptist tradition)
   Reprint of 2 works, the 1st published in 1946 by Kingsgate Press, London; the second published in 1952 by Carey Kingsgate Press, London.
   CONTENTS: Robinson, H. W. The life and faith of the Baptists.--Payne, E. A. The fellowship of believers.
   1. Baptists--England. 2. Baptists--Doctrinal and controversial works--Baptist authors.
I. Robinson, Henry Wheeler, 1872-1945. The life and faith of the Baptists. 1980. II. Payne, Ernest Alexander, 1902- The fellowship of believers. 1980. III. Series: Baptist tradition.
BX6276.B78   230'.6'141   79-52583
ISBN 0-405-12450-3

CONTENTS

THE LIFE AND FAITH OF
THE BAPTISTS

" If you will go with us, you must go against wind and tide; the which, I perceive, is against your opinion. You must also own Religion in his rags, as well as when in his silver slippers; and stand by him, too, when bound in irons, as well as when he walketh the streets with applause."

Christian to By-ends, in " The Pilgrim's Progress "

THE LIFE AND FAITH
OF THE BAPTISTS

BY

H. WHEELER ROBINSON
M.A., D.D.

PRINCIPAL OF REGENT'S PARK COLLEGE; PRESIDENT OF
THE BAPTIST HISTORICAL SOCIETY

LONDON:
THE KINGSGATE PRESS
4, SOUTHAMPTON ROW, W.C.1
1946

First Published in 1927
Revised Edition, 1946

Made and Printed in Great Britain by C. Tinling & Co., Ltd.,
Liverpool, London, and Prescot.

PREFACE TO FIRST EDITION

IN this book I have tried to do two things at once, and therefore may have failed to do either adequately. One aim has been to describe the life and faith of the English Baptists in a way that will be intelligible to sympathetic readers of other communions. This means that I have tried throughout to state Baptist convictions as a particular form of the consciousness of the Catholic Church; I should not remain a Baptist if those convictions were not for me the doorway into the larger fellowship of all who are loyal to Jesus Christ. On the other hand, I have also thought of Baptist readers who might benefit by the exposition of their own faith and practice, especially in its underlying principles, as well as by frank criticism of its limitations. Neither aim follows the methods of propaganda, which are apt to exaggerate difference and to conceal weakness; but truth, as a man honestly sees it, is always in the long run the best *apologia*. If there are some things in the book which the " average " Baptist may not like, he must regard them as an illustration of that individualism which characterizes the Baptists perhaps more than any denomination, and supplies the chief elements of both their strength and their weakness. Perhaps I may best put myself right with him by appropriating the reply of Dr. Chandler to a prelate who asked him why he did not leave the Dissenters, since he admitted that certain things amongst them were unsatisfactory: " My Lord, I would, if I could find a worthier body of people." [1]

It is easy for the outsider to see the weakness of any system of religion and to miss the strength; it is possible for the insider to know the strength and to be unconscious of the weakness. Every type of religion will eventually be judged by its efficiency in mediating the fellowship of God and man; *securus judicat orbis terrarum*. It does not follow that what is best for one man is best for another; that at least must be admitted by all who give individualism its full place in religion. But no man knows what a particular type of

[1] Stoughton, *Religion in England under Queen Anne and the Georges*, i, p. 332.

▼

religion can do for him until he has given himself whole-heartedly to it ; when he does, he discovers that fine paradox of ecclesiastical life, that catholicity is measured by depth of conviction, not by breadth of opinion. One truth boldly proclaimed was enough to make an Old Testament prophet ;[1] one truth held with sufficient intensity may bring a man into the circle of catholic Christianity, where he will find many other truths to learn.[2] But such a man must not be deterred by the imperfections of the Church and the faults of its members, existent under every system. If he looks for them he will easily find them, for the words " Seek and ye shall find " apply to evil as well as to good. The more difficult search for the good beneath the evil will discover the strength of religion within its apparent weakness. The simpler the system the more obvious the weakness, for an elaborate ritual and organization is better fitted to conceal the faults of our common humanity.

The plan of the book is somewhat unusual, but it has been deliberately chosen to give that emphasis of presentation which does more to create atmosphere than any particular thing that is said. After a brief statement of Baptist begin-nings, and a characterization of the general spirit of the Baptists, a number of more or less typical figures or scenes from the seventeenth and eighteenth centuries are employed to bring out some features of Baptist life in concrete form. (These studies are purposely based, for the most part, on manuscript sources or rare (books, not easily accessible.) These have not been continued into the nineteenth century, partly on grounds of space and partly because many assimila-tive influences were then bringing the different types of the Christian faith nearer to each other. Justification for the study of individuals, rather than of corporate history, may be found in the emphasis on individual experience which characterizes the Baptist faith and finds expression in the retention of the baptism of believers only (Chapter III).

[1] Cf. Robertson Smith, *The Prophets of Israel*, p. 182.
[2] If it be said that he may here find other truths more central than that with which he started, and logically calling for adhesion to another type of religion, then the certain loss through detachment from the old must be weighed against the possible gain from attach-ment to the new. But ever where conviction demands and obtains a new ecclesiastical life, gratitude for the service rendered by the old ought to remain.

From this follows the Baptist conception of the Church, as a fellowship of believers expressing that fellowship in worship and especially in the communion of the Lord's Supper, and nurturing it through specialized forms of that Christian " ministry " which is in itself incumbent on all (Chapter IV). It is further claimed that Baptists are conspicuous for two marked characteristics—their missionary spirit and their passion for liberty (Chapters V and VI). Finally, an attempt is made to estimate the value of their contribution to the Universal Church and their limitations (Chapter VII).

Several friends, to whom I am grateful, have helped me with criticisms and useful suggestions. My colleague, Professor A. J. D. Farrer, has read through the whole in typescript. Dr. W. T. Whitley, our leading authority on Baptist history (to whose book, *A History of British Baptists*, there is frequent indebtedness), has read the historical portions. The chapters dealing with Believers' Baptism and the Church have been read by the Rev. M. E. Aubrey, secretary of the Baptist Union. The chapter dealing with missionary work has been read by the Revs. C. E. Wilson and W. Y. Fullerton, secretaries of the Baptist Missionary Society. I have to thank the editors of *The Review and Expositor* (Louisville, U.S.A.), *The Baptist Quarterly,* and *The Baptist Times* for permission to make use of some material which has already appeared in their pages.

H. WHEELER ROBINSON.

REGENT'S PARK COLLEGE.

PREFACE TO SECOND EDITION

THE first edition of this book was published in 1927 by Messrs. Methuen and Co., Ltd., in their series "The Faiths: Varieties of Christian Expression", and is now out of print. The publisher's share of the copyright has been transferred to the Kingsgate Press, and I have to thank Messrs. Methuen and Co. for their courteous consent to this transfer. The opportunity has been taken to revise the text in a few small details, to bring the statistical information up to date and to add a short concluding chapter on "The Final Authority". I have to thank my former colleague, the Rev. A. J. D. Farrer, for the renewal of the help which he gave to the first edition, and Dr. J. H. Rushbrooke for providing me with the latest figures regarding Baptists throughout the world. I owe a very special debt to the Rev. E. A. Payne, who has not only made many useful suggestions, most of which I have adopted, but has also put me under deep obligation by preparing the bibliography, which is a new feature, and by seeing this second edition through the press at a time when illness has prevented me from incurring sole responsibility for this.*

H. WHEELER ROBINSON.

OXFORD, MARCH, 1945.

---

* Dr. Wheeler Robinson completed his notes for this new edition and drafted the above preface only a few weeks before his death which took place on May 12th, 1945. Care has been taken to make only such changes in the text as he had explicitly approved. The concluding chapter of which he speaks has been put as an appendix. —E.A.P.

CONTENTS

THE LIFE AND FAITH OF
THE BAPTISTS

I

THE ORIGIN AND PRINCIPLES OF
THE BAPTISTS

A CANDID inquirer from another planet, visiting this earth for the first time, might well be perplexed at the apparent multitude of differing religions in England. " I find half a dozen varieties ", he might say, " in a single street ; how am I to know which is right, and is it not far more likely that they are all wrong?   If they were working on right lines, surely by this time they would have reached a unity in the truth far more important than their diversity in the expression of it."   As a matter of fact, if our Martian took the trouble to attend the half-dozen Free Churches he might have found in the street he would realize that they *had* reached a practical unity, regardless of their notice-boards, and that the prayer and the praise and the preaching were largely indistinguishable by their denominational brand.   On the other hand, if he drew the hasty inference that the differences between the Free Churches were therefore negligible, because not very apparent to the superficial observer, he would be quite wrong.   Though they all belong to the Protestant, and for the most part to the Puritan, tradition of the Church, they represent different emphases, and have made different contributions to the Church and to the Kingdom of God.   They all carry on the witness of the Reformation, but they do it with varieties of accent and expression that are by no means to be ignored.   That witness is " the new conception of the relation of the individual soul to God, which found expression in [Luther's] distinctive doctrine of justification by faith ",[1] Then, as now, there were many contributory forces, such as the rise of nationalism, with its challenge of ecclesiastical imperialism ; the new learning, with its criticism of mediæval claims ; the consciousness of economic oppression, with its

[1] James Mackinnon, *Luther and the Reformation*, i, p. v.

revolt against the feudal system. But the central force was undoubtedly that which found its expression through Luther —the religious individualism which has been working out its consequences, for good and for evil, ever since. Of that individualism, the Baptists might fairly claim to be the extreme representatives, the very lance-head of the Reformation impact. The name they bear, which is the label affixed by others, calls attention to the fact that they retain the New Testament rite of baptism for the individual response of faith to the Gospel, and have not extended this rite, like other Churches, to those who are yet unconscious of the meaning of individual responsibility. That name, in the form of Anabaptist, or " re-baptizer ", was first given to the far-reaching and multi-coloured continental movement, which extended over Europe in the sixteenth century, and in some quarters issued in shameful excesses.[1] But though there are some points of possible contact between this movement in its more moderate forms and those Englishmen who became Baptists, whether in Holland or in England, the origin of English Baptists is to be found rather in their Puritan ancestry.[2] In history, as well as in idea, the Baptists carry forward the idea of the Reformation to its furthest issue, and have not unfairly been described as " Protestant of the Protestants ".[3]

This direct line of development is admirably illustrated in John Smyth, the first English Baptist, who occupies a place similar to that of Robert Browne amongst the Congregationalists, though unlike Browne he did not ultimately abandon his distinctive form of Church polity. Smyth was a Cambridge scholar who became the Puritan chaplain (as we should

[1] A brief account of the Anabaptist movement is given in my *Baptist Principles*, pp. 59-64. Further details will be found in Lindsay's *History of the Reformation*, ii, pp. 430 ff., or A. H. Newman's *History of Anti-Pedobaptism*.

[2] See the *Baptist Quarterly*, January, 1924, "Continental Anabaptists and Early English Baptists," by W. T. Whitley and A. J. D. Farrer ; the chapter on "The Anabaptists in England before 1612" in *The Early English Dissenters*, by Champlin Burrage ; the *Transactions of the Congregational Historical Society*, vols. xii and xiii, articles by D. B. Heriot; and R. J. Smithson, *The Anabaptists*, 1935. There is an explicit disclaimer of the name "Anabaptist" by John Murton in 1615 (see *Tracts on Liberty of Conscience*, Hanserd Knollys edition, p. 179).

[3] J. H. Rushbrooke in the collection of addresses by himself and others called *The Faith of the Baptists* (Kingsgate Press, 1926).

say) to the city of Lincoln, at the beginning of the seventeenth century. As a Puritan, he was still an Anglican, eager for the further reform of the Anglican Church, and working from within it to this end. Some years later he removed to Gainsborough, and after a protracted struggle decided that he must withdraw from the Anglican communion to realize his idea of the Church—that is, he became a Separatist. If he had remained at this stage of development his name would have been added to the list of Congregationalist pioneers, for it was the Congregationalist type of Church polity which his Church illustrated. Over against the parochial idea of the Church he and his comrades set that of a group of converted men, who had consciously based their fellowship on a covenant. John Smyth's covenant was remarkable because it pledged these Separatists " to walk in all His (Christ's) ways made known, or to be made known unto them, according to their best endeavours, whatsoever it should cost them ". They were ready to believe that " the Lord had more light and truth yet to break forth out of His holy Word ". As a matter of fact, John Robinson, who gave this better-known saying to the world, was a friend and assistant to John Smyth before they both went to Holland in search of freedom to worship God, and seems to have derived the great principle from him. In Amsterdam John Smyth obeyed his own Church Covenant by following the guidance of the New Testament into Baptist convictions ; he was led to maintain in teaching and practice that the true basis of the Church was not an arbitrary covenant, but the ordinance of baptism administered to believers only. Some of his followers, led by Thomas Helwys, came over to London in 1611-12, and there founded the first Baptist Church in England. It should be noticed that the baptism they then practised was by pouring, not by immersion. The mode was a secondary matter ; the primary truth was baptism as the basis of a regenerate Church—a Church, that is, according to the New Testament pattern and the Puritan ideal.[1] Anyone who thinks that Baptists then or now are primarily contending for the *mode* of immersion does not really know what their faith is. They stand for what they

[1] When the question of the mode was raised a generation later, it was speedily decided in favour of immersion, which has the advantages of New Testament support and eloquence of expression. See pp. 69f.

believe to be the logic of Separatist Puritanism, according to the example and practice of the New Testament. They refuse to obscure their testimony to the necessity for a converted Church by administering baptism to any but believers in Christ, whilst they are in sympathy with any expression of the responsibility of the Church for its young life which avoids this obscuration.

The Baptist movement begun by Smyth and Helwys issued in what came to be known as General Baptist Churches, viz. those which were Arminian in their theology, as contrasted with the prevailing Calvinism of contemporary Puritanism. But the main line of Baptist Church life moved along the lines of a Calvinistic theology, giving rise to what came to be known as Particular Baptist Churches, i.e. Churches holding the Calvinistic doctrine of election. According to this view (then prevalent in a great part of Protestantism), the Atonement was not made for all men, but only for those whom God had chosen for salvation ; it was particular and not " general ", i.e. universal. The first known Particular Baptist Church was also due to evolution from Congregational Separatism, like the first General Baptist Church. It arose in London between 1630 and 1640,[1] and here also baptism was at first by affusion or pouring, though immersion is prescribed as the true mode in the first Particular Baptist Confession, of date 1644. The General Baptists and the Particular Baptists have had separate histories ; the former have become negligible, the latter have gradually abandoned their original Calvinism, or at least its rigour. In 1770 there was a " New Connexion " formed amongst the more evangelical of the General Baptists which approximated to the main body, and in 1891 the distinction ceased to exist.

Baptist history now extends over three centuries, in the course of which they have become one of the largest Protestant denominations, with upwards of thirteen million communicants, chiefly in the United States of America.[2] In Great Britain and Ireland their communicant membership is nearly 400,000. In the seventeenth century they were prominent in the Puritan struggle for political and religious freedom, notably in Cromwell's army, though many of them

[1] See the chart given by J. H. Shakespeare in *Baptist and Congregational Pioneers*, pp. 184, 185.
[2] See Appendix III.

did not approve of the later developments in Cromwell's personal position and policy. In the eighteenth century they shared in the general lethargy of religion prior to the Evangelical Revival, but towards the close of the century they had the proud privilege of being pioneers in foreign missionary work, through William Carey. In the nineteenth century they carried on their twofold witness to the rights of conscience and the power of the Gospel through such men as are best represented by William Knibb and John Clifford on the one hand, and by Robert Hall, Alexander Maclaren, and Charles Haddon Spurgeon on the other. Now, in the twentieth century, they are facing those problems of corporate life which await every Church, however individualistic its origin and principle, and by voluntary effort have raised several great funds for the common welfare of Baptist Churches.

The Baptist contribution to the religious life of the nation during the last three centuries has not been spectacular, though it has had its great moments and has been very real. It has been less than it might have been, not only through the failure to maintain the high ideal of a regenerate Church, but also through the repression of Free Church life by ecclesiastical tyranny and political blindness, from which all the Free Churches have suffered in some degree. From that repression we have emerged slowly, and Baptists at any rate have not yet learnt to value the opportunities for larger education and the cultivation of the larger humanities as they ought.[1] But underneath the public life of the three centuries there has been flowing a steady stream of contribution to the common good —largely through humble homes and the conventicles of back streets.

Like all other Protestants, Baptists are thrown back on the Bible for the justification of their faith. It should never be overlooked that the English Reformation has its roots in the native soil, whatever it owed to the Lutheranism and the Calvinism of the Continent, and that this soil had been prepared by Wycliffe's work in making the Bible accessible. Thus Professor A. F. Pollard says: " The views of the English Reformers approach so much more nearly to those of Wycliffe

---

[1] See, however, the essay by E. A. Payne, " The Development of Nonconformist Theological Education in the Nineteenth Century with special reference to Regent's Park College " in *Studies in History and Religion* (Lutterworth Press, 1942).

than to those of Luther that the Englishman rather than the German must be regarded as the morning star of the Anglican Reformation." [1] T. M. Lindsay, in his general *History of the Reformation* (p. 316, vol. ii) points out that "Lollardy had never died out in England, and Lollardy was simply the English form of that passive protest against the mediæval Church which under various names had maintained itself in France, Germany, and Bohemia for centuries in spite of persecution ". [2] To the same effect writes G. M. Trevelyan in his *History of England*: —

Every important aspect of the English Reformation was of native origin. All can be traced back as far as Wycliffe, and some much farther. . . . A generation before Luther sprang to sudden fame, Lollardy, long suppressed, had come into the open once more. It was native to the soil of England, and had been faithfully preserved in cottage and workshop as a poor man's tradition by the spiritual ancestors of John Bunyan (pp. 250, 289).

John Bunyan and his fellow-Baptists had a special and distinctive reason for the appeal to Scripture. It was their one ground for the practice of believers' baptism which could be maintained against the appeal to the tradition of the Church. Now that constant appeal to Scripture for the distinctive denominational testimony, which is found with what many will think wearisome iteration, has had an important result. It has helped to make and keep Baptists a Bible-loving Church. The baptism of believers by immersion has not only emphasized conscious faith as essential to the Church, but it has also, by its symbolism, constantly recalled men to the foundation of the Gospel in history, the death and the resurrection of Jesus Christ, which, as Paul argued, are represented in the act of the believer's immersion and his rising from the waters of baptism. That act, constantly repeated before the eyes of Baptists, has taken the place of any formal creed, and helped to keep them an evangelical Church, without any authoritative confession of faith. Like the Lord's Supper, it has preached the Lord's death until He come, whilst leaving believers free, in successive generations, to interpret

[1] *Thomas Cranmer and the English Reformation*, 1906, p. 90.
[2] Hastings Rashdall, in the *Dictionary of National Biography*, s.v. "Wycliffe," p. 1133: "It may be broadly asserted that lollardy never quite died out in England till it merged in the new Lutheran heresies of the sixteenth century."

afresh the meaning of that redemptive death. Such liberty within loyalty is in the true succession of the religion of the Bible, which extended over a thousand years, and shows many changes of development, along with a true unity of growth.

This, of course, raises an important issue for the present day. Has not the criticism of the Bible, by which is meant not scepticism or unbelief, but the interpretation of Scripture in the light of all knowledge, and without any pre-conceived theory—has not the criticism of the Bible cut the ground away from beneath the feet of Baptists? Is it not out of date to insist on a Biblical rite at all?

This is not, of course, the place to attempt any adequate discussion of the modern attitude to the Bible in relation to evangelical belief in general. But the spread of education amongst Baptists as amongst other communities is bound to raise the issue of the nature of the authority which it is rightly felt must somehow be exercised by the Bible. On the lowest view, the Bible is the classic of Christian experience, and as such claims a permanent place and power in shaping the belief and practice of successive generations. Without it, as history has shown, the Church is apt to become an official institution, and individual experience is apt to lose its way in mere subjectivities. Whatever may be thought of the horizon and methods of " Fundamentalism ",[1] there can be no doubt that a true principle is embedded in the errors and prejudices of the movement. That principle is the reality of an " objective "

---

[1] We find a good deal of literalistic interpretation in the course of Baptist history, and a good deal of conservatism in this respect amongst Baptists at the present time, especially in America. This literalistic interpretation became politically important in the time of the Commonwealth. The " Fifth Monarchy " movement, in which Baptists were prominent, applied the apocalyptic visions of Daniel to contemporary events. After the monarchies of the four " beasts ", there was to be a fifth monarchy of the saints of the Most High (Dan. vii. 27). " The politics of seven years from 1653 were influenced gravely by this party " (Whitley, History of British Baptists, p. 85). They had previously desired the removal of Charles ; they opposed the " kingship " of Cromwell. The movement culminated under Thomas Venner (not himself a Baptist) in the insurrection of 1660-61, after which, as Dr. Whitley points out, " the millenarian tinge faded out ; but the literalistic temper remained, and attention being attracted to the fourth commandment, the Fifth-Monarchists transformed into Seventh-day Baptists ". These have had but a negligible existence in this country, and now hardly survive ; but in the United States the movement is still of some importance.

B

revelation of some kind to educate and to confirm the "subjective" experience of God, the necessity for a record of collective experience to guide and control the religious growth of the individual. We go astray only when we lay down beforehand the kind of revelation the Bible ought to be. The unprejudiced student will find that it is a "source-book" rather than a textbook of faith and practice. But to admit this is not to be deprived of the Bible as authoritative ; it is only to be driven back to the intrinsic evidence of God in human experience as recorded in the Bible. Behind the literature of the book there is the life that inspired it. If God spoke through the prophets and supremely in the Son, there will be evidence of His truth in the testimony itself. This throws us back on the Reformation principle of the *Testimonium Spiritus Sancti Internum*—the witness of the Spirit of God with our spirits.[1] This is not a phrase to conceal a weakness. The emphasis on the Spirit of God—that is, on the activity of His real presence in the inner and outer experience of men—has characterized the Christian faith from the beginning. The prophecy may be ventured that amongst the Baptists in particular there will be a growing recognition of this relatively neglected truth—a recognition to which they are already committed by their insistence on baptism in the New Testament sense. Baptism signifies the entrance into a life of fellowship with Christ, which means a baptism of the Holy Spirit.

If Baptists had contended for a rite without any central and permanent meaning, they would never have grown as they have. There must have been a deep appeal behind the rite, a central truth of permanent importance—as, indeed, practically all Churches virtually maintain by their retention of Baptism in some form or meaning. A baptism of *faith* takes us into the very centre of Christian experience, and is no bit of antiquated folk-lore. Further, the critical study of the Bible serves only the more to bring out the historical development of faith, and to show the emergence in the Bible history of those very contentions about the Church for which Baptists, along with other Free Churchmen, are standing. These are chiefly three, and I can do no more here than briefly indicate them.

---

[1] See my essay on " The Validity of Christian Experience " in the volume called *The Future of Christianity* (ed. by Marchant), reprinted and developed in *Redemption and Revelation* (1942).

First of all, there is the right of the soul to an immediate relation to God—the right which was reasserted in the Reformation by the doctrine of the universal priesthood of believers. In the earlier days of Israel there were many practices and beliefs, which we should call superstitions, coming between the soul and God.[1] In the latter, post-exilic, history of Judaism there was an elaborate priesthood which mediated God to men and men to God. But in the centre of the Old Testament development, as modern historical study has brought out clearly, there were the prophets and the prophetic consciousness. That consciousness asserts that God could put aside all barriers and limits erected by human hands and reveal Himself to men, as directly as, or even more directly than, in the ways of simple human fellowship, and that man could approach God with the same simplicity and directness. That is the core of the Old Testament religion, and the Christian consciousness of the New Testament follows on in that succession, under the guidance of the Prophet of Nazareth. Elaborate ways of worshipping God are described in the Bible, but the line of living development traceable through a thousand years is one of great simplicity. The truth which dawned upon the first believers was as startling as the dawn of day could be to eyes that saw it for the first time: "Our fellowship is with the Father and with His Son, Jesus Christ." Any human priesthood is apt to seem an irrelevance, if not an impertinence, for those who have once experienced that fellowship in its direct simplicity.

Second, there is the fact, also illustrated by the great prophets and continued in the apostles and disciples of New Testament times, that the chief content of this fellowship is moral holiness, that the believers are called to be saints, consecrated to the holy God by moral character. This was the vehicle of the Old Testament revelation through the prophets and the essence of the substance of that revelation. The plain duty of man to man was the highest offering man could bring to the God who desired mercy and not sacrifice. Without holiness no man can see God, but the pure in heart shall see Him. This inward and ethical emphasis stands in contrast with the externalism of the older idolatry and the later legalism.

Third, there is the principle of the regenerate Church

---

[1] E.g. the breach of taboo seen in Uzzah's death (2 Sam. vi. 6, 7), or the theory of the origin of circumcision given in Exod. iv. 24-6.

already to be found in the Old Testament before it was asserted in the New. Down from the times of Isaiah, who committed his testimony to his disciples, when the mass of his fellow-countrymen rejected it, we may trace this "little Church within the Church" of the nation on to the New Testament times.[1] In the dark days of Manasseh there were disciples of the prophets to whom we owe our Book of Deuteronomy, and the Reformation under Josiah. In the exile of Babylon there was a living nucleus, for which the latter part of the Book of Isaiah was written. In the fifth century those who feared the Lord spoke one to another, and formed a little Church. We see that Church in and behind many of the Psalms. We note its heroic revival and witness in the time of the Maccabees. It was to the successors of that long and faithful line that Jesus and His disciples appealed to fashion the new Israel. It was vital to the prophetic message to create such a community within the nation, for what whole nation has ever been a true Church? For that principle we stand to-day when we assert that the ideal of the Church must always be the community of the regenerate, a principle which is the life-breath of the Free Churches and is most emphatically expressed by the faith and practice of believers' baptism. May we not say, then, that critical study of the Bible, which has brought out these principles in their historical development so much more clearly than when the more priestly elements of the Old Testament were thought to be primary, has not weakened, but strengthened, the Baptist witness? We cannot, it is true, use the Bible to-day as Bunyan used it in *Grace Abounding*—as a body of oracles to be applied directly to life without any regard to the content of its truths. We are not likely to see in the Bible just what he did—a dramatic commentary on our own lives in all their personal details. But if we have lost the power of doing this, God has given us in the new knowledge of Scripture a more than adequate recompense. He has shown us that the Free Churches belong to a great historical development, with a nobler and more ancient lineage than even the Roman Church can claim.[2]

[1] See *The Cross of the Servant*, by H. Wheeler Robinson, p. 38, and cf. Isa. viii. 16, which suggests "an important epoch in the history of religion—the emergence of a spiritual, as distinct from a national, religious society" (Buchanan Gray, *Isaiah*, p. 155).

[2] See E. A. Payne, *The Free Church Tradition in the Life of England*, 1944, and *The Fellowship of Believers*, 1944.

But the real objection most men to-day might bring against the conception of the Church as the community of the regenerate (i.e. those who have experienced repentance and faith, which is what we mean by Christian conversion) is not that it is wrong, but that it is impracticable. " A beautiful theory," someone will say, " but is it really found in practice to be true? " Are the Churches which most emphasize the necessity for a regenerate membership conspicuously better than other Churches? Is it not as well frankly to recognize the limitations of human nature, and be content with a fair average, and to shape the polity of the Church simply by what is practically expedient? That is a line of argument which peculiarly appeals to Englishmen, who distrust ideas and love a practical policy. There is a good deal of truth in it, and we must not deny that truth. A wide gap separates the ideal of the regenerate Church from its actual practice. Discipline is now reserved almost only for those grosser sins which would create public scandal. The young believer often receives a shock of disillusionment as he comes to realize, quickly or gradually, how different the real of Church life amongst us is from the ideal. Would any of us venture to describe the particular Church he knows most intimately as made up of living temples of the Holy Spirit? Is there not a great appeal in the Catholic conception of the Church as a parochial Noah's Ark, a paternal gathering of those who are to be saved, rather than a select company of the saved?

Let us frankly admit the truth of this. Any Church we know is made up of men of like passions with ourselves, men for whom the saintly life is an ideal rather than the real. There are some in it struggling in the grip of passions, from the tyranny of which they have not yet wholly escaped, though they are striving to get out of the Slough of Despond on the right side, and though they struggle to their feet in the Valley of Humiliation wounded but fighting still. There are men with unconscious inconsistencies and weaknesses, men to whom the Parable of the Sower has an individual application, for in them there are tracts of ground on which the seed lies exposed, or on which the thorns grow, or where the soil is very thin. There are differences of taste that may annoy us more than these moral inconsistencies, differences of thought and expression that perplex us, genuine differences of conviction even within the same Church which it seems impossible to reconcile with our own. What shall we make of all these things in the light of the theory that the Church is the Body of Christ indwelt by the Holy Spirit of God?

This—that from the very beginning of God's work in the world He has worked in some sort of disguise. He hides Himself in Nature, so that He often seems cruel and relentless there. He hides Himself in grace, so that we still have to discover the Eternal Son of God in the guise of a Jewish peasant. He hides Himself in the Church, so that the real presence and activity of the Holy Spirit in the individual and in the society is not always or easily apparent. God the Holy Spirit accepts the limitations of human lives, even those of their moral imperfection, and works out His purpose in this mingled texture, wherein the golden thread of the pattern must be sought out. There must be personal faith, for it is by the hearing of faith that the Holy Spirit is received.[1] But faith does not ensure infallibility, intellectual or moral.

The Free Churches stand or fall by the doctrine of the Holy Spirit, as every kind of true Church must do. But in proportion to the simplicity of their worship and ecclesiastical machinery they offer themselves the more to criticism, and show the more plainly the contrast between theory and practice which is found in all men and in all Churches. If we bring the ideal and the real sharply together, we make our failures the more evident. It is easy enough with an elaborate machinery of officialdom, an elaborate ritual of pomp and power, to shift the emphasis from the human company to some remote and hardly visible entity. The red-robed cardinals of the Vatican are far enough away for *their* weaknesses to be unknown. The sonorous Latin of the Mass produces an emotional effect without any effort of intelligent thought, and has the dignity of ancient generations. Substitute a little company of villagers met for prayer in some ugly little chapel, and it is much easier to criticize the realization of a New Testament Church of saints. Yet are men to be slaves of their imagination? Is truth to depend on the mere picturesqueness of its expression? The ultimate issue is the same for all the Churches, and it is finely expressed by the words in which Alice Meynell bids us see in the communicant brother kneeling at our side the Real Presence of Christ, who speaks to us from that unknown heart

[1] Gal. iii. 2.

> . . . in all his strife,
> All his felicity, his good and ill,
> In the assaulted stronghold of his will,
>
> I do confess Thee here,
> Alive within this life; I know Thee near
> Within this lonely conscience, closed away
> Within this brother's solitary day.[1]

All this does not mean that any one form of Church polity is to be regarded as divinely ordained and prescribed for all time. The similar polity of Baptists and Congregationalists is open to improvement in many ways, and must be modified to meet new needs. It has learnt, and is learning, from both Methodism and Presbyterianism, and will doubtless learn more in the future, for we each of us have something to teach the rest. But this does not alter the fact that the Churches which present the ideal in closest and simplest contact with the real of life must expect to meet the sharpest criticism in their attempt to maintain the ideal. A. M. Fairbairn stated that ideal thus, in its four determinative elements: —

A church is (a) a society of the godly, or of men who truly believe and piously live. (b) It is a society instituted expressly to realize in the personal and collective life the religious ideals of Christ. (c) It is capable of extension only by means that produce faith, and of development only by agencies that create godliness. (d) It is autonomous and authoritative, possessed of the freedom necessary to the fulfilment of its mission, the realization of its ideals; and it is endowed with all the legislative and administrative powers needed for the maintenance of order and the attainment of progress (*Studies in Religion and Theology*, p. 215).

We may not argue for that ideal in quite the old way, by setting the examples of Scripture as authoritative precedents against the traditions of the Church. The modern appeal will be increasingly to the ultimate authority of experience —that Christian experience which both Scripture and Church express. But the appeal to experience need not dismay us, for it is the inner logic of the Reformation itself. In the long run it is the appeal to experience which will settle the argument, as it always does. We may serve the truth more by persistence in the ideal, whilst not concealing our present

---

[1] " The Unknown God " (*Oxford Book of Mystical Verse*, p. 462),

failure to realize it, than by sacrificing part of that ideal in the interests of expediency.

It may be convenient to summarize what has been said about Baptist principles in this chapter by quoting the statement of a leading American Baptist.[1] The angle of approach is naturally somewhat different, and we may find it necessary to make some modification of emphasis later on, but most Baptists would accept this as a fair statement of their position: —

The Biblical significance of the Baptists is the right of private interpretation [of], and obedience to, the Scriptures. The significance of the Baptists in relation to the individual is soul freedom. The ecclesiastical significance of the Baptists is a regenerated church-membership and the equality and priesthood of believers. The political significance of the Baptists is the separation of Church and State. But as comprehending all the above particulars, as a great and aggressive force in Christian history, as distinguished from all others and standing entirely alone, the doctrine of the soul's competency in religion under God is the distinctive significance of the Baptists.

[1] E. Y. Mullins, *The Axioms of Religion*, pp. 56, 57.

II

STUDIES IN BAPTIST PERSONALITY

THE aim of these brief studies is to give an inside view of Baptists as they thought and lived in the seventeenth and eighteenth centuries—Baptists in their weakness as well as in their strength, and in the unconscious humour of their ways, as well as in their abiding convictions. It would have been easy to make a much more impressive selection of names, e.g. to substitute John Foster the essayist, one of the few Baptist writers of real literary distinction, for the unknown Ann Dutton, who has no claim to be remembered except as a " type ". Moreover, two more names at least should have been added to show the thought and life of the nineteenth century, viz. those of Charles Haddon Spurgeon and John Clifford, so different and yet so complementary. But these are well known, and their lives can be studied in full-length biographies.[1] If these two be added mentally to this chapter, the reader will have a fair view, within the limits of space, of the course of the three Baptist centuries, more illuminative in its detail than any condensed consecutive history could be.[2] It is indeed characteristic of the Baptist faith that its emphasis should thus fall on the creation of personality in its individualism. Readers of other communions will perhaps think it chiefly wanting on the other side of personality—viz. sociality—at least so far as *formal* expression in organization and corporate emphasis is concerned. But voluntary co-operation has its own advantages.

(1) A BAPTIST HOME (CALEB VERNON)

On a late summer's day of the Plague Year, just when Samuel Pepys was publicly debating how to cope with it, and privately hesitating to wear his new periwig, " because the

---

[1] *C. H. Spurgeon*, by W. Y. Fullerton (1920) ; *Dr. John Clifford*, by Sir James Marchant (1924).
[2] The studies are more or less linked together by the people who emerge in them.

plague was in Westminster when I bought it", you might have seen a boat rowed down the Thames, with a consumptive boy of twelve lying in it. Even so short a journey as that from the pleasant country resort known as Battersea to the London of two and a half centuries ago had its perils ; it proved that both the waterman who rowed the boat and the servant who carried the light weight of Caleb Vernon from the river to his father's lodging were sickening for death by the pestilence. But the emaciated frame held a dominating purpose ; he would not be away from his father nor take his father away from his physician's work ; he wanted to sympathize with the sufferings of the Lord's poor visited people by being with them ; above all, there was a burning passion for the religious fellowship with which the garden-house at Battersea could not provide him. The story of this gifted and precocious life of twelve and a half years has been told by the father in a little book of great interest called *The Compleat Scholler* (1666).[1] This is the book which gives us incidentally so vivid a glimpse of a Baptist home in the seventeenth century.

Let us get to know this home at one of its most characteristic moments, that of family prayers. It is the first occasion after the boy's return, and the Scripture lesson is taken from the ninth chapter of Ecclesiastes. The father dwells very impressively on the tenth verse, and enforces its application : " Whatsoever thy hand findeth to do, do it with thy might ; for there is no work, nor device, nor knowledge, nor wisdom in the grave whither thou goest." It is not perhaps the point *we* should choose for the edification of a sick child, but those were more Spartan days'. The father himself is an old cavalry general, who once knew and wrote about horses, and has now, as a physician, transferred his knowledge to dealing with men. He has known intimately the richly varied life of the seventeenth century ; has been awakened from conventional religion to that passion for reality which such men as Gifford could kindle ; has fought the heresies of Quakerism and the presumptions of the Protector ; has tried in vain to establish a new constitution, when the Cromwell family disappointed hope ; now calmly continues to preach and to heal, though he has known what Newgate

---

[1] Two copies only are known to exist—one in the Bodleian and the other in the Angus Library of Regent's Park College.

meant, and warrants have long been out for his arrest, in these disappointing Restoration days.   Side by side with John Vernon is the wife he won from Devonshire in those great days of the forties, when he and William Allen were officers in the army of Fairfax and married sisters.   Perhaps Uncle William looks in sometimes and tells of the Windsor Prayer Meeting, which decided to call Charles Stuart, that man of blood, to account for the blood he had shed.   Another visitor of gentler spirit is Abraham Cheare, ready to repeat to the children some of his last-written verses.   Besides Caleb, there are his brother and three younger sisters, Mary of seven, Betty of five, and Nancy still younger.   Nor must we forget Honour, the maid, who has brought Caleb up from the cradle and taught him till he began Latin.   For this is not a home that makes piety a protection of ignorance.   Caleb at four could read the Bible, and at six was apt in doctrine and practice ; at seven he went to school, at ten had begun to add Greek to his Latin, and found time for some Hebrew.   But Caleb has already felt the clash between his classical authors and the teaching of his Bible ; he has already shown a remarkable religious development, very real in itself, though the forms of its expression will seem artificial and overstrained to us.   At ten Caleb wrote a letter about religion to an older friend, which raised grave doubts in the reader's mind as to its authenticity.   He replied with severe kindness.   " I received thine without date, but not without serious desire of the best things ", and went on to catechize him as to some of the terms used, such as " an outside professor ", from which catechism Caleb emerged with reasonable success.

We get another glimpse of this family as they sit round the table and the father calls on this or that child to say grace. The Puritans took their " grace " seriously.   Do we not remember that Roger Williams argued that an unregenerate child ought not to be allowed to say grace, whereupon an opponent retorted that since the thankless reception of God's gifts was certainly wrong, an unregenerate child should be given no food at all?   Here it is Caleb who overcomes his natural timidity and (repenting of a previous refusal) comes forward to encourage the others by his example.   Caleb's relations with his little sisters are tender and natural.   He gives them his toys towards the end of his short life ; it is good to know that there were toys in this grave religious home. When they were in the country, Nancy, aged five, would say to Honour, the maid, in the morning, "What mercy is it we are alive, and so many thousands taken away at London, and so many little children!" whilst Caleb says to Nancy as she sits by his bed, surely a demure and grave little nurse: "Nancy, the Lord make you a mother in Israel. Oh, how I long to see Christ formed in you!" But the old Adam is still in Nancy, for whilst Caleb lies ill, her childish voice rings up to the room, "Who shall have Caleb's bird when he is dead?" Caleb's sense of justice is seen in the fact that he instantly awards the bird, if he dies, to the younger Betty, because Nancy has one already. Caleb has a keen sense of justice. In one of his bad times, the noise of his little sisters and their cousin was more than he could bear, and he quoted Job at them: "To him that is in affliction pity should be showed by his friends". But he is soon sorry for this feeling of annoyance, and calls the children that he may cut them out some of his special jelly. The worst sins Caleb can remember are that once he disobeyed his mother by not going to bed when she had commanded it, and that "he had spent his time very childishly, and plaid away his convictions". We think of Augustine's stolen pears and Bunyan's tip-cat. But Nature has ingenious ways of thrusting in when we have thrust her out. Towards the end, when Caleb was very weak, "he desired some living creature might stand on the bed by him to prevent Melancholly thoughts, when he could not rest: being asked, what? He said a young Lamb, Pigeon, Rabbit or anything, but a Squerril being named (hoping it might easily be procured), he was earnest for that, having, he said, never seen any but once in the field". The squirrel could not be got, and the boy was much disappointed, for, as he told his father, "I find myself inclining to melancholy, and I think such a thing would be pretty company for me, and therein I may see the workmanship of God". One great though transitory temptation came to him in his sore pain—to curse God and die ; the intensity of his thought about it reminds us of Bunyan's "Sell Him!" But we must admit that there is something a little unnatural when a boy of ten desires to weep over the sins of his youthful days! It tempts us to say, though in this instance at least we should be wrong, that such repetition of phrases means no more than the curses which little children pick up with equal facility.

The central event in these simple annals of a Baptist home is Caleb's desire to be baptized—a desire to which his father and friends are all opposed because of the serious character of his illness.   There is something both admirable and, pathetic in the way this sick boy fights for his conviction that he ought to be baptized, yet bows reluctantly to the right of others to say the last word.   A representative meeting of the Church, numbering twenty persons, is held in his bedroom, candles being set on the bed, and they round about him, whilst this singular child begins his testimony, "God spake once, yea twice, yet man regardeth it not", and proceeds to apply this to two previous illnesses.   He confesses that his great sin is to have been "frothy".   He is carefully cross-examined on the faith—for example, on the priestly, kingly and prophetic offices of Christ—and he gives his reasons for desiring baptism, which are especially the words "He that believeth and is baptized shall be saved "; the example of Christ, Philip and the eunuch, "If thou believest with all thy heart, thou mayest", and the case of the jailer.   He is warned of the physical danger in his case, but is quite undeterred. It is of interest to notice the close contact of the home and the Church in the way the father deals with his own perplexity as to allowing this baptism.   He holds a prayer-meeting with others about it, "with prayer setting forth his great strait in the case ; and taking their answer one by one, upon what they had heard, both for and against it ".   Finally, the father decided to trust God with the issue.   But even then a physician friend came between the child's eager desire and its satisfaction, pointing out the danger and the scandal, and declaring that Caleb could not be carried alive to the place of baptism.   This friend is brought in to argue with poor Caleb, and makes use of a very unfair bit of exegesis: "It was said, all Judæa *went* out to be baptized, but he never heard that any were *carried* out."   I am glad poor Caleb had the wit to reply: "Christ bid his disciples go and teach all nations, baptizing them ; but never said, if they be sick and weak, do not baptize them."   At last Caleb prevails, and secures the promise of baptism on the next day, if the weather allows. "The night continued tempestuous, and he called often betwixt his slumbers to know what weather? " But the day was sunny and calm, and in the afternoon the whole company proceeded in three coaches, with some on foot, to the house by the river which had been prepared. Caleb would not lie on the pillows arranged on the knees of his father and mother, but insisted on sitting up. He is kept by the fire in the house whilst his father speaks from most suitably chosen words— they *did* know their Bibles in Bunyan's day—" And when he would not be persuaded, we ceased, saying: The will of the Lord be done ". The fulness of experiential meaning, the positive note of the divine gift in baptism, comes out in the father's exhortation, who " desired now to witness to it as the will of God, showing the Commands for it, Signification of it, and ends that should be proposed in it, desiring they might be in them, and that Presence which might make it to both his Sons the Communion of the Death and Resurrection of Christ to such a putting him on (in virtue of all his Offices), as might manifest their being as it were—thenceforth new-died [dyed] with, or tinged into Christ, to their favour of him in all things, in newness of Nature and life ". The two boys, Caleb and his brother, were then baptized, and Caleb was received by his father into a warm blanket, saying as soon as he could speak, " I am very well, father ", as he had said to the doubtful administrator, " I am not afraid ". On his way home in the coach he told his mother and father: " He had very great joy in Communion with God coming up out of the Water, when he could not express it, his breath failing through some water that went into his mouth (which he merrily said, he had forgot to shut) ". The next day but one a meeting of the Church was held in his room, that he might have the privilege of the Lord's Supper with them, " wherein to the eye of Faith Christ would be evidently set forth, crucified before him, for his consolation ".

Naturally enough, the mother is not so prominent in this record as the father, who is both physician and minister as well. But she moves in and out of the sick-room, and sits with her boy in fullest communion. " Mother," he says to her once, " I love your company dearly." It is the mother who, like another mother, treasures these things in her heart, and writes them down secretly, so that we have some of the material for this record through her. " God loves me, mother, and sometimes I love the Lord." Does not that bear the hall-mark of truth upon it? It is pleasant to hear of the service rendered by Abraham Cheare, the Baptist verse-maker, who was a friend of the family. Caleb is fond of repeating his verses. After some of them his mother says: " And do you remember, Child, what he saith of young Isaacs? " " Yea, Mother," said he ; and then further repeated some of these concerning youth:

> Young Isaacs who lift up their eyes,
>   And meditate in fields ;
> Young Jacobs who the Blessing prize,
>   This age but seldom yields.
> Few Samuels leaving youthful playes,
>   To Temple-work resign'd ;
> Few do as these, in youthful dayes
>   Their great Creator mind.
> How precious Obadiahs be
>   That fearèd God in youth:
> How seldom Timothys we see,
>   Vers'd in the Word of Truth. . . .
> Few tender-hearted Youths as was
>   Josiah, Judah's king ;
> Hosannah in the high'st, alas,
>   How seldom children sing !

It is worthy of note that even in those stern old days they were making the same complaints about the degeneracy of youth as we hear to-day and as our great-grandchildren will hear in their turn. And they *were* stern old days. There is something rather grim in the attitude of the father to the son, something Spartan and Stoic at least, as when the child says that his bones are sore, and the father replies, " Ay, Child, but your soul is not " ; or when Caleb asks, " Do not you think that death is troublesome? " and the old Cromwellian replies, " Yes, Child, a little to the flesh." Yet there is deep feeling beneath this religious Stoicism. The boy can thank God for tender parents on earth as in heaven. Even if there is respectful timidity when the sick boy says to his father, writing in the room, " Father, will it not disturb you to talk with me? " there is surely the heart's knowledge of affection sure and deep when the sufferer looks up from his bed of affliction and says: " Father, you be my dear father." That. I think, is significant of the whole book. We turn away from the stilted language of the " anagrams " and " acrosticks " with which the older and younger friends of Caleb Vernon adorn his hearse ; they leave us cold, if not repelled ; most people to-day would turn away also from the unnaturalness of the experience of a Bunyan, as it seems, on the lips of a boy of twelve. We have more patience to-day with literary precocities than with religious, though as we judge we shall be judged by a later generation.   But underneath these forms alien to our expression there is the common human nature and the sincerity of a religious experience akin to ours.   The strength of such a home was in its religion, and its religion did inspire and sustain a loyalty to the home ties and the home duties which is the true consecration of such human relationships.

(2) A Baptist Soldier (William Allen)

One of many services rendered by Dr. Whitley's *A History of British Baptists* is to have brought out the great place taken by Baptists in Cromwell's " New Model Army ".   A typical figure amongst them, about which we are exceedingly well informed, is that of William Allen,[1] whose name appears more than once in Carlyle's *Letters and Speeches of Oliver Cromwell*.   To Carlyle, Adjutant-General Allen was " a most authentic earnest man . . . a strenuous Anabaptist . . . a rugged, true-hearted, not easily governable man ; given to Fifth-Monarchy and other notions, though with a strong head to control them ".   This impression is confirmed when we identify him with the Trooper Allen (as Carlyle wrongly refused to do) who brought the letter of the soldiers to Major-General Skippon in 1647.[2]   Allen stated then, in his examination, that he was a Warwickshire man who had been a felt-maker by trade in Southwark.   He had served in Essex's army under Colonel Holles, till he was taken prisoner at Brentford.   After seven days of captivity, he was condemned with seventeen others to be hanged ; then every tenth man was drawn out to be hanged ; finally he was dismissed with the others.   He was wounded at the first battle of Newbury and again at Henley, when Skippon rewarded him with five shillings.   If only Allen had written for us a few " letters from the front " the historian would have been more grateful to him than for what he did write—with the one exception of the account of the famous " Windsor Prayer Meeting ".   Carlyle's pages have made us familiar with that gathering of army leaders meeting for three days of prayer in the *impasse* to

---

[1] Uncle of the Caleb Vernon who was the subject of the preceding study.
[2] See *The Clarke Papers*, ed. Firth, i, p. 432 and A. S. P. Woodhouse, *Puritanism and Liberty*: *Debates from the Clarke MSS. with Supplementary Documents*, 1938.

which ar impracticable Parliament and a shifty king have
brought them, retracing their steps to the point at which they
had exchanged straightforward action for political scheming,
and led at last to the historic conclusion " that it was our
duty, if ever the Lord brought us back again in peace, to call
Charles Stuart, that man of blood, to an account for that
blood he had shed and mischief he had done to his utmost,
against the Lord's Cause and People in these poor Nations ".

Military movements brought William Allen and John
Vernon into Devonshire, where they married sisters of the
name of Huish, their father being James Huish, of Sidbury.
The names of Allen and Vernon stand on the church-roll of
Dalwood, in Dorset, and often recur together in later records
and books, as in the prefaces they both contribute to the
religious autobiography of Deborah Huish, their sister-in-law
(which is entitled *The Captive taken from the Strong*, and
was written down from her lips by William Allen). But this
was in later days of sorrowful leisure, after Allen had been so
disappointed in his leader. His first disillusionment with
Cromwell appears in an intercepted letter of his of 1654,[1]
written soon after the Protectorate began, in which he says:
" As to the person in chief place, I confess I love and honour
him, for the honour God hath put upon him, and I trust will
yet continue ; I mean that of uprightheartedness to the Lord,
though this last change . . . hath more stumbled me than ever
any did ; and I have still many thoughts of heart concerning
it." He was, in fact, coming to think of the Lord Protector
as Labour has often thought of its official leaders—who need
watching, to say the least. Yet at the same time he will not
resign his commission, and argues against a friend who has
done so, on the ground that he can exercise more effective
influence where he is: " I trust I shall not, upon the account
of honourable or other worldly respects, stay a day longer in
employment than I judge I may do more good in than out."
Allen was then in Dublin[2] whither he had gone as " Adjutant-
General of the Horse " in 1651, and he also appears as a com-

---

[1] Thurloe, *Collection of State Papers*, ii, p. 214 (App. 6).
[2] Allen's services in Ireland were very great, as may be seen in
Dunlop's *Ireland under the Commonwealth*. He was also one of the
thinkers and organizers who suggested grouping all the Baptist
Churches into associations ; the military led to the ecclesiastical
organization (Whitley, p. 90).

missioner for the settlement of Ulster. But it was not long before his dissatisfaction with Cromwell led to an open collision. They had an interview in London which, according to Allen, made the Protector very angry, though Allen complains that he was not allowed to say as much as he wanted to, since the Protector did most of the talking. Allen came down to Devonshire, where his movements and talk aroused suspicion that he was plotting. Finally he was dramatically arrested when in bed at his father-in-law's house by several soldiers armed with sword and pistol. Allen writes in defence of himself and in protest against such treatment after thirteen years of faithful service. His defence was hardly likely to smooth the ruffled plumage of his old commander, for he says, in the course of a letter[1] to Oliver:—

You are also pleased to tax me with having as light an esteem of you as of C. S. [Charles Stuart], though neither did any word in my letter nor any action of mine ever give you ground for such a surmise. What my esteem hath been of you in some verticall forsaking [sic] days I believe you can remember ; and I can truly say, if I have erred, it hath been, I fear, in esteeming too highly of you. The different esteem I yet have of your Lordship from the other part is this ; I could freely engage against the other as formerly, but I durst not lift a hand against you, nor join with or advise the doing of it.

Cromwell's own view of the situation is given in the letter to his Exeter agent: " Adjutant-General Allen doth very ill offices by multiplying dissatisfaction in the minds of men to the present Government." Nevertheless Allen was permitted to return to his post in Ireland, though difficulties were not ended. How could they be for two such men? In 1657 we hear of Allen's resignation to Henry Cromwell, who records the impression Allen made on him [2]:—

Subtile and grave Mr. Allen brought up the rear and was more ingenuous than the rest in declaring that the ground of his dissatisfaction took its rise from the first change of the government, foreseeing that they should be no way able to answer the end for which they were first engaged ; and being now more fully convinced of it, and looking upon himself as formerly discharged by his highness, he thought it best for him to draw to a more retired position.

[1] Thurloe, op. cit., iii, p. 140.
[2] Thurloe, op. cit., v, pp. 670-2.

We hear of Allen and Vernon again in Devonshire just after the death of the Protector. Sir John Coplestone has his eye upon them,[1] as the late Protector had commanded, for they are men who must be watched: "Certainly they are persons of as much venom and revenge as any whatever and will not spare to adventure on anything that may give them the least hope of success." Allen's displacements from military service, like the repeated banishments of Athanasius, reflected the vicissitudes of the time, for he was made a colonel of horse by the restored Long Parliament in 1659, only to be removed by Monck in 1660. Soon after this he was imprisoned for " endeavouring to debauch some of the soldiers from their obedience, and likewise suspected of being dangerous to the State ". In the following year he and John Vernon were sent into exile, and the last we hear of Allen is an elegy over his brother-in-law's death in 1666.[2] Some of its lines surely express the writer's own disappointment with the times : —

> His soul did mourn in secret for such pride
> He found with many long before he died :
> To see a worldly, formal, selfish spirit
> 'Mongst men professing Heaven to inherit.

But the fullest account of his attitude is to be found in his *Word to the Army*, a pamphlet of twenty pages issued in 1660. In this, as in his *Faithful Memorial* of the preceding year (which gives the account of the Windsor Prayer Meeting), he reviews the decline of the true cause, and speaks of Cromwell in his virtual kingship as " a ghost from the grave " of the Stuarts. The army has been guilty of " King-craft and worse than Bishop-like trapannings ". He sees a grim meaning in the taking away of the Protector on the very anniversary of his victories at Dunbar and Worcester. The only true way to a Magna Charta is to acknowledge God.

We may sympathize with this Baptist condemnation of Oliver as a "worldly politician " (the phrase is S. R. Gardiner's) without for one minute thinking that Allen could have succeeded where Oliver had failed, even though he had been Oliver. There are situations in which events demonstrate

---

[1] *Ibid. op. cit.*, vii, p. 385.
[2] *Bochim* (British Museum, Lutt. I, 153).

their power over men,[1] and the situation becomes too big for them, as recent events have taught us. There is no short cut to a kingdom of the saints, as the Fifth-Monarchy men thought, and the Parliament supposed to be made up of saints was at least as ineffective as any other. But through human failure, as well as human success, we can recognize and admire the presence of great aims, pursued with conscience and with courage. William Allen and his comrades can claim an interest of eternity as well as of time. As S. R. Gardiner remarks: " It was because the spear of Parliamentarism was tipped with Puritanism that the strife appeals to all who are attracted by the spectacle of unselfish human emotion resolving itself into action ".[2] The militant Puritanism of that age was largely Baptist.

(3) A BAPTIST REFORMER (THOMAS LAMBE)

If Carlyle had come across a little four-page tract, the only known copy of which seems to be that in the Angus Library,[3] he might have treated it in the same manner as *The Chronicle of Jocelin of Brakelond,* and made it the basis of a miniature *Past and Present.* The title of the tract is, *An Appeal to the Parliament concerning the Poor, that there may not be a Beggar in England.* It is signed "T. L.", the initials of Thomas Lambe, a well-known Baptist of the seventeenth century, who has found his way into the *Dictionary of National Biography,* though at the cost of some confusion with another Baptist of the same name. It bears the arresting date of 1660, the year of the great "Settlement", upon which Carlyle pours such scorn in the book I have named. That date gives significance to the opening words of the tract: "In the midst of many and great Undertakings, let not a Settlement for the *Poor* be forgotten." The surprising thing about this tract is its modernity. Here we have proposals for Labour Exchanges, Parish Councils (of a sort), and the drafting of unemployed labour to industrial centres. Even the pressure on the middle classes, which we think peculiarly our own

---

[1] Cf. Lord Grey, *Twenty-five Years,* p. 51: " There is in great affairs so much more, as a rule, in the minds of the events (if such an expression may be used) than in the minds of the chief actors."
[2] *Cromwell's Place in History,* p. 22.
[3] Reprinted in the *Baptist Quarterly,* i, 3, pp. 128-31.

difficulty, is in view, for the writer compares them with
" small Iron Creepers in a chimney " (the iron " dogs "
which supported the burning wood on the hearth) " who
bear the burden and heat of the Fire, until they be wasted to
Sinders ".

Thomas Lambe believes with Carlyle that everything
depends on the men you put in office, and he believes also
that the problems of poverty and unemployment must be faced
locally.   Each parish is to " agree with some Able Man, or
Men, that rightly understandeth their Work ".   These representatives of the parish will divide their problem into three
parts.   They will assist the old, the impotent, and young
children by a parish levy ; they will help those whose work
does not bring in a living wage ; they will group the unemployed in tens or twenties and arrange either for them to be
supplied with work from some employer, or for them to be
drafted to centres in which there is need of hands.   The social
problem is envisaged as the disproportionate distribution of
potential workers and the need for a proper distribution of
them.   But it is also recognized that " though there may be
work enough, yet the Idle will not come for it ", so that
authority will be necessary.   In some parishes a decayed
industry must be replaced by something new.   In others,
where there is no poverty (instances near London are given),
contributions must be raised for more necessitous districts.

The Labour Exchange proposed is to be a centre trough
which would-be employers and the unemployed can be
brought into contact, where boys can find masters to whom
they may be apprenticed, where girls may find apprenticeship
or service.   But in regard to such service for girls, Thomas
Lambe is singularly up to date in his fear of " blind alleys " ;
the girls are not to go to service " until they be first Taught
to Spin, Knit, Sew, learn some Trade, or way of livelihood ;
who else are neither fit for Service, nor can in aftertimes do
any thing for themselves ".   Further, there is to be ready
access to Justices of the Peace for complaints of neglect or
oppression, and the judges of assizes and sessions are to
enforce justice in this matter and to publish the law in regard
to it.   The wants of the poor must be supplied before legal
measures are to be taken against them.   Part of Lambe's
scheme is a census of city populations.   He urges that all this
is everybody's business and not simply the concern of Parlia-

ment men. " If any Object the Trouble: To have such Multitudes of Beggars in this fruitful Kingdom, is not that trouble? To hear them cry and not give, is not that trouble? To hear their cry and give, is trouble also ; not knowing whether it doth good or harm."

The little tract is a good example of that " social conscience " which is by no means such a discovery of yesterday as is sometimes thought. It illustrates the sense of serious moral responsibility,[1] as well as the social sympathies which are certainly promoted by Baptist principles.

(4) A BAPTIST TEACHER (BENJAMIN KEACH)

On a certain autumn Thursday in the year 1664, between the hours of eleven and one, groups of people stood in the market-place of Winslow (in Bucks) curiously or sympathetically watching the pillory and a young man who had his head and his hands fixed in it. Over his head, as over his Lord's so long before, was an inscription which the more learned spelt out to their neighbours: " For writing, printing and publishing a schismatical Book, intitled, *The Child's Instructor, or a New and Easy Primmer.*" Some of them had seen his face turned and his hands outstretched to them before, in the less constraining attitude of the pulpit, for he was a preacher ; others were perhaps wearing clothes at which he had stitched, for he was a tailor. Presently there was a little stir as the hangman came forward and kindled a small bonfire in front of the captive. When it was burning sufficiently, he thrust into it a very little book—the book to which the inscription referred. No copy of that edition has come down to us, but Benjamin Keach lived to re-write and republish it, just as Jeremiah, through Baruch, re-wrote and re-published his own burnt prophecies. A characteristic little frontispiece in the earliest surviving edition (that of about a quarter of a century later) depicts two godly youths on the narrow way, one praying and one advancing, whilst a vener-

---

[1] Cf. the remark made in a letter by Thomas Arnold of Rugby: " When I look round upon boys or men, there seems to me some one point or quality, which distinguishes really noble persons from ordinary ones ; it is not religious feeling—it is not honesty or kindness ; but it seems to be moral thoughtfulness " (Stanley's *Life of Arnold,* end of chap. viii).

able friend, comfortably seated, holds out the open page of Scripture.   Below is the alternative, where a horned and clawed devil lurks in a pit at the end of the broad way ; inset are two episodes of the journey, in one of which the foolish youth has his mincing steps escorted by two gaily bedizened damsels, whilst in the other, three players are gathered around the card-table.   They did not leave much to the imagination in those seventeenth-century days.

The book is of considerable interest to the educationist, and amply deserves the commendatory preface by Hanserd Knollys.   We begin with the alphabet and a short series of spelling lessons.   Then follow " Precepts for Children " in verse, which mingle with the Christian appeal adjurations to spell rightly ; that mixture, with a preponderance of the appeal, is characteristic of the whole book.   After a few Scripture sentences broken up into syllables, we come to the first of a series of three catechisms, suited respectively to the ages of " between three and four ", " ten ", and " mature age "—quite on the principle of the " graded school " of our days !   These are of interest as giving cross-sections of the presumptive religious capabilities at these several ages.   The child of three or four learns that Methuselah was the oldest man that ever lived, that God is a Spirit, and that salvation is by conversion ; the moral lessons he needs are put into verse, evidently to be memorized.   He is zealously warned against giving his mind to play.   Next comes his brother of ten, who is plunged into deeper waters of theological inquiry.   Keach must have felt this, for when the father asks " Who is God? " the child is at least taught candour in his reply : " I do not know very well ; is he not an old man? ", the reason being that " God made Man in his own Image ".   But the child's chief difficulty, as his instructor conceives him, is in the serious temptation to defer religious decision to a later age.   "Father," he says plaintively, " I am very young " (ten!), " may I not do as other Children do, and defer the minding of these things, until I am older? "   But the father promptly ascribes such thoughts to the inspiration of the devil, and grimly counters with the words, " Do you not see many *little* Graves as well as great ones? ", and recounts the experience of pre-cocious infants and young children, including a girl of nine, who rises to the ripe experience of a Bunyan, and after long waiting for an answer to prayer says, " Well, I venture my

Soul upon Christ." Here the father does not mince matters. " Are you," he says to this pathetic child of ten, " old enough to be damn'd and too young to be sav'd? " No wonder that the child's last word is, " My dear Father, I can hold out no longer, my Heart is smitten, and my Soul trembles ", and forthwith chants the ten commandments in a versified form. There is now a digression, in which the father addresses his daughters and warns them against the worldly life of the Restoration, with its " rowling Eyes and amorous Glances ". Again there is a plaintive interjection, for one daughter says, " Doth not God allow some Things for Ornaments? ", and the father is honest enough to remember Rebekah. For the versified duties of the daughters Benjamin Keach feels that he cannot do better than borrow from Abraham Cheare, the contemporary Baptist verse-maker, whose verses were sung by little Caleb Vernon also:

> When by Spectators I am told
> What Beauty doth adorn me,
> Or in a glass when I behold
> How sweetly God did form me:
> Hath God such comeliness display'd
> And on me made to dwell,
> What pitty such a pretty Maid
> As I should go to Hell.

The Youth's Catechism which follows is a whole body of divinity, too long for notice and for most men to-day too tedious, followed by an exposition of the Lord's Prayer. The subject of Believers' Baptism is well handled, without bitterness against " our Godly Brethren, who differ from us ". The " Advice to Youth ", in verse, gives an interesting glimpse of the pious youth and his beginning of the day. He thanks God for preservation during the night, and prays for grace during the day. He goes downstairs, salutes the other members of the family, and proceeds to wash his hands (at the pump) and comb his head, paying due attention to the cleanliness of his clothes. After the reading of Scripture and prayer, he is ready either to sit at table or to wait on his parents. He is particularly careful neither to talk nor to stare in the faces of his parents. The rest of the book is mainly concerned with worldly information, " Thirty days hath September ", the writing of a receipt, punctuation, weights and measures, and a dictionary of hard words. But we return to the theme of the frontispiece at the end, where both the Devil and Christ solicit an ungodly youth. Then Christ passes from the scene, and is replaced by a doctor, whose only prescription for aching head and cold feet is " Call upon God for you will die ", and the Doctor is duly followed by Death. They made it all very plain in those days of our forefathers.

Keach eventually became a leading figure amongst London Baptists, and, as we shall see, the pioneer of congregational hymn-singing. He returned to the theme of " War with the Devil ", or the Young Man's Conflict with the Powers of Darkness, in 1673. In this use of religious allegory he was, as Dr. Whitley has pointed out,[1] a precursor of Bunyan. But Keach's narrative, though reaching twenty-two editions within a century, lacks that insight into the realities of human life which has given Bunyan his place amongst the immortals.

(5) A BAPTIST CHURCH
(THAMES STREET, NEWGATE STREET, CRIPPLEGATE)

Some aspects of Baptist personality in the seventeenth and eighteenth centuries are best revealed by the study of a Baptist Church of those days. Here we shall see the social interaction of Baptists within the little world of religious fellowship which they created for themselves, the disputes which agitated them, the methods of their corporate life as expressing their convictions, the human passions that beset the Christian minister. All these aspects are illustrated in a Church-Book of the Baptist Church gathered by the well-known Hanserd Knollys about 1642, though its continuous record does not begin till a year or two before his death in 1691.[2] The manuscript, in many different hands which belongs to the Angus Library of Regent's Park College, is found in a vellum-covered volume, with clasps, its size being 16 in. by 6 in. The book is not the Minute-Book of the Church (to which reference is occasionally made), though for part of the period

[1] *A History of British Baptists*, pp. 132, 133.
[2] Before it reached Thames Street, it had met in Colman Street, Wapping (Tower Street), Artichoke Lane, Booby Lane. It never owned a building and is now extinct (Whitley).

covered it seems to have been used as a Minute-Book ; originally, the record might better be called a Discipline Book, in
which the more private and personal matters were recorded.
The earliest date is September 26, 1689, and the latest
Christmas Day, 1723. Four regular pastorates are included,
though we have only the first year of the fourth, viz. those of
Robert Steed, who became co-pastor with Knollys in 1689,
and died whilst still in office in 1700; David Crosley, who
was ordained in January 1702-3 and expelled on August 14,
1709 ; John Skepp, ordained September 7, 1714, died in office,
December 1, 1721 ; Humphrey Barrow, ordained June 5,
1723, died in office, 1727. The Church had 113 members in
1689 and 212 in 1721. It was one of some twenty-six Baptist
Churches of all types to be found at this time in London,
Southwark, and Westminster, which together had a population of over half a million.[1] Probably its inner life and
problems may be taken as fairly typical of a " gathered "
community at the time, of what we now call the Congregational polity.

(a) *The Discipline Book*

The first point to be made is that the study of such a record
is the best way to realize with accuracy and proper emphasis
what the principles of a denomination really mean. Instead
of conventional and colourless statements, which admit of
very different applications, we have here a picture of real life,
with men and women acting under the stress of living convictions. In the meeting-place, first in George Yard, Thames
Street (1688), some years later at the Bagnio, Newgate Street,
and a little later still at Curriers' Hall, Cripplegate, we listen
to the speech of a solemn and intensely earnest group of men
and women, and we find where their interest really lay. It
was not the fact, as is often supposed, that their chief concern
was the negative one of " independency ", i.e. of repudiating
any interference from without ; their concern was the positive
one of maintaining what they held to be the Christian
standard of faith and conduct within. We may feel that
their microscopic examination of the lives and thoughts of their
fellow-members was not wholly healthy, and had grave perils ;

---

[1] Whitley, *History*, p. 181.

yet even when we criticize their methods, we must admit that the endeavour to maintain a high quality of Christian life was itself a noble one, and the logical and necessary outcome of their principles. They were a separated Church of men and women ; they were bound to insist on a Christian ethic, the expression of a Christian faith which should stand out emphatically from the conventionalism and loose morals of the age.

For convenience, we may confine ourselves under this head to the Discipline Book kept by Robert Steed from 1689 to 1700.[1] There seem to have been only about a score of cases of discipline in the course of the dozen years, which is a remarkable testimony to character, when we consider the rigorous scrutiny and the social level from which most, perhaps all, of the membership was drawn. The occupation of some is characterized in the list of members: —

> A Taylor in Hungerford Market.
> A chambermaid to Squ. Barrington.
> The daughter of her that keeps the meeting-house.
> A schoolmaster in Gravell Lane.

Half a dozen of the cases of discipline illustrate the Scriptural truth that the love of money is a root of all kinds of evil. Two women members were convicted of having obtained money under false pretences from another woman—her little all of £40 saved up for old age. They told her that her capital would be increased if she lent it, but, in fact, the money was needed by one of these delinquents to pay her debts. They were both excluded from membership. Brother Brooksby, as a result of a transaction in hops with a member of another church, called him a rascal and a knave, and brought a law-suit against him. The matter received careful attention, but Brother Brooksby overreached himself by putting in a document that was proved to be a forgery ; exit Brother Brooksby. Brother Leeson not only failed to meet what was due to his father-in-law, but aggravated this by behaving " as a rude Hector ", as witnessed by a letter of threats duly read to the Church. Brother Hind also failed to pay his debts, but the trouble here was intemperance in drink.

---

[1] Published in the *Baptist Quarterly*, July and October, 1922.

Sister Foster was found guilty of a breach of trust in regard to some goods deposited in her keeping and was proved a liar. In two cases the trouble was between husband and wife. A journeyman shoemaker was excluded for wife-beating and for failing through idleness to make proper provision for his family. In another instance the husband complained of the wife's bad language to him. After due examination, it was decided " that deep distressing poverty had afflicted her through his incapacity or negligence to get a livelihood or subsistence, whereby great provocations had been given her to speak and act unadvisedly " ; the case was admonition and temporary suspension. Another set of domestic problems meets us in the relations of master and apprentice. Brother Hake, an apprentice to Brother Dennis, a scrivener, was charged with negligence and disobedience and with calumniating his master and mistress to their neighbours. Young Hake was brought up before the Church to express his repentance, but threw out a hint that he was not content with the food he got, and was eventually again brought up by his master. This time he had thrown down and beaten another apprentice and threatened this youth's master when he came to his rescue. When found about the place next morning and told to be gone, " he held up his fists against Mr. Reep, and told him it was well it was Sunday morning, otherwise had it been another day he would have beaten Mr. Reep ". This young swashbuckler's fault was aggravated because Mr. Reep had been friendly with him. It was testified that Hake " had idly spent his time at Coffee houses playing at draffts. And that one time Mr Reep aforesaid playing with him and having won the game of him, He making him pay the forfeit which was a dish of Coffee, He fell out with Mr. Reep and sayd as soon as he was gone that he had about him that which would do Mr. Reep's business which he could find in his heart to make use off ; which was a penknife he had in his pocket to stab him withall ". It was unfortunate for young Hake that he was born before the time of the Boy Scouts ; they might have made an excellent fellow of him. But the stern Church sent him into the outer darkness, to flourish that scrivener's penknife of his beyond our ken. Another apprentice in trouble was called Joseph Faircloth, a haberdasher, who did not live up to his first name if he did to his second, for he became too intimate with a cheesemonger's wife, who kept him out late.   These London 'prentices must have given their masters a world of trouble.   (Another apprentice case of the same kind is reported.)   There are two instances in which action is taken for non-attendance at meetings ; the defence was the experience of spiritual temptations, which should have been regarded as a reason for attending, not for stopping away ; in two others there were frustrated attempts to get back on the Church roll without due warrant.   The only instance of excommunication for heresy—that of a man and his wife who denied the divine nature of Christ—was quite fairly dealt with.   The only other type of case left unnoticed is that of a man who persisted in preaching elsewhere at the public meetings, then called " Lectures ", without seeming to the Church to have competent gifts for it.   The way in which the Church dealt with him is both drastic and ingenious, though I do not suggest that *they* saw the subtle humour of it. They condemned him for preaching without formal approval by the Church, for neglect of his business whilst he went preaching, with the result that he had to compound with his creditors, and also for failing to be in his place in the Church to which he belonged whilst he was away preaching elsewhere! His exclusion, after admonition, only served to harden him in his evil courses, for we read that " instead of repenting he turned from the truth and, joyned with them that sprinkl infants, is ordained the pastor of a pbiterian [i.e. Presbyterian] congregation at Epping in Essex ".

These details are of interest in themselves, and help us to reconstruct a living picture of the life and relations of a Separatist Church of the congregational order at the close of the seventeenth century.   But the purpose for which they are here mentioned is to show how seriously these people took what is, after all, the foundation principle of a separated or gathered Church—the character and conduct of its membership.   Whatever we may think about the perils or the impossibility of exercising any such discipline to-day, at least we ought to realize that the discipline was an honest attempt to carry out the principles theoretically expressed in the self-governing polity.   As long as that polity is retained, it would seem that both Baptists and Congregationalists are committed to the principle underlying it, and this Discipline Book shows us what that principle really means when taken as seriously as it was in Newgate Street.

The best example, however, of the thoroughness with which questions of discipline were handled is contained in a record of the Church Book subsequent to that Discipline Book of which I have been speaking. The particular example is a painful one, and some of its details could not well be made public. It is the story of the downfall of David Crosley, of which this is the only full record. He and his cousin, William Mitchell, had done a great evangelistic work in Yorkshire and Lancashire, and the Baptist Churches that ultimately sprang from their joint labours were many. He came into prominence in the south through a sermon preached at a Presbyterian church when he was twenty-two. He had been staying in the house of John Strudwick (where Bunyan had died three years before), and opposite him as he sat at the dinner-table was a tapestry depicting Samson in combat with the lion he slew. This seized his imagination, and led to the sermon called "Samson a type of Christ", in the manner of the allegorical preaching of the time. A bookseller who heard it there and then proposed to print it, and a thousand copies were sold in six months. After the death of Robert Steed in 1700 he was invited to succeed him, and was ordained at the Bagnio in January 1702-3, being then about thirty-three. His ministry was eminently successful, as we might have expected from his record; but from about 1707 rumours were in circulation that the popular minister was drinking too freely, even for that tolerant age, and that his behaviour towards women gave rise to grave suspicions. For a long time the rumours were discredited by most, who felt, as is said, that "he could not if guilty be so helped in his ministry". It is the story of Hawthorne's *Scarlet Letter* over again, though on a lower and coarser level. At length the Church was bound to deal with it.

I have been greatly impressed by the thorough and just manner in which the leaders of the Church dealt with this painful scandal. The affidavits of the witnesses are given in full; their evidence was carefully tested, and full opportunity was given to David Crosley to defend himself. He acknowledged drunkenness, and was convicted of lying in the course of the very deliberate proceedings, but he maintained to the end his innocence in the gravest features of the case. There can be little doubt, however, in the mind of anyone who reads the documents and follows the course of events, that

David Crosley was guilty of immoral conduct, and that the
Church was fully justified in its ultimate act of excommunication, in which there was full unanimity. After prayer, there
was a careful statement of the charges proved by " the Brother
that was the mouth of the Church ", with references to the
Scriptures that bore on each point. The brother then
proceeded : —

You, the Church of Jesus Christ, having judged him guilty
of these gross sins, and having also judged it not for the glory
of God, nor for the honour of this Church that such a one should
be continued in the communion of this Church (and after silence,
the Brother appointed expressed the sentence in these words) : —

Therefore, we do in the name of our Lord Jesus, and in the
name and authority of this Church, withdraw from our Brother
David Crosley, for his disorderly walking, and we put him out of
union, and Communion, of this Church, until the Lord give him
repentance to the satisfaction of the Church.

The Church at Tottlebank, Lancashire, of which Crosley
had been minister for nine years before coming to London,
refused to believe him guilty, but they never had the evidence
before them. If we needed confirmation, it would lie in the
fact that similar charges were brought against him in the
north again in 1719, and he was virtually excommunicated in
the following year. Yet his powers as a preacher remained,
and at the age of seventy-two he could hold an open-air
audience of four thousand people. He died in 1744,
bequeathing us one of those perplexing problems of human
inconsistency—or human frailty. As I turn over these manuscript pages of his story, I seem to see a man temperamentally
weak by the very qualities that made him effective as a
popular preacher, poised in unstable moral equilibrium, and
the more able to understand the struggles of other men—till
the habituation of evil thought made evil act easy, and the
finer edge of moral judgment was blunted. As an older man,
when the passions of youth were left behind, he seems to
have won and kept the respect of others, and George Whitefield writes a preface to the republication of his famous
sermon on " Samson a type of Christ ". Strudwick's tapestry
was a prophetic foreshadowing of his own life, for David
Crosley was something of a Samson in his strength and in his
weakness.

(b) *The Controversy about Hymn-singing*

The past is strewn with the ashes of controversies where the fires of passion once burnt fiercely, and at least one interesting example of this is afforded by the book before us. At the beginning of 1693 a group of twenty-two malcontents from the Church of Horsley Down, Southwark, under the ministry of Benjamin Keach, sought fellowship with the Bagnio Church under Robert Steed, " being dissatisfied with their setting up of common set form singing after it had been exploded by the Baptized Churches as a humane invention ; and also being grieved with the manner of their proceeding with them when they declared their dissatisfaction with their introducing that innovation ". Thereon hangs a tale of some length. The honour of first introducing hymns into the regular worship of an English congregation, established or dissenting, belongs to Benjamin Keach,[1] and his book of three hundred hymns, called *Spiritual Melody*, and published in 1691, was the first hymn-book to be so used, though he had published hymns for children to learn as early as 1664. None of his hymns has survived in common use, and had the leaders of this " split " from his Church argued that Keach's hymns were doggerel, instead of arguing against the general principle of hymn-singing, we might have sympathized with them. Here are some specimens:—

> Our wounds do stink and are corrupt,
>   Hard swellings we do see ;
> We want a little ointment, Lord,
>   Let us more humble be.   (p. 173.)

> Repentance like a bucket is
>   To pump the water out ;
> For leaky is our ship, alas,
>   Which makes us look about.   (p. 254.)

> Here meets them now that worm that gnaws,
>   And plucks their bowels out ;
> The pit, too, on them shuts her jaws,
>   This dreadful is, no doubt.   (p. 312.)

[1] Cf. Whitley, *op. cit.*, pp. 187, 188.

However, it was not the quality of the hymns, but the principle of hymn-singing (as distinct from singing Scriptural psalms) that was at issue. Benjamin Keach's practice of hymn-singing, first introduced at the Communion Service, was spreading amongst Particular Baptist Churches, though vigorously attacked. In the same year as Keach published the first hymn-book, he issued an *apologia* for his practice, entitled *The Breach Repaired in God's Worship*, in which he elevates the practice to a *Sacred Truth of the Gospel* (p. vi), and couples its neglect with that of the ministry as the two chief causes of " our sad witherings ". A favourite proof-text of his was Exod. xxxii. 18, " the noise of them that sing do I hear ", and he argues quite reasonably that " one man's voice could not have made such a noise ", therefore the singing must have been congregational ; nor is he deterred by the fact which his opponents gleefully pointed out, that this congregation was singing to the praise of the Golden Calf. One of these opponents was Robert Steed, which explains why the group of malcontents with Keach sought refuge at the Bagnio Church. In 1691 Steed published *An Epistle . . . concerning Singing*, denouncing the practice on the following grounds. Singing by a set stinted form is an invention of man, being of the same quality as, if not worse than, common stinted set-form prayers, or even infant sprinkling. It is artificial, and therefore alien to the free motions of the Spirit of God. We should have the true and spontaneous song if we had more of the Holy Spirit. As for arguments drawn from the music of the Old Testament, all *that* is done away in Christ. Moreover, some cannot sing, not having tunable voices, and women ought anyhow to keep silence in the churches. I think we must admire Robert Steed's ingenuity, whilst we differ from his conclusions. But the most important point to notice in this ancient and long-settled controversy is that both sides seem to us wrong-headed in their arguments. To us, hymn-singing is neither a Gospel ordinance to be neglected at our soul's peril, nor a wicked innovation, displaying the policy of Satan ; it is of practical use in worship, and that settles the matter. We have moved away from the ground of Scriptural authority in such matters to the modern ground of the evidence of religious experience. It is these great changes, often unrecognized, that do settle most of the controversies, not the particular arguments employed. The dispute about hymn-

D

singing and many another bone of contention lies forgotten ; but it is worth while to hunt it out from the dark corner where it lies to remind us that some of our own issues may suffer the same fate, and be settled, not by our arguments, but by the inevitable course of things and their intrinsic worth. This does not mean any lack of respect for the seriousness displayed in the endeavour to refer details of practice to evangelical principles.

(6) A BAPTIST WRITER (ANN DUTTON)

The Baptist passion for liberty which characterized the seventeenth century and the Baptist awakening to the need for missionary work shortly before the nineteenth century are like two great waves, which have between them the trough of the hyper-Calvinism and the spiritual lethargy of Baptist life in the eighteenth century. It is only fair to show the general character of this period, as it is reflected in a particular life, in order to bring out the perils and weaknesses of this type of religious experience, whether Baptist or not. We take as our example a copious writer, whose monument once recorded " twenty-five volumes of choice Letters to friends and thirty-eight Tracts on Divine and Spiritual Subjects ",[1] though they are doubtless entirely unknown to the present reader. Her revealing account of herself is interesting as a " human document ", but the study of it will also test our power of sympathy, for underneath all the vanities and frailties that are so apparent within the narrow theological frame, there is still a genuine passion for God; in her own phrase, she was " an ascending Spark in Christ's vehement flame ".

If Ann had been born a couple of centuries later she would doubtless have become a leading lady on the denominational platform. If Ann had been born in the Court circles of her own day she might have become another Countess of Yarmouth, by her good looks, her lively imagination, and her sensuous disposition. As it was, " she aspired to be the

---

[1] J. C. Whitebrook in *Transactions of the Baptist Historical Society,* vol. vii, Nos. 3 and 4, pp. 129 ff. He devotes himself chiefly to her controversies and correspondence with Wesley, Whitefield, Cudworth and others. The present study is confined to the volume of autobiography.

Countess of Huntingdon of the denomination ".[1] Her portrait suggests a Court beauty rather than a Baptist minister's wife—though, indeed, she was never quite that, for Mr. Dutton would always be " Mrs. Dutton's husband ". Here is an accurate description of the portrait as given by a caustic biographer: " It represents her tossing a very shapely little head, on which her own hair is tired high, to fall in large curly ringlets on either side of a smooth, well-poised neck. A silk gown, tight in sleeves and waist, is rucked in rolled chiffon, décolleté, with gathered sleeves ribboned at the insertion. Her expression is what our ancestors would have called ' sprightly ', and quite explains much of the airiness which she laments ".[2]

There was nothing Ann enjoyed so much as writing about herself, and she has left us her autobiography in three parts, dealing respectively with her conversion, the special providences of God, and the publication of her books, to the number of about fifty. The autobiography is entitled *A Brief Account of the Gracious Dealings of God with a Poor, Sinful, Unworthy Creature,* the respective dates being 1743 for I and II, and 1750 for III. A " Letter " is appended, defending the right of a woman to print her message, notwithstanding that unfortunate saying of the Apostle's about a woman keeping silence in the churches ; the writer concludes with the remark that she can at least pray for those who will not read her.

Ann Williams was born in Northampton in 1692, brought up in a religious home, and attended the Independent Church at Castle Hill under the Rev. John Hunt (1698-1709). She blames herself for the early pharisaism which said, " I have been at Prayer, while others are at Play "—though it is doubtful whether she ever outgrew that fault. She was converted at thirteen by a deepened sense of the meaning of eternity, in glory or misery, and says, " I pray'd, read, heard in a very different Manner than I had ever done before ". She records the thought, so illuminative of the pressure of Calvinism, " if I must go to Hell at last ; I desire I may be holy there ". She was afraid to speak about her spiritual troubles to her parents, though her father sought to give her an opportunity. And so often the spiritual strain of these

[1] Whitley, *History of British Baptists,* p. 214.
[2] Whitebrook, *loc. cit.,* p. 132.

four months issued in physical breakdown, from which she was relieved by the potion of "a very skilful, tho' a very prophane Person". The peace that came through trust in Christ was disturbed by the thought "that all the Experience I had had of the Lord's loving Kindness was but mere Delusion" (we may compare the modern trouble about auto-suggestion). Like Bunyan (whose *Grace Abounding* has influenced her narrative), the hero of the *Scarlet Letter*, and so many others, she is tempted to utter blasphemous thoughts and naturally does not know that this is but an inevitable psychological reaction from excessive religiosity. But she gains a true sense of faith: " I saw that believing was venturing, casting, trusting my Soul in the Hands of Jesus ", i.e. an act of will, "a holy Venture" like Esther's. She recognizes that the experience of the saints may vary in particulars, though agreeing in general ; the great thing is to "come as thou canst, tho' with a trembling heart". Prevenient grace was at work "in giving thee a new Nature before thou began'st to breathe after it". The note of genuine experience rings through all this, in spite of the stereotyped religious vocabulary and of the dependence on Bunyan and Rutherford.

The second part of the autobiography enables us to trace her outward movements, which are all more or less regarded as "special providences", and are specially linked to opportunities for worship and edification. It begins in 1709 with the removal of her minister, the Rev. John Hunt, and the succession of the Rev. Thomas Tingey (1709-29), whose ministry did not edify her, as she did not fail to inform him. She accordingly removed to the open-membership Baptist Church [1] in College Lane, then under the ministry of the Rev. John Moore, where she found "fat, green Pastures. . . . . The Sanctuary-Streams ran clearly ; and the Sun shone gloriously. . . . . Mr. Moore was a great doctrinal Preacher: And the special Advantage I receiv'd under his Ministry, was the Establishment of my *Judgment* in the doctrines of the Gospel". Her *Brief Hints concerning Baptism* (p. 27) show that it was not till she was a member of College Lane that she was baptized on profession of faith (which incidentally shows the educative value of an open-membership Baptist Church

---

[1] *I.e.* a Church in which there *may* be membership on profession of faith without the requirement of baptism.

when the minister is, like John Moore, himself a convinced Baptist).

In 1714, at the age of twenty-two, she was married to her first husband, and this led to her removal to London, where she had communion with the Church at Cripplegate, under the ministry of the Rev. John Skepp. In the Cripplegate Church Book[1] there is a Register of letters, with an entry of date about 1715, " No. 18 Ann Catle from Northampton for Transient ". This means that she was not fully transferred, but received into temporary communion, retaining her membership at College Lane. Her full transfer was made more than two years later, for we read in the Cripplegate book: " 31st of the 1st mo. 1718. Same time one M^S Ann Cattle and M^S Martha Bass, members of the Church of Christ under the care of B^r Moor of Northampton, presented a letter of dismission to the Church which was read . . . M^S Ann Cattle gave a Large and very choice account of the Work of the Spirit of God on her soul to the great joy of the Church." Note the " Large "—very comprehensible to those who have waded through some of her writings. How Ann must have enjoyed herself on that occasion! She gives an interesting analysis and comparison of the preaching of Moore and Skepp ; the latter went beyond the former in " Quickness of Thought, Aptness of expression, suitable Affection, and a most agreeable Delivery ; . . . his Ministry abounded in Similies . . . the special Blessing I received under it was the more abundant Life and Power of the Truths known ". Skepp's book on *Divine Energy* will explain this judgment ; he left his mark on Ann, though her husband's business called them away for some time to Warwick. Here she found another climate: " I thought, when I came first, ' Surely, this People worship without the Blood of Jesus '. They stood at such a Distance from God in Prayer." She writes enthusiastically to Mr. Skepp that *he* does not " make a Composition of Matter, merely out of other Men's Judgments, and then commit it to a few dead Notes to read to the

---

[1] This is the Church Book which was the subject of the preceding study. Her husband's name is given by Mr. Whitebrook as " Coles ", but this must be a mistake for " Cattell " or " Catel ". In the College Lane Church Book, under date August 18, 1715, there is an entry: " Ann Cattell dismissed to Mr. Skepp's Church near Cripplegate in London."

People! " They soon returned to London, where, after five years (i.e. in 1719 or 1720) her husband died. She then returned to Northampton, and within a year or so married Benjamin Dutton, who had been apprenticed to a clothier and draper, had then studied for the ministry, and now, on their marriage, returned to his trade. She greatly missed Mr. Skepp's ministry, but after his death in 1721 transferred her spiritual affections to the Rev. William Grant, of Wellingborough. She evidently gave her husband no peace until they removed to Wellingborough, though this was long delayed for business reasons. There is an evident want of proportion when she compares herself with Abraham going out, not knowing whither he went, and with Ruth migrating to a strange land, for, after all, Wellingborough is only ten miles from Northampton. The fact that Mr. Grant was once "ill of a Quinsy" leads to pages of religious debate. She did not wholly exclude her husband from her anxieties, though we hear much less of him than of her favourite ministers. She was greatly upset when business kept him away three days beyond time, and had a great struggle to resist looking into the newspaper to see whether he was drowned—but that was not to be until a quarter of a century later. Finally, the Duttons got to Wellingborough, and Ann could listen to Grant on the Canticles to her heart's content. But again came disappointment. Business necessitated a removal to Whittlesey (near Peterborough), where her spiritual exile brought on an illness, during which she characteristically chose a text for her funeral discourse. We can see Ann, with her lively imagination, ecstatically imagining that scene as she lay in bed. Her friends decided (probably not without some prompting) that " it was necessary for me, for the Recovery of my Health, to return again into my own Air". They lived in Wellingborough for about three years, till in 1732 they removed to Great Gransden, in Huntingdonshire. This removal was not for business reasons. Mr. Dutton had been preaching for some time, and was now called to become minister of the Church there—a struggling cause. Her long debate as to whether she ought to go makes it plain that she regarded the call as one to herself even more than to her husband.

Her activity as a writer, already begun, formed her dominant interest in Great Gransden, to judge from the third part of her autobiography. This consists of a long and detailed account of the publication of her successive books. She is eager to tell both how she came to write them and how the way was miraculously cleared for their publication, even " in the Exuberance of His love, *Three at once*! " She speaks of herself as " a Favourite of Heaven, a special Favourite ", and as one who " has a great name among some of [God's] children ". She is specially eager that her books shall circulate in America, and when other matters take her husband to America, she enlists him as her distributing agent. Scripture is made to testify its confirmation of her desires at every point ; thus the text " the Woman fled into the Wilderness " is a divine hint that her books would be used in the American Wilderness. She finds, of course, Scriptural warrant for an attack on Wesley's false doctrine, and Jael's example warrants a hammerblow at the Christians of Philadelphia. She calls her books her children (" How often have I admired divine Kindness, in that freedom from worldly encumbrances! "), and can thus appropriate the text " Leave thy fatherless children " for her MSS. But enough has been said to show, underneath the religious vocabulary, the kind of monomania which possessed this ambitious woman. Her husband remained in America from 1743 to 1747, and was drowned in returning. (Mr. Whitebrook rather unkindly suggests that he needed rest and peace.) It is a little startling to find that this extraordinary woman is partly comforted for his loss by the way being now open to the declining Church to get another minister! It ought to be said that she endowed the cause at Great Gransden, and " left the repute of a singularly patient, well-living old woman to survive her in the memory of friends who loved her ". [1] Human nature is often a perplexing blend of many qualities.

The faults and limitations of the character thus revealed are obvious to all. Ann regarded her writings as a divinely directed means of evangelism, yet her spirit and attitude towards the great evangelists of the century is not unfairly described as " censorious ", [2] We are conscious of the narrowness and provincialism of her outlook, her misuse of Scripture

[1] Whitebrook, *loc. cit.*, p. 140. She bequeathed her Bible to the only other notable woman in Baptist circles of the time, Ann Steele ; it may be seen at Broughton (Whitley).
[2] Whitley, *op. cit.*, p. 214.

as a Delphic oracle to confirm her own desires, the unpleasant sentimentality of her use of Canticles, her conspicuous egoism. On the other hand, we ought to recognise that some at least of these faults belong to her age rather than peculiarly to herself. In spite of them, she is honestly seeking God, and trying to serve Him, and it is her misfortune that she belongs to a period and a religious circle of which the life has become artificial and self-absorbed. The moral of her story is drawn for us by history. The new life came through the new evangelism, liberated from outworn dogma, and the new duties which that evangelism inspired.

(7) A BAPTIST STUDENT (JOHN COLLETT RYLAND)

William Newman, the first Principal of Stepney (Regent's Park) College, who was an assistant in the school kept by John Collett Ryland at Enfield, has told us [1] two incidents of John Collett Ryland's boyhood which may be taken as fully characteristic of him: "At twelve years of age he teazed his father so much for a gun that he knocked him down with a stick ; and then, to make it up with him, he gave him one. Soon after, as he was setting it down (not regarding the trigger) against a box, the whole charge went into the ceiling. After this his father gave him a horse. He bought spurs; and the faster the horse galloped the more he spurred him. At length the horse threw him against a bank, and left him there bleeding most profusely." This was the headstrong and passionate youth, born of an impetuous ancestry, who was captured for Christ and Calvinism by the young pastor of Bourton-on-the-Water, Benjamin Beddome. Here is what the youth wrote of his minister (in the diary which is the basis of this study[2]) when through Mr. Beddome's interest and influence he had reached the Baptist Academy at Bristol:—

June 25th., 1744. M 6½. Surely Mr. Benj. Beddome is an instance of the Existance of God and the Truth of the Christian Religion. Wt. Could Change his Heart, and induce him to leave his Profession or Trade—which was much more Profitable—and what could move him to Stay at Bourton rather yn go to Exeter, to which he was strongly sollicited—what is it yt moves him to

[1] *Rylandiana*, p. 2.
[2] Now in the Angus Library of Regent's Park College.

preach, Pray and be so active? is it not ye Delight he finds in ye Work—Tis plain that tis not Worldly Interest.

Here we see the aspect of religion which chiefly appeals to a young man—the unselfish and generous devotion to some high cause. Young Ryland was not so happy (or thought he was not) in the minister and teacher whom he found at the Bristol Academy, Bernard Foskett. Mr. Foskett, who also acted as minister of the Broadmead Church, won the enthusiastic praise of his colleague, Hugh Evans, for his character and devotion to duty during nearly forty wears of service ; but Dr. John Rippon, whilst quoting this praise, goes on to admit that " his method of education was limited rather than liberal ; severe rather than enchanting ; employing the memory more than the genius, the reasoning more than the softer powers of the mind ; . . . Mr. Foskett was not the first of tutors ".[1] So we find John Collett Ryland, eager and impetuous in temper, inquisitive and speculative in mind, rather discouraged by the training of this elderly disciplinarian who could not appeal to his pupil's enthusiasms : —

June 15. 2 in the Afternoon. If God dont bless me wth Abilities for ye Ministry I'll Get me a place to be an outrider for a Bristol, Coventry, or London Tradesman—when this year is finish'd with Mr. Foskett. I shall partly See how ye Matter will go—and if I dont Engage in ye Work of ye Ministry, I'll Endeavour to return ye Money Paid for My Board—and any More they Expended on My Account,—and what they Desire for Interest—and Engage in ye Business I served my Apprenticeship to Learn—and if Please God I am able I'll also Make Mr. Fosket a Handsome Present for bestowing his Pains on such a Dull Fool as I have been, and I am afraid shall ever be.

But the gratitude to Mr. Foskett here expressed gave way to other feelings. On April 1, 1745, after nine months' more experience of his teacher, he writes : —

This day when Mr. Foskett he chid me exceedingly—and spoke some Severe Words which make a lasting impression on my Soul. —but if he knew my desires and endeavours to approve my Self Sincere in the Presence of God, and the doubts I do—and have for a long time labour'd under—about some of the Fundamentals of all Natural and Reveal'd Religion--I believe he would not be so Severe in his Reflections upon me.

[1] *An Essay towards an History of the Baptist Academy at Bristol,* p. 22.

The next day, however, we read: " Mr. Foskett was in a good temper and us'd us kindly." That such an attitude should be chronicled suggests that it was the exception rather than the rule—which is rather hard on a college Principal! (Perhaps it is a good thing that students no longer keep college diaries.) A couple of months later (May 30, 1745) there is a rather enigmatic entry: " Note what Mr. B. Beddome told me last Saturday—that the Day before, i.e. on Fryday, Mr. Foskett *spoke to him again, about my going in the Country.*" Over this is written in specially large and distinctive characters, " Bernard Foskett's Ignorant Cruel Hardness of Heart to me ". This unfavourable judgment of his tutor was no passing mood of indignation, for nearly forty years after (March 18, 1784, Thursday evening) John Collett Ryland wrote down this deliberate verdict on his college days: " Foskett should have spared no pains to educate our souls in grandeur, and to have enriched and impregnated them with great and generous ideas of God in His whole natural and moral character, relations and actions, to us and the universe. This was thy business, thy duty, thy honour, O Foskett! and this thou didst totally neglect." [1] That is a fairly sweeping condemnation, characteristic of the man who wrote it. Perhaps the truth was that the teacher's way of comprehending and handling divine truth was not the pupil's, and that the pupil was passing through his years of storm and stress, whilst the teacher had forgotten his own.

These spiritual struggles of a student's heart are reflected in not a few pages of the diary. Thus he writes (May 25, 1745), five days before the last-named entry: " I thought: If there was no God nor my Soul was not Immortal, no Death, Judgment, Heaven or Hell, yet I would not live beneath the Dignity of the Hunan Nature." Quite early in his college life he systematically analyses his condition:—

Inward man, for the most part, very dark, weak and wicked. My memory greatly failed me. My understanding very much blinded with sin. My conscience very stupid and unfaithful. My affections very carnal and corrupt. My reason almost ruined, and had little power to exercise itself. My thoughts exceedingly vain, corrupt and trifling, wild and ungovernable, unsteady and unfixed. Unbelief very strong indeed ; atheism, and every other

[1] Newman. *op. cit.,* p. 37.

corruption, working strongly in my heart. Sometimes ready to deny the being of God and of Christ, etc.[1]

Such condemnation of himself, in one form or other, constantly recurs throughout the diary. Introspective analysis is carried to an altogether morbid degree ; wherever the fault may lie—with himself, with his college, with his theology— no one who reads these pages to-day could claim that he was taught to see life steadily and to see it whole. The seminary life can be as unhealthy as the monastic, and we are frequently reminded of the records of life in monastic communities by the diary of this Baptist student. Again and again he blames himself for having a good appetite for his meals, in such terms as these: " From 1½ till 2. Spent at Dinner: very greedy and after the Creatures. My rapacious appetite may well make me blush, and O ! what Darkness, Atheism, Ignorance, Unbelief, Enmity, Madness, Distraction and folly, Selfishness and Uncharitableness Dwells within me in every Power of my Nature." (Feb. 15, 1744-45.) This morbidity was evidently reflected in his outward behaviour, for he records (Feb. 4, 1744-45): " Evg. at Supper. *Mrs. Heritage and Mrs. Evans gave me a hint about my strange, Stiff, unmannerly Conduct towards Mrs. Ev., and towards many of our Friends, etc. when I pass by them."* On the other hand, this shy and awkward youth from the Gloucestershire farm was apt to let himself go too much when it came to extempore prayer. Two days before this incident he writes: "Mr. Foskett gave me a hint to Day about expressions in Prayer—not to be too rash." The hint from the ladies evidently bore some fruit, for two days later we find the note, " God helping, Provide better for Table Conversation ". Later (April 19, 1745) we find the resolution carried out: " This day at Dinner happily fell into a Strain of Telling remarkable Stories and Events—O ! that I may be assisted to provide suitable, seasonable, pleasant, Profitable and usefull Entertainment this way, whenever I've an opportunity." He developed the methods of the expert *raconteur,* for farther on we read (May 13th): " The afternoon spent in finishing the Abstract, and in Collecting some little stories ; The evening after Supper spent in Reading and telling Little Stories." This facility in anecdote

---

[1] This is quoted by Newman, *op. cit.,* pp. 29, 30.

became quite a characteristic in the after-days, as his school-assistant, William Newman, records; one way of rewarding good conduct in the school was to fetch Mr. Ryland to tell a story. This is rather an interesting example of the way in which the consciousness of a defect may actually lead to the acquirement of a marked characteristic—when there is sufficient resolution. In Ryland's case that quality of resolution comes out most notably in what is known as the Bristol vow, which has often been quoted, first, I think, in the funeral sermon over John Collett Ryland preached by John Rippon in 1792 (p. 41). The original is written in large characters on a piece of worn and folded paper which has been pasted into the diary:—

June 25. Ev. 10—1744. Aet. 20 yrs 8 Months 2 Days.
If there's ever a God in Heaven or Earth, I Vow protest and Swear in God's Strength—or that Gods permitting Me, I'll find him out and I'll know whether he loves or hates me or I'll Dye and perish Soul & Body in the Pursuit & Search.
Witness   Jno. Coll. Ryland

Nobody but a thoroughgoing Calvinist, face to face with the definite issues of a limited Election and an alternative Reprobation, the love or the hate of God, could state the issue quite like that, and nobody but one of Ryland's eager, passionate, extravagant temperament could so fling himself into the search for God and ultimate truth. Yet the words do not rise to the noble height of that somewhat similar cry of Bunyan's, as he faced the prospect of death: "If God doth not come in, thought I, I will leap off the ladder, even blindfold into eternity, sink or swim, come heaven come hell. Lord Jesus, if thou wilt catch me, do; if not, I will venture for thy name." John Collett Ryland's strong Calvinism was proof even against Charles Wesley's eloquence. Under date April 2, 1745, we read:—

After meeting was over We went to hear Mr. Cha: Westley at the Room; he was preaching or expounding John 5, 1 to 14 verse, on Our Lord's healing the Impotent Man, and charging him to sin no more, Lest a worse thing should befall him. Mr. Cha. Westley positively asserted falling from Grace, in the strongest Terms. I thank the Lord I thought at yt Time on Mr. E. Coles Discourse on Final Perseverance, also coming home, and at Prayer and at

Supper, with an unusual Impression, and it seem's to Strengthen, Comfort and enlarge My heart in Thankfulness and Praise.

So the terrible heresy of Charles Wesley did him some service after all—by confirming him in his previous belief.

We get a glimpse of this student's meditations (quite unconsciously touched with humour):—

June 22d. Ev. 10. Laus Deo. I fell into a Beautifull Scheme of Reasoning as I sat Musing wth my head down and my eyes shut—Thus—How comes Man to be endow'd with those Various powers and properties wch I find in myself, viz.

I can cast my Eyes all around me in ye Day Light and see Coulers, Shapes, Motions. I can Look up and See the Sun with his cheering Rays in ye Daytime & ye Moon and Stars by Night, ye Sky, ye Clouds, etc.

Down upon this Terraqueous Globe I can see such a Sort of Beings as Myself, and also Females wch are some of them Sweet & Lovely Creatures, but who gave them & us of ye Male Sex our Existance ; Did We our Selves? No ; then we must be and not at the Same time.

Did our parents? No ; For wheres the Father or ye Mother yt will or Can Say that they—either Father and Mother Fashion'd their Sons or yr Daughters in ye womb. They neither of them knew wch Sex ye Child would be or wt. Shape, whether Strait or Crooked, Wise or Foolish, Ugly or Handsome.

To this interesting meditation there is appended the word " Unfinish'd ", and in that word much virtue lies. Elizabeth Frith, of Warwick, was probably not yet within his horizon.

No one could say, after reading this diary, that John Collett Ryland faced his life-work with a mean and impoverished conception of its intellectual demands. He drew up a most ambitious programme for a year's work at college.[1] It must be here sufficient to give another and briefer summary of his aims (June 7, 1744. M. 6¼):—

I beg if ever the most High God sends me forth into the Publick Work of the Ministry, I may go well Qualified, if it please his gracious Majesty to give me Large and Exact Skill in 5 Languages, and Large Skill and Knowledge of about 20 Arts and Sciences, Including that one which is above them all, viz. DIVINITY—this, this is what I would Excell in, Both in the Theory and Practice of Every Branch from the Greatest to the Least.

[1] Reproduced in the *Baptist Quarterly* for April, 1925.

He shows a very laudable ambition that he and his fellow-students may beat the college record, and "excell all the young Students that have ever been before us" (July 8, 1744). Already he cherishes thoughts of authorship, which he was destined to carry out almost too copiously. "N.B. Make a Little Greek and a Little Hebrew Gramr., if ever thou livest to have Skill enough" (July 10th). It is good to read that on going to bed on July 12th he "long'd to know more of the Hebrew Tongue". His methods of study are good, and his self-made "Rules for Daily Examination" might be profitably employed by the student of to-day:—

1. Wt New Words have I gain'd in the Eng. French, Latin or Hebrew Languages or in any Part of Grammar in those Tongues.
2. Wt. New Ideas in the Human Sciences. Especially Rhetoric, Logic, Ontology, History, Chronology, Geography or Natural Philosophy.
3. Wt. New Words or Ideas in evr'y Book that I have Read this Day, whether Human or Divine Subject.
4. Wt. Have I gain'd in Divinity either in ye Theory or Practice Part, in Keach, in Vincent, in Confession of Faith, in Dr. Ridgley's Body of Divinity, but more Especially wt have I gain'd from the Holy Scriptures Old or New Testaments.
And be sure Examine ev'ry night at Least ; how much of Self has been in all thy Thoughts, words and works that Day, whether Natural, Sinfull, or Righteous Conduct (July 10, 1744).

He forms the excellent purpose of committing to memory select portions of the Bible, and tests himself by making himself repeat such passages whilst kneeling on his bed (July 3rd and 4th). He also constantly analyses the books he reads, and a good part of the diary is filled with such analyses. It may be of interest to quote in full a sample day from the diary, which shows him as an "introvert" and not an "extrovert" like Pepys, who was so full of zest for things without:—

Feb. 1. Friday. 1744-5. M. 6½ awoke. M. 7 arose, very dead, dark, hard and miserable. O! I am for ever Miserable, if Christ dont appear in rich Mercy to me. Pray'd & yn [then] read Genesis I.—at 7½ was call'd down to Breakfast & Prayer till 8¾ ; then came up Stairs ; from 9 to 11 engag'd as usual ; from 11 to 1, wth Mr. Foskett ; from 1 till near 2 at Dinner ; my heart too

much engag'd in the Creatures, etc. ; from 2 to 4½, Putting my
Papers & Books in good order ; very dark & dull all the time,
tho' some Sorrow at bottom for my past sins and follies and
present deadness & stupidity ; from 4½ down by the Fire, reading
over my Quotidianas from June 16 to Dec. 31, 1744. Some things
in them worth another Review—at 5 Begun Mr. John Reynold's
Confirming Catechism—5th. edit. 12mo. 1734. About 6, Began
his Book Entituled Enquiries concerning the State and Oeconomy
of the Angelical Worlds.—8vo. 1723. A curious Treatise.—at 7
Began & took a Cursory View of it thro'out Mr. John Hurrion's
Scripture Doctrine of the Holy Spirit, in 16 Sermons. 8vo. 1734.
A Most Excellent & Glorious Performance. at 8 engaged wth our
Family in Usual Service—and then till near 11, reading Mr.
Hurrion's aforesaid noble Treatise.—O! for a Heart to embrace
this glorious Lord God the Spirit in all his Operations. ev. 11—
up Stairs. Read as follows (viz) Promises To the Fatherless and
Widow, pag. 45—Of the Means of Grace, page 77 to 81. To
Faithful Servants.—Sect. 4. 202—Ps. I. Matth. 1—I thank the
Lord I hope I had a little more Light to night. I hope God the
Spirit has not quite forsook me—went to bed more Comfortable
and Lively than for some time past—near 12 oClock.

It will be seen that the diligent student of those days got
through an enormous amount of reading, including much more
study of " theology " in the narrower sense than is done by
the average student of to-day. If we ask how he found time
for it, the answer lies in the story of such a day as we have
just had. He concentrated on the one thing and had few
distractions. We can count on the fingers of one hand the
references to public events in the diary before us. There is no
reference to social and philanthropic activities such as take
no small part of the time and energy of a Christian man
to-day. The sight of the " outsiders " in the streets of Bristol
does not stir this young Calvinist to evangelistic or missionary
ardour towards *them* ; he writes: " When out in Town, saw
many poor objects—N.B.—God assisting Improve by them—
and Stir up others—and constantly " (Mar. 30, 1745) ; or
again: " N.B. this morning *going to Mr. Day I had such a
sense of Distinguishing Goodness of God to me—above the
100ds & 1000s yt Walk about ye Streets that it exceeded my
Belief. My Soul was almost overwhelmed at the Sense of it* "
(May 8, 1745). There we have the unhappy side of the
doctrine of predestination as held in the earlier part of the
eighteenth century before the Evangelical Revival. We cannot forget that it is John Collett Ryland who opposed young

Carey's missionary enthusiasm so long after these Bristol days.[1] Ryland was an enthusiast himself, but then enthusiasts about different things always find it hard to understand each other. The truth is that the sharp cleavage between the Church and the world which is so well illustrated in this diary, and characterizes the religious life of the time, meant narrowness of judgment as well as concentration of aim. The faults that Protestants can see in Catholic asceticism have belonged often enough to Puritanism, which is indeed Protestant asceticism.

It would take us too far to trace the subsequent life and work of this young Bristol student, in his double capacity of Baptist minister and schoolmaster. The same characteristics remained, and the promise of his gifts and ardour was amply fulfilled. It must be sufficient to recall two passages to illustrate this. One is an account of the education of his son, John Ryland, who succeeded him as the minister of College Lane, Northampton, and afterwards became the Principal of Bristol Baptist College: —

John is now eleven years and seven months old ; he has read Genesis in Hebrew five times through ; he read through the Greek Testament before nine years old. He can read Horace and Virgil. He has read through Telemachus in French! He has read through Pope's Homer, in eleven volumes ; read Dryden's Virgil, in three volumes. He has read Rollin's ancient history, ten volumes 8vo. And he knows the Pagan mythology surprisingly. (August 28, 1764, as quoted in the funeral sermon by Rippon, p. 43.)

There is more than paternal pride in those words ; there is the sense that he is giving to his boy that which he was once so eager to win for himself.

Better known is the story told by Robert Hall of his being taken by his father as a little boy to Mr. Ryland's school at Northampton. It was the time of the American War of Independence, and Mr. Ryland sided with the Americans against his own Government. Finally Mr. Ryland burst out characteristically with the declaration that if he were General Washington he would call for his officers and have them all bled into a punch-bowl, himself the first, and then all should dip their swords into the bowl, and solemnly swear never to

[1] See Chapter V, p. 113.

sheathe those swords whilst an English soldier remained in America. "Only conceive, Sir," said Robert Hall in telling the story, "my situation ; a poor little boy, that had never been out of his mother's chimney corner before, Sir, sitting by these two old gentlemen, and hearing this conversation about blood. Sir, I trembled at the idea of being left with such a bloody-minded master. Why, Sir, I began to think he would no more mind bleeding me, after my father was gone, than he would killing a fly. I quite expected to be bled, Sir "[1] There we have Ryland of "the Bristol vow", still eager, passionate, extravagant, still young at heart in his enthusiasm. Whilst I do not attach much importance to "last words ", I think that there is something appropriate in the last words of John Collett Ryland,[2] "I'll go and try."

(8) A BAPTIST PREACHER (ROBERT HALL)

The "new boy" at Mr. Ryland's school was destined to become one of the foremost preachers of his time. Backward and weakly at first, he had learnt his letters in his nurse's arms from the gravestones of a burial-ground ; later on this had been his study, whither he carried in his pinafore his little library, to lie amongst the long grass and quench his passionate thirst for knowledge. At nine he had read and re-read with keen interest Jonathan Edwards on the *Affections* and the *Will,* together with Butler's *Analogy*. After his school-days in Northampton he went, like his teacher, to the Bristol Academy as a scholar, helped by the benefaction of Dr. James Ward, and from Bristol to King's College, Aberdeen (1781-85), where (Sir) James Mackintosh was his inseparable student companion. He held pastorates at Bristol, Cambridge, Leicester, and again Bristol, where he died in 1831.

Here is the impressive description of his oratory by one of his Cambridge hearers who became his biographer:—

From the commencement of his discourse an almost breathless silence prevailed, deeply impressive and solemnizing from its singular intenseness. Not a sound was heard but that of the preacher's voice—scarcely an eye but was fixed upon him—not

[1] John Greene, *Reminiscences of the Rev. Robert Hall* (1832), pp. 93, 94.
[2] Newman, *op. cit.*, p. 22.

E

a countenance that he did not watch, and read, and interpret, as he surveyed them again and again with his rapid, ever-excursive glance. As he advanced and increased in animation, five or six of the auditors would be seen to rise and lean forward over the front of their pews, still keeping their eyes upon him. Some new or striking sentiment or expression would, in a few minutes, cause others to rise in like manner ; shortly afterwards still more, and so on, until, long before the close of the sermon, it often happened that a considerable portion of the congregation were seen standing —every eye directed to the preacher, yet now and then for a moment glancing from one to the other, thus transmitting and reciprocating thought and feeling:—Mr. Hall himself, though manifestly absorbed in his subject, conscious of the whole, receiving new animation from what he thus witnessed, reflecting it back upon those who were already alive to the inspiration, until all that were susceptible of thought and emotion seemed wound up to the utmost limit of elevation *on earth,*—when he would close, and they reluctantly and slowly resume their seats.[1]

It is difficult, if not impossible, to recapture anything of this experience by reading the six solid volumes of Hall's collected *Works*. Their eloquence is stately and dignified, the vocabulary copious and well chosen, the intellectual mastery of the subjects treated very marked. But the style is that of a bygone day, and is too measured and elaborate for our modern taste, nor is the originality of thought sufficient to claim a permanent place in theological literature. To read the sermons is to be made conscious of the changing fashions of oratory and its inevitable dependence on the mental world and outlook of the hearers. Moreover, we must admit the criticism made even by his contemporary fellow-Baptist, John Foster, in a lengthy and searching characterization of Hall's preaching—that it was wanting in individualization, the direct and particular application to life, and dealt with man rather than with men.[2] We miss that power to see and represent the universal in the concrete particular which may make an ordinary sentiment memorable, and, in the copious wealth of Bunyan's imagination, creates literature. Yet Hall was a great figure of his day, a recognized genius as an

---

[1] *Memoir of Robert Hall*, by Olinthus Gregory, prefixed to vol. vi of Hall's *Works*. The biographical details of this study are drawn from the memoir ; cf. also the brief sketches in the *Encyclopaedia Britannica* and the *Dictionary of National Biography*.

[2] This follows Gregory's Memoir in vol. vi of Hall's *Works*, pp. 143-88.

orator, described by an editor of his time as "perhaps the most distinguished ornament of the Calvinistic dissenters".[1] An Anglican contemporary, Dr. Parr, even compared him with Jeremy Taylor, as sharing "the eloquence of an orator, the fancy of a poet, the acuteness of a schoolman, the profoundness of a philosopher, and the piety of a saint".[2] His popularity is witnessed by the fact that the sermon on the death of the Princess Charlotte went into sixteen editions of a thousand copies each. His *Apology for the Freedom of the Press and for General Liberty* is quite in the Baptist tradition and attracted much attention ; its denunciation of Pitt, beginning "A veteran in frauds while in the bloom of youth", leaves nothing to be desired in vigour.[3] Hall was prominent in a controversy within his own denomination as to the terms of communion with those who had not been baptized on profession of faith, his antagonist being Joseph Kinghorn, of Norwich. His own catholicity of outlook is seen in the protest against organizing a Church with a specific view to the propagation of some particular truth, which is, as he rightly says, a perversion of the original end and design of Christian societies. The result would be disastrous to truth : —

Every denomination will exhibit some portion of it, in a distorted and mutilated form ; none will be in possession of the whole, and the result will be something like the confusion of Babel, where every man spoke in a separate dialect. As the beauty of truth consists chiefly in the harmony and proportion of its several parts, it is as impossible to display it to advantage in fragments, as to give a just idea of a noble and majestic structure, by exhibiting a single brick.[4]

There is, however, something more memorable than Robert Hall's oratory, and that is his undaunted courage and resolute character, in spite of extreme suffering. From early childhood to the very end he suffered more or less acute pain, which the post-mortem proved to be renal calculus. The surgeon who performed it writes : "Probably no man ever went through more physical suffering than Mr. Hall ; he is a fine example of the triumph of the higher powers of mind exalted by religion, over the infirmities of the body".[5] To

---

[1] *Op. cit.*, vi, p. 132. [2] *Op. cit.*, p. 131. [3] *Op. cit.*, iii, p. 65.
[4] *Op. cit.*, ii, pp. 475, 476.   [5] *Op. Cit.*, vi, p. 134.

the strain of this agony was doubtless due the mental breakdown of 1804 and 1805. A letter of April 11, 1805,[1] reflects
the deep effect which this humiliation had upon him ; it is
addressed to John Fawcett, one of the Baptist leaders in
Yorkshire :—

I have undergone the severest affliction that ever befel me.
The Lord has shewn me terrible things in righteousness. It has
graciously pleased him, however, to restore my captivity, and to
recover me to the perfect exercise of my reason. Assist me, my
dear Sir, to magnify the name of the Lord. May a sense of the
goodness of God be indelibly imprinted on my mind. Bless the
Lord, O my soul, and all that is within, bless his holy name. I
am a monument of astonishing meɪcy. May the goodness of God
lead me to repentance and stimulate me to obedience.

It is significant of the man's sincerity that in the increasing
paroxysms of pain towards the end his mind dwelt on the
sufferings of Christ. He remarked to his doctor that " a con-
templation of the sufferings of Christ was the best antidote
against impatience under any troubles we might experience ;
and recommended me to reflect much on this subject when in
pain or distress, or in expectation of death ".[2]

Readers of Lord Lytton's novel, *The Caxtons,* may recall
the fine tribute there paid to Robert Hall by a soldier who has
read the memoir :—

What I have seen in this book is courage. Here is a poor
creature rolling on the carpet with agony ; from childhood to
death tortured by a mysterious incurable malady—a malady that
is described as " an internal apparatus of torture " ; and who
does, by his heroism, more than *bear* it—he puts it out of his
power to affect him ; and though (here is the passage) " his
appointment by day and by night was incessant pain, yet high
enjoyment was, notwithstanding, the law of his existence."
Robert Hall reads me a lesson—me, an old soldier who thought
myself above taking lessons—in courage, at least.—(Part ix,
chap. vi.)

[1] The manuscript is in the Angus Library of Regent's Park College.
[2] J. M. Chandler, *Authentic Account of the Last Illness and Death
of Robert Hall,* p. 28.

BELIEVERS' BAPTISM AND THE EMPHASIS
ON INDIVIDUAL EXPERIENCE

A RELIGIOUS community is never a merely logical or theoretical construction, based on and fully explained by a paper constitution. Like a State or any other form of continuous social life it is shaped on the anvil of history by repeated blows and varying temperatures, so that its distinctive nature emerges but slowly as the product of many factors. Thus the *emphasis* on believers' baptism which distinguishes Baptists is from one point of view an accident of history for which they are not responsible. It is due to the simple fact that others have lost a feature of New Testament Christianity which Baptists have kept. In this particular respect they are a projecting " shelf " on the rock of the Church, *because the other strata have " weathered "*.

(1) The Meaning and Justification of Believers' Baptism

It is neither possible nor necessary to enter on a detailed examination [1] of the New Testament references to baptism in order to show that this was (a) the baptism of believers, (b) by immersion. So far as historical exegesis goes, these two points are usually conceded by competent scholars, as, for example, by Sanday and Headlam in their paraphrase of Rom. vi. 4 : —

When we descended into the baptismal water, that meant that we died with Christ—to sin. When the water closed over our heads, that meant that we lay buried with Him, in proof that our death to sin, like His death. was real. But this carries with it the third step in the process. As Christ was raised.from among the dead by a majestic exercise of Divine Power, so we also must from henceforth conduct ourselves as men in whom has been implanted a new principle of life.—(*International Critical Commentary*, p. 154.)

[1] A fuller statement of this and the following paragraphs will be found in my *Baptist Principles* (Kingsgate Press, 1925), from which I have quoted some sentences in what follows.

Believers' Baptism seems to have been an invariable accompaniment, if not a definite sign, of entry into the Christian society.

It may, indeed, be argued that what was natural or, inevitable for the first Christian missions ought not to be prescriptive for a Christian community in which children are brought into relation with the Gospel from their earliest days —or that the silence of the New Testament about the baptism of infants leaves us free to infer and to practise it—or that the difference of East and West, the ancient and modern world, warrants us in modifying the practice or dropping it altogether. But no one has the right to argue that the baptism of the *New Testament* is less than the immersion of intelligent persons, as the expressive accompaniment of their entrance into a new life of moral and spiritual relationship to God in Christ. It may further be argued that it is more than this, since the symbol in the ancient world usually carried an *effective* as well as a declaratory or expressive meaning, and to this point we shall return in the closing chapter. Christian baptism in the New Testament certainly means four great things, in the sense that these are its normal accompaniments. It implies a cleansing from sin ; it is associated with the gift of the Holy Spirit ; it is administered to believers and no others; and for Paul, at any rate, it meant an experiential union with Christ in His redeeming acts, deeper in meaning than words can express. [1]

We must distinguish quite definitely the *subject* of baptism (i.e. the believer) and the *mode* of baptism (i.e. immersion), for there can be no comparison of their importance for those who realize what New Testament faith means and are not mere literalists. The ancient mode may be defended on various grounds, especially that of its expressive character and its impressive influence ; but if this were all, or even the chief point, there would be absolutely no justification for the existence of the Baptists. Nothing shows more clearly a failure to understand the faith of the Baptists than the frequent idea that they are a peculiar sect which insists on baptizing " adults " by immersion. They baptize not " adults ", but " believers " on profession of their personal faith in Christ, and this is their primary distinction, though it has a very

---

[1] E.g. Acts xxii. 16, x. 47, ii. 38 ; Rom. vi. 4.

important bearing on the constitution of the Church into which such believers enter by their faith; as a quite subsidiary point, they practise the most ancient form of baptism,[1] because they find this the most eloquent expression of the essentials of that faith—the death and resurrection of their Lord. As a matter of fact, it may be repeated that neither of the two kinds of Baptists, the "General" and the "Particular", at first practised immersion, so that the mode was historically, as well as logically, an afterthought.

We cannot here follow the historical development by which the Church gradually came to substitute the baptism of infants for that of believers.[2] A sentence by a quite impartial historian of dogma accurately sums up the facts: "Infant baptism, first demonstrable in Irenæus, still contested by Tertullian, was for Origen an apostolic custom".[3] Even so, it was not until the fifth century that infant baptism became a general practice.[4] That practice influenced and was influenced by many other developments of the life and thought of the Church which evangelical Christians deplore. In contesting it, Baptists are testifying against much more than an isolated and relatively unimportant custom ; they are testifying against the whole complex of ideas of which it was a symbol, out of which grew the conception of the Church as primarily a great sacramental institution, administered by a body of officials vested with spiritual powers in which ordinary Christians could not share. We cannot, indeed, trace such testimony in the early centuries, and have therefore no right to infer its existence, but we do find believers' baptism practised among the Paulicians of the East about A.D.

[1] As is recognised in the rubric of the Anglican service, which prescribes immersion as the proper form of baptism, unless the child is certified to be weak. An amusing instance of confusion between the mode and the subject is recorded in connection with H. B. Swete. As a curate, he publicly baptized an infant by immersion. But this unheard-of act created a commotion in the parish, which led the old parish clerk to say, with grave shaking of the head: "Mr. Henry ought never to have done such a thing ; that were believers' baptism" (*Henry Barclay Swete*, p. 27).

[2] See *Baptist Principles*, chap. ii: "The Abandonment of Believers' Baptism ".

[3] Loofs, *Dogmengeschichte*, ed. 4, p. 212.

[4] On the other hand, the substitution of other *modes* of baptism for immersion is shown by the *Didache* to have begun at least as early as the first part of the second century, though immersion is there regarded as the preferable mode.

800, and amongst the Petrobrusians of the West in the twelfth century.[1]   The practice also gave a name to the great "Anabaptist" movement of the sixteenth century, which extended over Europe, though here it was allied with a number of ideas and practices which have nothing to do with the principle which believers' baptism represents.[2]

It may be freely recognized that infant baptism, *considered apart from its historical context,* is a harmless and even useful rite, at least in *some* of its modern adaptations.   In the significantly bare form of the *Book of Congregational Worship* the essential things are a promise by those who present the child that he shall be brought up in the nurture and admonition of the Lord, and a declaration of trust by the minister that " hereafter he shall not be ashamed to confess the faith of Christ ".   That is dedication at its simplest, and no explanation is offered of its connection with baptism, except for words borrowed from the Anglican liturgy, though hardly in the same meaning: " We receive this child into the congregation of Christ's flock."   The same words appear in the Wesleyan order, with the addition " that he may be instructed and trained in the doctrines, privileges and duties of the Christian religion ".   The prayers for a change in the child's nature *follow* instead of preceding the act of baptism, and the emphasis falls on the covenant of the parents to be subsequently realized in the personal covenant to be made by the child when he comes to responsible years.   The Presbyterian order emphasizes the doctrine that baptism is a sign and seal of the covenant of grace, which includes children as well as parents.   Baptism is a divine pledge that God will fulfil His part in giving grace.   All these types of teaching may be regarded as legitimate expressions of evangelical Protestantism, apart from their connection with a rite which belongs to believers only, according to the New Testament.   The Anglican service takes us into a different realm, for it prays *before* the act of baptism, " sanctify this water to the mystical washing away of sin ", and declares *after* the act that " this child is regenerate and grafted into the body of Christ's Church ".   The emphasis here falls on the actual activity of divine grace in water-baptism, not on the pledge of future activity.   The underlying doctrine that baptism cleanses the

[1] *Baptist Principles*, pp. 53 ff., 57 ff.
[2] *Op. cit.*, pp. 59-64 ; cf. pp. 11, 12, of the present book.

child from the guilt of original sin (i.e. the sin involved in his descent from Adam), finds fullest expression in the canons of the Council of Trent, which frankly make baptism necessary to salvation. [1]

The common element in all these interpretations of baptism is the necessary *passivity* of the infant baptized. Whether baptism be called dedication, or covenanting by 'parents, or the sealing of a divine covenant, or an actual regeneration, it is throughout something done to, nothing done by, the baptized. So far as he is concerned, all of them are non-moral acts, though the act of the parents or sponsors is properly moral. The Baptist position is not simply a new phase of this succession of interpretations ; it stands outside of them all as *the only baptism which is strictly and primarily an ethical act on the part of the baptized.* As such, it is the only type of baptism which is properly consistent with the logic of " Separatism " and the whole idea of a separated Church of believers. John Smyth, the first Baptist, saw this point when he said that " the Separation must either go back to England (i.e. the Anglican Church) or go forward to true baptism ". A pædobaptist Separatist is always in unstable equilibrium, so far as this point is concerned. This explains why baptism falls into a relatively insignificant place, or drops out altogether, as it frequently does, amongst Congregationalists. The Baptist stands or falls by his conception of what the Church is ; his plea for believers' baptism becomes a mere archæological idiosyncrasy, if it be not the expression of the fundamental constitution of the Church. We become members of the living Body of Christ by being consciously and voluntarily baptized in the Spirit of Christ—a baptism to which witness is borne by the evidence of moral purpose and character as the fruit of the Spirit.

But loyalty to the past is never an adequate ground for present usage, though many an abuse still stands upon it—to form the " slum property " of history. When a symbol ceases to have real and valid meaning, its retention can work nothing but mischief, such as a superstitious reliance on the mysterious as such. Our concern should be whether the

[1] At the other extreme, we find the total rejection of water-baptism by the Quakers ; their attitude is that, as Robert Barclay says, " we do always prefer the power to the form, the substance to the shadow ", and " we find not anything called the pledge and seal of our inheritance, but the Spirit of God ".

symbol in itself and in its usage admits of such interpretation as would justify its continued use. What is the intrinsic worth of believers' baptism by immersion, apart from any question of loyalty to the original form and significance of the rite? What is there in this ceremony that makes it worth while to retain it, in terms of present moral and spiritual value? We may distinguish (1) its psychological value, (2) its emphasis on individual conversion, (3) its confessional value as the dramatic and efficient substitute for a verbal confession of faith.

Modern psychology has thrown into brilliant relief the importance of *acts* as influencing thoughts. "Actions speak louder than words." There must be some definite act to register and make memorable the experience of repentance and faith if they are not to become increasingly obscure and inoperative in retrospect. We live largely by memory, but memory depends upon landmarks. Hence the New Testament, with intuitive instinct, anticipates our psychology, and says: "With the heart man believeth unto righteousness ; and with the mouth confession is made unto salvation." [1] Doubtless Paul is here referring to the confession of faith made in and with baptism. Now the baptism of believers asserts more emphatically than any words can do that which the believer also confessed at his baptism in words, viz. the repentance and faith, the conversion from darkness to light which is one half—the human half—of the meaning of baptism. It should be remembered that the apostle appeals again and again to the baptism of believers, especially in the sixth chapter of Romans, as the foundation of his moral or religious exhortations. "You know what you were then," he virtually says; "see what you ought to be now." Baptists alone in the Universal Church can make such an appeal to baptism, for to all other Churches baptism predominantly means something which can never be remembered by the infant. No really moral appeal to the grown man can be based on that which others did to him as an unconscious infant.

(2) THE IMPORTANCE OF CONVERSION

The emphasis of believers' baptism on individual conversion is unmistakable. "Believers'" baptism does by contrast with the practice of other Churches emphasize a particular

[1] Rom. x. 10.

aspect of faith, viz. its individuality, its personal initiative, its consequent variety. By contrast—for if all Christian Churches had retained baptism in the Baptist way, the *distinctive* emphasis now characterizing Baptists would be lost (cf. p. 69). As it is, the Baptists are left to emphasize in a unique, though conservative, manner the individuality of Christian experience—a real truth, though by no means the whole truth. The one-sidedness of this emphasis (for which they are not wholly to blame) has had interesting results for their history and general development. It has inevitably accentuated the qualities of initiative and individuality. Baptists tend to be individualists in both thought and action. They claim liberty of thought for themselves, and on the whole have been ready to give it to others ; they may co-operate amongst themselves for practical ends, but always with a reserve of individual freedom, and usually with a reluctance to delegate executive authority. We shall see that both the strength and the weakness of the Baptists may be traced to this emphasis on the individuality of their experience of God in Christ.

This emphasis on individuality may be specially seen in the place given to " conversion ". Wherever conversion is taken seriously (as it must be when it is real), it is a lonely, because a unique, experience. John Bunyan (who was a Baptist, though of the broader type) has sometimes been foolishly blamed for the " selfish individualism " of his pilgrim, who started on his spiritual journey without wife and children. But it could hardly be otherwise. Within the same family group each member lives his own life, known or unknown to the rest. The modern " social emphasis ", however laudable and necessary in itself, has tended to obscure the primary foundation of religion in the individual experience. A distinguished contemporary philosopher usefully and impressively reminds us that " religion is what the individual does with his solitariness ". . . . " The great religious conceptions which haunt the imaginations of civilized mankind are scenes of solitariness: Prometheus chained to his rock, Mahomet brooding in the desert, the meditations of the Buddha, the solitary Man on the Cross—it belongs to the depth of the religious spirit to have felt itself forsaken, even by God." [1] It may be admitted, indeed it must often be urged, that personality is a

[1] Whitehead, *Religion in the Making*, pp. 47 and 19, 20.

much bigger thing than individuality, yet it certainly includes it. When we discover God, and respond to that discovery with any reality, it must be each for himself, however true it be that Christian conversion is always the discovery of others in God, others whose life is ours, for Christ's sake, others for whom we have become responsible. It is also true that conversion is a social outcome as well as a social inlet—that it is shaped and moulded by a thousand subtle influences and traditions passed on by the surrounding group, and that it is often directly linked with the adolescent stirrings of body and mind towards union with others. But all these things, to which the psychology of religion has devoted so much recent attention, are like the political and social and economic factors of the Reformation—they depend for their functioning on the vital spark of a personal, and therefore individual, experience of God.

It is not open to any well-informed man of to-day to treat conversion as an antiquated survival, an artificial "technique" of evangelicalism. The particular contents of any experience of conversion may be antiquated enough, for centuries of development may separate two men who walk along the street together. Again, it is easy enough to stimulate certain formal reactions by mass-suggestion and reiteration. But the comparative study of religion, in freeing us from the provincialism of ignorance about these things, has also shown us how universal and how significant in religion the experience of conversion is. [1] We must, of course, put aside the idea that conversion necessarily means a startling and dramatic experience. The favourite comparison in the Bible is with the dawn of light. But though there may be scenes in which "the dawn comes up like thunder out of China 'crost the bay", the normal dawn is gradual and almost imperceptible in approach, even if there will always be some significant moment at which the man could say, "Whereas I was blind, now I see". That awakening of human personality to the presence and power of the divine, however achieved, is of the greatest significance and importance. In this large sense of the term there must always be conversion in Christian experience, and the baptism of believers, marking (amongst other things) this crucial readjustment, is emphasizing that which deserves to be emphasized. Those who have assigned another meaning to

[1] See *Conversion, Christian and Non-Christian*, by A. C. Underwood.

baptism, yet agree as to the significance of conversion, sometimes become conscious of the lack of any significant expression of it in the institutions of their Church. They find that there is a real difficulty in getting one who is brought under Christian influence to register his experience through some definite and memorable act from which to make his new start. Unless this is done in some way or other the experience is apt to fade away. But where can we find a more impressive and memorable register of the birth of a new purpose than that which is provided by believers' baptism?

On the other hand, Baptists ought frankly to admit the tendencies of this strong emphasis on the act of decision. Just because believers' baptism has for them this primary significance, and is a unique act, expressing a unique experience, all that went before and all that comes after may easily become subordinate and secondary to a degree that is perilous. The normal convert is one who has grown up under the influence of the Christian home, the Sunday-school, and the services of the Church. Only where such influence is efficiently brought to bear on the growing life is the responsibility of the Church faithfully discharged. Many Baptists are conscious of a danger here, and the frequent use of the " Cradle Roll " in connection with the Sunday-school, and the increasing introduction of " Dedication Services " in connection with the Church, show them moving towards the fuller recognition of this responsibility. The danger subsequent to the impressive act of believers' baptism is that nothing, not even the Communion Service as usually conducted in Baptist Churches, seems comparable with it, and the baptized believer may easily come to think that the rest of his Christian life may be taken more or less for granted. Of course, ministers and teachers are always urging the contrary, and pointing out that believers' baptism is a beginning rather than an end, but the very frequency of their warnings shows that the peril exists.

(3) THE CONFESSIONAL VALUE OF BELIEVERS' BAPTISM

The confessional value of believers' baptism *by immersion* is that it becomes an " acted parable " (like the broken bread and the poured-out wine of the Communion Service) of the Lord's death, burial, and resurrection, which are the cardinal verities of evangelical faith and the historical basis of Christianity. The expressive acts by which the believer identified himself with Christ were accompanied, apparently, by the oral utterance of a confession of faith in its simplest form, viz. " Jesus is Lord ", [1] and baptism was into the name of the Lord Jesus. [2] Towards the close of the New Testament period this was expanded into the formula of baptism into the name of the Father, and of the Son, and of the Holy Spirit.[3] Later still, as is generally agreed, this simple confession was further enlarged into the Apostles' Creed (the baptismal confession of Rome) in the West and the Nicene Creed (the expanded form of the baptismal confession of Cæsarea) in the East. So far as the general substance and aim of these historic creeds are concerned, it may safely be asserted that Baptists are as loyal to them as are any of the evangelical Churches. Yet it is equally true that Baptists hold a very detached position in regard to creeds and formal confessions of faith *as such*. The only approach towards a creed held in common by Baptists[4] in this country is the " Declaration of Principle " in the Constitution of the Baptist Union of Great Britain and Ireland, which reads as follows :—

The basis of this Union is :

1. That our Lord and Saviour Jesus Christ, God manifest in the flesh, is the sole and absolute authority in all matters pertaining to faith and practice, as revealed in the Holy Scriptures, and that each Church has liberty, under the guidance of the Holy Spirit, to interpret and administer His Laws.

2. That Christian Baptism is the immersion in water into the Name of the Father, the Son, and the Holy Ghost, of those who have professed repentance towards God and faith in our Lord Jesus Christ who " died for our sins according to the Scriptures ; was buried, and rose again the third day ".

3. That it is the duty of every disciple to bear personal witness to the Gospel of Jesus Christ, and to take part in the evangelization of the world.

The student of creeds and confessions of faith will recognize that this is not a creed proper, as it makes no attempt to analyse and define the exact content of the Christian faith, but, as its heading says, a " Declaration of Principle ", expressing, as well as a brief statement can, the common ground of union on which the individuality of Baptist faith is left free to work itself out. The first clause posits personal

---

[1] Rom. x. 9 ; cf. 1 Cor. xii. 3.   [2] Acts viii. 16, xix. 5.
[3] Matt. xxviii. 19.
[4] Excluding "Statements of Faith" made by Free Churchmen in common.

loyalty to Jesus Christ as God manifest in the flesh for man's salvation. This, of course, excludes a "Unitarian" or "humanitarian" view of the Person of Jesus Christ. His authority over each believer is based on the divine character of His personality. But there is no attempt and no intention to frame a particular Christology, and each believer is purposely left free to interpret both the authority and its theological basis "as revealed in the Holy Scriptures", whilst each group of believers forming a Church of Christ is left free, within its corporate loyalty to Christ, to govern itself.

This may seem to afford no guarantee of what is usually known as an "evangelical" faith, for many heresies condemned by the Church in ancient or modern times might plausibly shelter themselves within such a declaration. The reason that Baptists are, generally speaking, homogeneous in their evangelicalism is to be found in the second clause, defining Christian baptism. There is here an implicit reference to the symbolical character of the baptism of believers by immersion, according to the teaching of Rom. vi., which Baptists regard as a charter of their distinctive faith and practice in regard to baptism. They find there a triple reference: (1) The historical facts of the death, burial, and resurrection of Jesus ; (2) the symbolic reproduction of those facts in the actual going down of the believer into the water of baptism, his submersion, and his rising from the water ; (3) the experiential parallel implied by faith in Christ, a spiritual union with Him in which the believer dies to sin and rises to newness of life. This, it may be said, is an ideal experience, never perfectly realized in any believer, not even in the Apostle who set it forth. But from this ideality comes the potency of the act for those who have been enlightened as to its meaning.[1] Every time such an act of Christian baptism takes place, the Pauline statement about the broken bread and the poured wine becomes equally applicable to the initial rite—"we preach the Lord's death until He come". Both the Supper and the Baptism in their different ways have an evangelistic function—they preach the cardinal facts on which

---

[1] We may say of it what William James has rightly said of the whole conversion experience, "that it should for even a short time show a human being what the high-water mark of his spiritual capacity is, this is what constitutes its importance" (*The Varieties of Religious Experience*, p. 257).

an evangelical faith rests, viz. the death and the resurrection of Jesus Christ.   More impressively than by any verbal recital of a creed, the historical basis of *every* Christian creed is constantly brought before a Baptist Church.   The cumulative effect of this repetition, even from a purely psychological point of view, must be very great.   To this must be ascribed the general continuity of " evangelicalism " within the Baptist community.   They are repeatedly brought face to face with the facts of the death and resurrection of Jesus Christ as the salient articles of their faith—an epitomized " Apostles' Creed ".   Yet, on the other hand, they are left free, indeed they are expected, to reach a personal interpretation of the meaning of those facts for Christian faith.   They are guided to such an interpretation in the classes of instruction held wherever a Baptist minister faithfully discharges his duty. But they are not required to accept any form of words as the authorized statement of that interpretation.   If this makes a high demand on personal intelligence (which is by no means universally satisfied), its very challenge is educative.   The Baptist, moreover, is free from the embarrassment of ancient forms of words, which can no longer be held in their exact ancient meaning.   He is committed to a living loyalty as the only adequate reproduction of the ancient faith.   He is allowed full scope for the individuality of that loyalty, its necessary individuality if it is to be personal.   Yet he is brought into personal relation with the essential facts of history, on which all Christian faith must build, if it is to keep its spiritual continuity.   This—whether Baptists themselves always realize it or not—is the secret of that reluctance of Baptists to bind themselves by the historic creeds of the Church.   They hold the contents of those creeds, it may safely be said, as loyally as any other body of Christians to-day.   But they feel the peril of stereotyping that which must be living to be real, and the peril of substituting a formal assent for what is of value only as a personal conviction.[1]

[1] It is naturally difficult for those committed to formal creeds to realize that they are not indispensable, and may be replaced by an "atmosphere" which supplies health and vitality.   I remember, when a student in Strasbourg, having a keen argument with a narrow-minded Lutheran lady on the one hand and a vehement Catholic Pole on the other, and I remember how impossible it was to make either of them understand the Baptist emphasis on a spiritual experience symbolized in believers' baptism, without the fetters of a rigid statement of its interpretation.

In the foregoing statement of believers' baptism I have said little of the motive which in practice appeals most powerfully to many Baptists, viz., the desire to obey a direct command of Christ (Matt. xxviii. 19) and to imitate His own acceptance of baptism at the hands of John (Mark i, 9, 10). I do not doubt (whatever be the date of Matt. xxviii. 19) that our Lord instituted the baptism of believers, but I believe it is in accordance with His spirit to emphasize the intrinsic meaning of the rite, rather than its extrinsic aspect as an act of formal obedience.

The third and remaining clause of the "Declaration of Principle" calls for notice here only as individualizing the responsibility of the Church for missionary work in the largest sense. As will be shown in a subsequent chapter, the consciousness of this responsibility is strongly developed amongst Baptists, and they are justly proud of their contribution to the evangelization of the world. It is not an accident of history that they have led the way in foreign missionary work ; it is a logical and obvious deduction from their emphasis on individual faith. The measure of personal conviction is seen in its vigour of expansion, its zeal of propagation.

IV

THE BAPTIST DOCTRINE OF THE CHURCH

THERE was something to be said for the old "Dissenting" distinction of the "Church", as the community of believers, from the "chapel", as the building used for worship by that community—a distinction by no means yet extinct. It kept the big name for the essential fact. It recalled the time when the Church was not yet the owner of useful property, and had no abiding city, yet was the Church. The change of terminology has come about inevitably through the need to counter the contemptuous use of "chapel", as though it were not the home of a true Church. But it remains necessary always to assert that men are more than things, and principles are more than utilities.

Let us try to imagine the different conceptions of "Church" in the minds of those who glance at some ecclesiastical building in a city street. To one man it is simply an architectural feature of the street in which he has no further interest (indeed, a landowner not far from London who had no church steeple in the landscape seen from his windows went to the expense of erecting a wooden one on a barn to satisfy his æsthetic instinct). To another man a Church is a survival from a past age of faith, maintained in the interests of a particular social group; it is a purely sociological phenomenon. To another it is chiefly a philanthropic agency, to be encouraged on purely practical and utilitarian grounds. Even those who bring a definitely religious connotation to the term "Church" from their own experience will often emphasize some relatively superficial feature in explaining the difference of one Church from another. What are the principles which Baptist Churches express?

(1) MEMBERSHIP AND POLITY

The Baptist Churches arose historically as a special development of Puritanism, and their conception of the

Church is a special form of the Puritan doctrine in general, when this had been passed through the sieve of "Separatism" (see Chapter I). The special feature is due to the retention of believers' baptism, with its emphasis on individual experience (see Chapter III). The most recent formal statement of the Baptist doctrine of the Church is that which formed part of the reply of the Baptist Union Assembly [1] to the Lambeth "Appeal":—

We believe in the Catholic Church as the holy society of believers in our Lord Jesus Christ, which He founded, of which He is the only Head, and in which He dwells by His Spirit, so that though made up of many communions, organized in various modes, and scattered throughout the world, it is yet one in Him.

We believe that this holy society is truly to be found wherever companies of believers unite as Churches on the ground of a confession of personal faith. Every local community thus constituted is regarded by us as both enabled and responsible for self-government through His indwelling Spirit, who supplies wisdom, love, and power, and who, as we believe, leads these communities to associate freely in wider organizations for fellowship and the propagation of the Gospel.

We reverence and obey the Lord Jesus Christ, our God and Saviour, as the sole and absolute authority in all matters pertaining to faith and practice, as revealed in the Scriptures, and we hold that each Church has liberty to interpret and administer His laws. We do not judge the conscience of those who take another view, but we believe that this principle of the freedom of the individual Church under Christ has the sanction of Scripture and the justification of history, and therefore we cannot abandon it without being false to our trust. Moreover. it is plain to us that the headship and sole authority of our Lord in His Church excludes any such relations with the State as may impair its liberty.

Here the three paragraphs respectively declare (1) the diversity in unity of the Catholic Church of all believers, (2) the right of the local Church to be self-governing, (3) the sole authority of Christ within the Church. These claims are explicitly based on the principle that the Church is a society divinely controlled, and implicitly on the assumption that the "Congregational" polity here stated is adequate to the operation of that divine control. It is always the implicit assumptions of such a statement that need most carefully

[1] At Leeds on May 4, 1926.

watching, because those made explicitly are usually common ground. All who belong to the Christian Church in any recognizable form would assert the *ultimate* Headship of Jesus Christ over it ; the point that needs discussion is not this, but its implications and the manner in which it is conceived to be administered. It is these assumptions and implications which are so hard to express because they make the real life of the community.

Let us take the normal and typical " convert " who proposes to " join " an English Baptist Church. He has probably passed through the Sunday-school ; he may not have received definite religious instruction from his parents, possibly not Baptists. He has joined a Bible-class because one of his friends took him, and for the same reason he comes, more or less, to the Sunday services. Perhaps he also belongs to the Society of Christian Endeavour or a Young People's Guild. He feels he wants something to live for and something to live by, and all around him there are people suggesting that this something may be found through faith in Jesus Christ. He may often lack clear ideas as to what such " faith " means, but he has enough confidence that Jesus Christ is a true Leader of men to put discipleship to the proof, and he responds to the appeal of his teacher or minister, and says he wants to be a Christian. He goes to the minister's Preparation Class, held from time to time as there are candidates for baptism, and receives some instruction as to Church Membership and Discipleship, Baptism, and the Lord's Supper, in which the minister will follow no prescribed form.[1] His name is brought before the Church, the report of " visitors " on his fitness for fellowship is heard, and a vote taken. Finally, he comes forward with others to profess Christian faith in baptism, and is admitted into Church Membership[2] by being given the " right hand of fellowship "

---

[1] It must be frankly acknowledged that this duty is often neglected by ministers. I once asked a class of twenty students how many had received what they would now call adequate instruction in Baptist principles, and found that seventeen had not, though some of these had heard occasional addresses on the Baptist faith.

[2] Entrance into the Church is regarded as distinct from baptism, though in practice usually combined with it. Believers' baptism is not infrequently administered to Christians of other communions, who have no intention of joining a Baptist Church.

at the next observance of the Lord's Supper. He is now expected to attend the monthly Communion service, to be regular in attendance at the services, to make some regular contribution to the funds of the Church, if he is earning a living. He is encouraged to take up some form of Christian service, such as Sunday-school teaching. He will depend for further instruction in the faith on the sermons or addresses he may hear. He will go to the Church Meeting from time to time, where he will be called upon to give his vote on matters which the " deacons " bring before the Church. He may eventually become a deacon himself by the election of the Church, one of a committee which virtually manages the affairs of the Church, though always with theoretical reference to the directions and judgment of the whole Church. By such apparently " casual " paths a man is brought to face the highest issues.

Our young friend thought he was " joining " the Church ; he may awaken to the much more serious discovery that he is helping to " constitute " it—that the Church, according to Baptist faith, is not a hierarchy of officials, with an appendage of laymen, but a society of men and women drawn together by common convictions and needs, and entering into a social experience of the Christian faith for which their individual experience has so far prepared them. It is possible, of course, to say that this conception of the Church lacks dignity and fails to elicit reverence adequate to its true idea. In practice that may be perfectly true ; the outer form and the inward idea are always tending to react on each other, and the idea is the more malleable of the two. It *is* difficult to keep the august and majestic conceptions of the Epistle to the Ephesians alongside of the friendly and natural intercourse of the first disciples with one another and with their Lord. Yet it should always be remembered that the Church grew out of human fellowship and friendship, and that it is never true to its origin when it ceases to be in some sense a family. The worst type of Baptist Church is that in which this human side of the relationship has somehow been lost, but fortunately such a Church will extinguish itself and cease to exist. Where there is real and helpful fellowship, even though there is a lack of reverence and a certain superficiality in regard to deeper truths, we have at least one vital element of the Church of the New Testament pattern.

It will be seen how entirely the spiritual efficiency of such a Church as this will depend on the quality of the individual convictions on which it rests. In the days of clear-cut Calvinism there was a definite body of religious doctrine with which everyone started, together with a certain neglect of what seem to us not less definite social duties. To-day there is usually the practical desire to be of use in the world along the lines of Christ, and a good deal of indefiniteness as to doctrine, or at least a very superficial response to it. But in itself the principle of a regenerate Church is sound, when we allow for the inevitable conditions of a union of " body " and " soul ". " St. Paul's conception of a Christian community is a body of which the Spirit of Christ is the soul."[1] As Christ by His Spirit makes a temple of the individual body, so Christ by His Spirit may make a temple of the collective society. The society is a larger opportunity for the activity of the Spirit of God. That activity, however, is not guaranteed by a society any more than by an official or group of officials.

The idea underlying the congregational polity of a Baptist Church could still be sufficiently expressed in the words of Dr. Joseph Angus: " The Christian Church is founded on the double principle, that all true religion is a personal thing, and that the Churches of Christ are associations of religious men— of all such and of none besides."[2] But the four-score years since those words were written have brought some considerable changes to all the Churches. It is no longer possible to " prove " the case for a particular form of polity by a string of Scripture texts. For one thing, our general attitude towards the Bible has changed or is changing. It betokens no lessening of reverence and loyalty towards the moral and religious ideas of the Biblical revelation to say that the *forms* of its life are not necessarily those most suited to the needs of to-day. Indeed, we have no right to assume that these forms were ever intended to be authoritative for all time. They are experiments rather than precedents ; they show life active and vigorous, creating its own means of expression as each need arose. Why, then, should we stereotype one particular stage in the development, whether it be early or late? Moreover,

---

[1] Lindsay, *The Church and the Ministry in the Early Centuries*, p. 69.
[2] *Christian Churches*, p. 70 (1863).

even from the earliest times there are the germs of many later developments. It is perhaps historically true to say with Lindsay that " we see a little self-governing republic " in such a Church as that at Corinth[1]. But, on the other hand, the authority of the Apostle Paul is very real, and is firmly exercised ; he is far from being the self-effacing chairman of a democratic society. The modern study of the New Testament has taught us to see more and more clearly that the emphasis falls on the life of the Spirit creating these transient forms rather than on the forms themselves. It is not sufficient, therefore, to prove that there were Congrega-tionalist or Presbyterian or Episcopalian forms of Church government in the New Testament times ; the previous question must be faced—what authority, if any, have these forms over the present life of the Christian Church? Against those who insist on organization as of the essence of such a Church it is perfectly legitimate to argue that the gathering of the Upper Room was a fellowship rather than an organization; on the other hand, is there any valid reason, other than practical convenience, why the Church in Jerusalem should be "independent" of the Church in Antioch? The whole issue seems to be transferred from the theoretical to the practical—what is the best and most efficient way of expressing that conception of the Church which we hold to be true?

The conception of the Church as a society of believers is assuredly no unworthy one, nor is it lacking in majesty and dignity for those who know what faith means. Faith is a spiritual adventure, a challenge of the seen in the strength of the unseen. Christian faith in its simplest expressions always implies the great underlying unities of all the Churches, "one Body and one Spirit, even as also ye were called in one hope of your calling ; one Lord, one faith, one baptism, one God and Father of all, who is over all, and through all, and in all ".[2] It argues a poverty of spiritual imagination when we fail to see in the human temple, individual or social, a worthier sanctuary than any material shrine. We may say that the ideal of a society of holy believers is never fully and adequately realized in men and women of flesh and blood, but this is a quite different thing from saying that the ideal

---

[1] *Op. cit.*, p. 57.   [2] Eph. iv. 4.

itself is wrong or inadequate. Newman asks in one of his books "what there is venerable, awful, superhuman in the Wesleyan Conference to persuade one to take it as a prophet ". Certainly nothing is venerable or awful or superhuman that plays fast and loose with history [1] but where two or three are gathered in the name of Christ, and therefore with His promised presence, who is the Truth, there is ample room for veneration and awe and faith in the supernatural guidance of those two or three, even though they be no more than a village prayer-meeting. " Where Christ is, there is the Church." John Smyth could say of his little group of fellow-believers, in replying to a contemporary :—

If you knew but the comfort and power of the Lord's ordin-ances of admonition and excommunication as we do (blessed be our good God) in some measure, and that growth and reformation which is in some of us thereby, you would be so wonderfully ravished with the power of God's ordinances that you would acknowledge the Church to be terrible as an army with banners, and yet amiable and lovely, comely and beautiful.—(*Works*, ii, pp. 441, 442 ; quoted by Burgess, *op. cit.*, p. 91.)

Baptists hold, then, that the congregational polity of a Baptist Church is one legitimate way amongst others of ex-pressing the fundamental idea of the Church. [2] The theoretical centre of its activities is the " Church Meeting ", usually held monthly. Here all members of the Church are at liberty to speak on matters affecting its common welfare, but the control of the meeting is naturally in the hands of the " deacons " and the minister, who presides. These usually form an Executive Committee, with a good deal of variety in the powers assigned to them, so that in practice they often become a sort of " Kirk-Session " ; indeed, it might be argued that in a really efficient congregational polity it is necessary that they should. The deacons combine, however, the spiritual functions of " eldership " with the financial functions of the diaconate in the Presbyterian Church (though many Baptist Churches have a separate Finance Committee). In

---

[1] As when Newman speaks of the Virgin Mary as going to Mass (*Discourses to Mixed Congregations*, p. 356).

[2] Many Baptists, perhaps a majority, would not be content with this statement ; they would urge that because it is nearest to the historical beginnings of the Church it is the form obligatory upon us.

the seventeenth and eighteenth centuries the Church Meeting was largely concerned with matters of "discipline", i.e. the faith and conduct of its members. No one with any capacity for human sympathy can turn over the pages of one of these old Church-books without feeling the tragedy and the comedy of it all—the vision of a great principle and not infrequently the misinterpretation of that vision for want of any true perspective.[1] This little group of men and women of whom we may be reading is so very much in earnest, so authoritative in its interpretation of Scripture, so fearless in the application of its authority, that we cannot but be impressed. Yet we feel also that it *is* a little group, divorced from the life of the great world about it, and inevitably to have its faith modified when that world is taken into full account. This is what has happened to English Baptists as to other religious communions of the Free Churches. Discipline has necessarily been relaxed, for no religious community could make such demands on the attendance or even the conduct of its members as were made in the seventeenth century ; many Baptists think discipline has been relaxed beyond what is right or reasonable. In practice, discipline is now confined to grosser moral evils ; a Baptist Church would not tolerate sexual immorality or habitual drunkenness or proved dishonesty in business relations in any of its members. Such cases are dealt with by personal investigation, usually by the minister and deacons, by private remonstrance or appeal, by suspension of membership for a time, until there is credible evidence of true penitence, finally by exclusion from the fellowship of the Church. Formal suspension and exclusion naturally require the vote of the Church, but in practice voluntary withdrawal is often counselled by the minister to avoid scandal.

Except for the more critical moments in the history of a Church, as when a call to a new minister has to be given or some change of general policy or activity introduced, the Church Meeting at the present day tends to become an ordinary service, differentiated only by the fact that "the minutes of the former meeting were read and confirmed". Many Baptists are seriously troubled by this frequent decline

---

[1] Examples have been given in the historical sketch contained in the second chapter (pp. 43-49).

in the place given to the Church Meeting, since it is the pivotal centre of the Church consciousness and gives the really distinctive character to a Congregational polity. The decline is partly due to the rivalry of other forms of organization, started with the best of intentions—Christian Endeavour Societies, Young People's Guilds, and the like, together with the very large number of special organizations not linked to any one Church, yet drawing their supporters almost exclusively from the Churches. The truth is that the Baptist of to-day has a great many other interests, religious and secular, which lie outside the circle of the Church, to a much greater extent than even the Victorian Baptist. His conception of the relation of the Church to the Kingdom of God has subtly changed, for he no longer identifies them in the way Baptists (like their fellow-Puritans) once did. The Kingdom of God is inevitably seen to be much larger than the Church, with many " values " for life which the Church consciousness does not touch. This is probably one of the main factors in the present drift from all the Churches, at least so far as serious-minded people are concerned. There seems no remedy for it but to widen the conception of Christian activity until it includes much more of life. The very phrase " Christian worker " calls up a narrow and impoverished picture of some two or three types only—the district visitor, the Sunday-school teacher, the secretary of some religious organization. But Christian service is being rendered by every Christian, in whatever vocation, who applies his faith to the affairs of his daily occupation. It is just this practical service which the Church has allowed to pass beyond its horizon, to its own great detriment. I do not see any prospect of a revival in the Church Meeting, which means in the Church consciousness of Baptists, apart from such recognition of the work of the Kingdom in a larger sense and of the leadership of the Church in the work of that larger Kingdom. An ideal Church Meeting of to-day would be one in which member after member of the fellowship spoke of the helps and hindrances of his daily life in the light of great Christian principles—in which the Christian magistrate and the Christian lawyer, the Christian manufacturer and the Christian shopkeeper, the Christian typist and the Christian errand-boy, all pooled their Christian experience for the common good, and learned to think of themselves as being

Christian workers and what they did as Christian work.[1] Our ecclesiastical theory and practice have not kept up with the changes in our practical philosophy. Our outlook on life as men and women is bigger than our outlook as Baptists or Wesleyans or Anglicans. Who does not feel something of that in reading a denominational newspaper?

The self-governing independence of the local Baptist Church obviously does not, and ought not to, preclude some sort of voluntary association with other Baptist Churches. From the beginnings of Baptist Church life in the seventeenth century right on to the present day successive forms of organization have been evolved to meet new needs, though the independence of the local Church was always jealously guarded and explicitly recognized. No one can understand the life of the denomination who does not realize that all larger groupings of Baptist Churches are for common action by representatives, not for the exercise of authoritative control. The local Churches join or withdraw from these as they see fit, though in practice there is stable union and a large measure of joint activity. Baptist Church life is thus expressed in three stages of representation, which indicate a growing world-consciousness and the sense of larger problems. The first grouping is that of the " Associations ", of which there are 30 in England, 14 in Wales, making with the Unions of Scottish and of Irish Baptists a total of 45. These Associations usually include smaller local groups, which need not concern us ; it is the grouping of the county (or practicable area) which forms the first effective unit beyond that of the local Church.[2] Each Association carries on its own denominational life in its own way, though there is naturally an increasing tendency to assimilation. A President is elected

---

[1] Cf. the address by Professor Barry on "The Holy Spirit in the Church", delivered before the Church Congress at Southport, October, 1926 : " Religion to-day is, in the large, simply one activity side by side with all the others, not standing even in vital relation to them. Religion is ceasing to be the inspiration of life's best ideals and activities, and obviously that spells a double loss. They are losing their quality and ' saltness ', and religion itself is left thin and bloodless, with no strong roots and spreading out into life. The Churches as we know them to-day are mainly *devotional* associations ; they are not fellowships of life and work.'' (The address is given in full in the volume *The Eternal Spirit*, edited by Canon Raven, pp. 116-136.)

[2] The earliest of those now existing is the Bristol Association (from 1640).

annually, very often a layman, and the annual meetings of the Association (usually held near Whitsuntide) form the centre of its ecclesiastical year. Almost all of these are in membership with the "Baptist Union", the second kind of grouping. This was first formed in 1813, though it did not become of much importance for the next eighteen years. Its "Assembly", meeting annually, is constituted by representatives of the Baptist Churches in voluntary membership with the Union, together with personal members (whose voting power is conditional on the consent of the rest). Such an "Assembly" is naturally too large to deal with any but the broadest issues of policy, and in practice the direction of common interests is in the hands of the Council of the Union, consisting of 165 members, elected partly by the Assembly and partly by the Associations. (There are, of course, a large number of special committees.) The President of the Union is elected annually, and a layman frequently fills this office, as with the provincial Associations. There are upwards of 1,500 Churches in membership with the Baptist Union. There are as many more of one sort or another remaining outside in the exercise of their freedom, though the main stream of Baptist Church life flows through the Baptist Union. About 600 Churches, unable to pay their ministers the minimum salary of £160, are helped to do this by the "Sustentation Fund". In connection with this, and for other purposes also, the country is divided into ten Areas, with a "General Superintendent" in charge of each, but the name must not be taken to imply more than moral and persuasive authority. It would quite misrepresent their position and work to regard them as "bishops"; but they are more than travelling secretaries. They are encouragers and advisers, and are at the service of the Churches and ministers for all spiritual purposes.

In 1905 a further step in representative organization was taken by the formation of the Baptist World Alliance, which has held its Congresses in London, Philadelphia, Stockholm, Toronto, Berlin and Atlanta. Its latest returns show about ten millions of (communicant) members, eight and a half millions of these belonging to North America.[1] There are over 72,000 Baptist Churches, over 51,000 pastors and

[1] See Appendix III.

missionaries, and upwards of eight million Sunday scholars.
Baptists form, therefore, one of the largest of the Protestant
Churches, indeed the largest Free Church communion in the
world. This fact is a remarkable testimony to the vigour of
the ideas they express, especially when we remember the lowly
beginnings of Baptist Church life in the seventeenth century,
the absence of social or political support, and the presence
indeed for a long time, and even now in some countries, of
social and political repression or persecution. The organization of American Baptists follows the same general principles,
as may be seen from the following statement: —

We have the district Associations or voluntary assemblies of
messengers from local churches covering a limited district. We
have our State Conventions, which include messengers from all
parts of the State, and our general conventions among English
and continental and other Baptists. Our organization, therefore,
in its amplitude and geographical extent is equal to that, say,
of our Presbyterian brethren, but without imitating them in the
introduction of the principal of indirect authority. None of these
bodies is legislative or judicial. Christ is the sole authority in
all. They are for advisory and administrative purposes.
Then, too, our superintendents and secretaries of missions perform the work of bishops without any of the authority of bishops.
They visit the fields and lend a helping hand by means of suggestion and in other ways. But they have no semblance of authority
over any congregation, however small. We have also a great
variety of Boards and Councils. Congregationalism is capable of
great diversity in this respect. These are not rigid in form that
they may not be changed when occasion arises. Thus there is all
needful flexibility.[1]

(2) WORSHIP

An Anglican, entering a Baptist Church for divine worship,
might often be alienated by the seeming want of reverence.
There is no visible altar, and an obtrusive pulpit takes its
place. The choir is too visible, and does not seem greatly
concerned with anything but its own function. Deacons walk
about unnecessarily, and even come to chat with people in the
pews. The secretary gives out notices at an alarming length,
and may intersperse a few remarks. The preacher, who wears

[1] Mullins, *The Axioms of Religion*, pp. 147, 148.

no distinctive dress, follows no particular order in his prayers, and may be wearisomely long in his sermon. People stay about in clusters talking when the service is over, and the minister may come down and join them, or stand in the vestibule shaking hands with people. As for the Communion Service—— !

There is some truth in this impression, though not as much as is imagined. It would be better for Baptists to cultivate more reverence in the forms of worship, and to think more intelligently about the meaning of those forms, since thought and feeling are always being shaped by their own expression in deed as well as by word. It is all too easy for those who protest against a fixed ritual to slip into a pseudo-ritual of their own, slipshod and provincial, instead of dignified and comprehensive. Yet it must be remembered that the Church is a family as well as a building or a body, and that the vital warmth of human fellowship can be sanctified to high spiritual ends. Even if some of these people talk when it would be better for them to be silent, or err unconsciously in matters of taste, yet the weightier matters of Gospel fellowship may be theirs. The Church is their spiritual home in a real sense, with all the " homeliness " of familiar association. The many organizations and activities of the week provide human fellowship for them and their families. Whilst the increase of these for special objects has, as we have seen, its unfortunate side, in depriving the Church Meeting of part of its significance, we must not fail to recognize that these various activities provide an outlet for energies in useful employment, and, above all, provide opportunities for Christian fellowship in the wider sense of the term. We may admit, as I think Baptists ought to admit, that there is something wanting on the side of reverence in our expression of worship, but we ought also to claim that a very real side of Church life does find expression in this homely fellowship.

What are the ideals of worship which ought to control the practice of the Baptists, given their general standpoint and conception of the Church? The fundamental fact in all worship is the bringing of the soul face to face with God ; in this sense, as William Penn says, "worship is the supreme act of human life". Calvin began his " Institutes " by the words, " Almost the whole sum of our wisdom, which ought to be reckoned true and solid wisdom, consists of two parts, the knowledge of God and of ourselves ". Newman tells how early Calvinistic influences acted upon him, " making me rest in the thought of two and two only absolute and luminously self-evident beings, myself and my Creator ".[1] A. M. Fairbairn, in a brief study of worship which is one of the best expressions of the Free Church ideals,[2] says: " Worship in its fundamental idea may be said to be the speech of God to man and of man to God. . . . Where the specific Christian elements appear is in the quality and character of the beings related." [3]

The new feature of " public " worship as compared with private devotion is the corporate and collective quality, which introduces no alien element, since sociality is as much an attribute of personality as individuality. We are what we are because we have grown up in a society, from the earliest influences of the home. When men come together for a common purpose that unites them, their powers for that purpose cannot be reached by the arithmetic of mere addition of the units ; they are a new unit, whether it be a political meeting or a religious service. As the players in an orchestra must learn to limit themselves, yet thereby are able to reach new results—which the composer can achieve only through their combination—so for ourselves and God corporate worship opens new possibilities. Both in common praise and in common prayer—the two elements of such worship on the human side—the individual gains something new by the subordination of his individuality to the social thanksgiving and petition.

The forms which worship ought to take are ruled by no authoritative principle, save that of the Apostle, " Let all things be done decently and in order, for edifying ", i.e. " building up " man's conscious relation to God. The development of the centuries has naturally been from simpler to more elaborate forms. The primitive Christian meeting followed the synagogue rather than the temple, and was controlled by what has well been called a " liturgy of the Spirit ".[4] From the subsequent elaboration of Church worship Protestantism returned to more democratic forms,

---

[1] *Apologia*, p. 4.
[2] *Studies in Religion and Theology*, pp. 253-82.
[3] *Loc. cit.*, p. 264.
[4] Duchesne, *Origines du Culte Chrétien*, p. 48.

especially in the Puritan movement. Early Baptist worship is described for us as it was carried out in Smyth's Separatist Church in Amsterdam:—

We begin with a prayer, after read some one or two chapters of the Bible ; give the sense thereof and confer upon the same ; that done, we lay aside our books and after a solemn prayer made by the first speaker he propoundeth some text out of the Scripture and prophesieth out of the same by the space of one hour or three quarters of an hour. After him standeth up a second speaker and prophesieth out of the said text the like time and space, sometimes more, sometimes less. After him, the third, the fourth, the fifth, etc., as the time will give leave. Then the first speaker concludeth with prayer as he began with prayer, with an exhortation to contribution to the poor, which collection being made is also concluded with prayer. This morning exercise begins at eight of the clock and continueth unto twelve of the clock. The like course of exercise is observed in the afternoon from two of the clock unto five or six of the clock. Last of all the execution of the government of the Church is handled.— (Letter of Hugh and Anne Bromehead, given in Burgess, *Smith, the Se-Baptist*, etc., pp. 170, 171.)

It will be observed that there is no singing, even of psalms, in this order. But, as was shown in an earlier place,[1] Baptists became pioneers in congregational hymn-singing. In modern times the chant and the anthem (not always to advantage) have followed the hymn, and there is an increasing tendency to break up the " long prayer " into shorter and more intelligibly followed petitions, though there is no general movement amongst Baptists towards a liturgy which would displace this " free " prayer.

To this prayer and praise the divine response may be conceived to come in three ways—in the reading of Scripture, which is the record of man's experience of God through many centuries, and has proved its power to recreate that experience in new settings ; in the sermon, whether expository of the meaning of Scripture, or " prophetic " as the utterance of the preacher's new experience of God or outlook on contemporary life (both becoming the vehicle of the Spirit of God, " a hammer that breaketh the rock in pieces " on lines of cleavage prepared by the Providence of God) ; and in the

[1] See p. 48.

third place, the voice of the Spirit may sound in uncovenanted ways, through the incidental phrase of hymn or prayer, through the cumulative effect of worship, when custom is vitalized, as in the synagogue of Nazareth, into one of its rare moments, or in the unspoken message of the Spirit: —

> . . . the breath
> Of God in man that warranteth
> The inmost utmost things of faith.

God is Spirit, and worship is free to choose whatever forms may best lift men into the realm of the Spirit, since all forms, whether of Jerusalem or Samaria, are subordinate to the reality of that inner experience of God's presence, which is worship in spirit and in truth.

(3) The Communion of the Lord's Supper

"The ordinance of the Lord's Supper", or "the Communion Service", is generally observed in English Baptist Churches monthly, after the first evening service of the month, though many Churches also observe it after one of the morning services for those who find this more convenient. The choice of name is characteristic ; " the Lord's Supper " implies that it is the commemoration of the simple meal in the Upper Room, whilst "the Communion Service" implies that it is an act of fellowship—the fellowship of believers with one another and with their Lord. This is the justification of the place assigned to it in the present book. For Baptists the Lord's Supper is the supreme expression of the fellowship of the Church as created by, and maintained in, the fellowship of individual believers with Christ. They believe that special significance for all time was given to the last meal of which Jesus partook with His disciples, through His own words and actions, and that He made the broken bread and the poured-out wine the symbols of His body to be broken on the Cross, and of His blood sacrificially outpoured, in the manner of the symbolic acts of Hebrew prophecy. That which the word more clearly articulates the deed more graphically presents.

This primary conception of the Lord's Supper makes it a close parallel to the rite of believers' baptism, another " acted parable " when by immersion. The unrepeated act of baptism is the rite of initiation, the repeated act of communion

G

that of continuation, in the community of believers, but both proclaim the Lord's death. Dr. Denney's impartial statement has a special significance for Baptists: " Modern Christians try to draw a broader line of distinction between the Sacraments than really exists. Partly, no doubt, this is owing to the fact that in our times baptism is usually that of infants, while the Supper is partaken of only by adults, whereas, in New Testament times, the significance of both was defined in relation to conscious faith."[1] Those who practise infant baptism, with any serious doctrine of baptismal regeneration attached to it, are quite logical in following this up, as they sometimes do, with a " Children's Eucharist ". On the other hand, Baptists approach the Lord's Supper in the light of believers' baptism as neither more nor less requiring personal faith for its benefits to be enjoyed. Thus the two ordinances illuminate and reinforce each other.

The Lord's Supper becomes, in the first place, a pledge of fidelity renewing the vow of loyalty made personally in baptism. The honour of the Lord's guests is pledged by their continued and repeated presence at His Table. They are bound to come in humble penitence, asking the pathetic question of the first disciples, which is so characteristic of a truly sacramental hour. When Jesus spoke of unfaithfulness in their midst, they did not resent the charge with Petrine indignation. Their hearts were too much subdued ; they were brought too close to the sorrowful possibilities of human nature, under the solemn influences of the farewell. They could not look at others asking, " Is it *he*, Lord? " They looked at their own hearts, saying humbly, " Is it *I*? " It seems fitting that the first act in the Communion Service should be a confession of sin and a prayer for pardon.[2]

The elements employed in the two rites are complementary in their spiritual symbolism. The water of baptism is the symbol of moral and spiritual cleansing ; the bread and the

---

[1] *The Death of Christ*, p. 136.

[2] But for a general service there is truth in Martineau's criticism of the Prayer Book order: " The profound sense of sinful imperfection is not ready on the surface of even the humblest mind ; and it is not till the spirit has felt its way through the mists and dimness in which Prayer begins, and emerged into the clear presence of the Infinite Holiness, that the abasing consciousness of spiritual poverty is awakened, and the sad interval is seen between what we are and what we ought to be " (*Life and Letters*, i, p. 383).

wine are the symbols of moral and spiritual support. But the reality set forth is in both rites the work and gift of the Holy Spirit. Without His presence and activity, sanctifying the obedience and the manner of it, creating that fellowship of faith which is, as the Benediction implies, His peculiar work, there can be no sacramental communion. Fellowship means activity on both sides, and the fellowship of God in Christ with man is always mediated by the Holy Spirit. It is fitting, therefore, that at the Communion Service we should offer such a prayer as the *Epiclesis* of the Eastern Church, an invocation of the Holy Spirit.

The Lord's Supper expresses the spiritual unity of the Body of Christ, that Body into which believers are baptized in one Spirit. As they are made one by baptism in one and the same Spirit, so they renew that consciousness of unity in the acts expressive of the fellowship of the Spirit. It is fitting, therefore, that we should offer prayer at the Communion Service for " the communion of saints " and give thanks for those departed who still belong to the general assembly and church of the first-born.

The interpretation of the Lord's Supper most common amongst Baptists at the present time would be technically described as " Zwinglian "—though it must be remembered that there was a recognition of mystical union with Christ in Zwingli's teaching which did not find full expression in his controversies. There have always been Baptists whose interpretations of the Lord's Supper is Calvinistic rather than Zwinglian, and there is to-day a growing consciousness that this rite has not taken the place amongst us which belongs to it, and that it should be celebrated with greater reverence.

Whilst the Communion Service is fundamentally a memorial rite—" This do in remembrance of me "—it is much more than this for all who receive spiritual blessing through it. It renews obedient loyalty, and it establishes and mediates fellowship, both with God in Christ and with fellow-members of His Body. It implies the real presence of the risen Lord by His Spirit, and Baptists might join the great theologian and humble believer, Richard Hooker, in saying, " The real presence of Christ's most blessed body and blood is not, therefore, to be sought for in the Sacrament, but in the worthy receiver of the Sacrament " (V, lxvii, 6).

Baptists have no prescribed form of Communion Service, as they have none for baptism or for worship in general.' But the words of institution are always read, prayers are offered, and the elements are distributed by the deacons to the communicants.   Any member of the fellowship, permanent or temporary, may conduct the service, but in practice the minister almost always presides.   A voluntary offering for the poor of the Church is always taken at the regular Communion Service, and this is afterwards distributed by the deacons.   The attendance of Church members is recorded by a ticket system, which enables those absent to be noted and visited.

The relation of believers' baptism to the Lord's Supper raises an issue on which Baptists are divided, i.e. as to whether the communion of the Table should be " strict " (in the sense of being confined to those who have been baptized on profession of their faith) or " open " to believers in general.   The issue has been argued at much length, as between Kiffin and Bunyan, representing the " strict " and the " open " position in the seventeenth century, between Booth on the narrower and Robinson and the Rylands on the broader basis in the eighteenth, between Joseph Kinghorn and Robert Hall in the nineteenth.   For the greater number of British Baptists the issue is now practically settled.   At the beginning of the nineteenth century Robert Hall could write: " Strict Communion is the general practice of our Churches, though the abettors of the opposite opinion are rapidly increasing both in numbers and respectability."[2]   At the beginning of the twentieth Charles Williams could write: " Charles Haddon Spurgeon, with the majority of British Baptists, invited all who loved the Lord Jesus Christ to commemorate with them His love in dying for them."[3]   That result has come about by the larger logic of the essential unity of the Church over against the narrower logic that a man is not fully a Christian

[1] The order of service outlined above is rather more detailed than that of most Baptist ministers.   It begins with a hymn, is followed by (1) prayer of confession, (2) invocation of the Holy Spirit, (3) words of institution and prayer of thanksgiving, (4) distribution of the elements, (5) prayer for the communion of saints, followed by the collection for the poor of the Church and a closing hymn.

[2] *Works*, ii, p. 16.

[3] *The Principles and Practices of the Baptists*, p. 25 (1903).

unless he has been baptized according to what Baptists regard as the New Testament baptism. To exclude a fellow-Christian from the Lord's Table does seriously reflect on the quality of his Christianity.

The question of "strict" and "open" communion at the Lord's Table should be clearly distinguished from two other issues with which it has frequently been confused. It has nothing to do with the doctrinal difference between the "Particular" or Calvinistic and the "General" or Arminian Baptists, though the combination "Strict and Particular" has been common. Neither has it anything to do directly with the further question of "closed" or "open" membership of the Church. This concerns the requirement of baptism by immersion as a condition of entrance into the Church. The great majority of Baptist Churches throughout the world are in this sense "closed" to any but believers baptized on profession of faith. But there are a number of English Baptist Churches which allow membership on profession of faith without baptism. It would certainly be a curious result if the practice of "open" membership should become as predominant amongst Baptists as that of "open" communion. Our dictionaries might then define a Baptist Church as the only one which did not make baptism a condition of admission! But the issue is hardly to be settled by the analogy of the open-communion question. The Lord's Supper is the Lord's gift to the Church; it lies outside our jurisdiction in a sense in which the administration of the affairs of a local community does not. It may be regarded as a matter of expediency rather than of principle that other Christians not personally pledged to the practice of believers' baptism should share with Baptists in the administration of a Church. Under the present constitution and polity each Church is entitled to judge for itself as to what is expedient, whilst equally the majority would be justified in refusing to recognize as a Baptist Church one in which the testimony to believers' baptism ceased to be effective. It cannot be denied that there is a certain peril in the increase of open-membership Churches (though the peril is not so great as it might seem, provided the minister is himself a convinced Baptist). It may also be argued, as is done by American Baptists generally, that clear-cut testimony is always more effective than compromise.

(4) MINISTRY

As the Lord's Supper expresses the fellowship of the Church in its dependence on Christ, so the "ministry" denotes the service rendered within and through that fellowship for Christ's sake. "Pastors are, in a word, the servants of the Church. The Church, indeed, is not their master; but they are, nevertheless, its servants."[1]

In any statement of the nature and function of the Christian ministry which is based on the New Testament principles and practices there. are certain questions of historical exegesis which meet us on the threshold, and to which a definite answer must be given. Does the New Testament insist on any *form* of ministry at all? Does the emphasis fall on *office* or on *gift*, and how are they related? Is the later "monarchical" bishop the product of elevation or localization—is he, for example, an exalted presbyter or a settled apostle? Finally, what does apostolical succession mean, in the light of the earliest history of the Church? Obviously there can here be no argued discussion of these themes, on which so many volumes have been written, and they are named only to bring out the essential Baptist position, which finds support in the critical scholarship of all schools. That position is an emphasis on the inner, spiritual, and intrinsic nature of Christian ministry, its particular forms being accidental and occasional, evolved to meet particular needs as they were felt, such as the ministry of the seven at Jerusalem.[2] The ministry was richly varied in its contents, ranging from the itinerant work of an apostle to the word of exhortation spoken by the member of a local Church, yet it was regarded in all its forms as a "gift" of the Holy Spirit.[3] The office grew out of the gift, and not vice-versa. Paul, for example, became an apostle because, as he tells us, "God thought well to reveal His Son in me".[4] Against the theory that Christianity is "the establishment of a visible system of means for realizing the end of human life",[5] and the statement that "All authority was concentrated in the upper room of Pentecost. Thence it has been devolved",[6] it is sufficient to point out that the natural

---

[1] Angus, *Christian Churches*, p. 47; cf. 2 Cor. iv. 5.
[2] Acts vi. 1-6.   [3] 1 Cor. xii. 4-11, 28-31; Eph. iv. 11 ff.
[4] Gal. i. 15, 16.   [5] Gore, *The Church and the Ministry*, p. 313.
[6] Lacey, *Unity and Schism*, p. 127.

meaning of "they were all together in one place" includes the hundred and twenty disciples who have just been mentioned, as well as the Apostles, and to say, with the Bishop of Gloucester, that the Apostles "represent ' discipleship' in its highest form . . . they are not primarily the appointed rulers of the Church, but the nucleus of the Church out of which it grew ".[1]   As for the evolution of the monarchical episcopate, the general principle framed by Bishop Lightfoot (apart from particular theories of its operation) seems to have stood the test of the searching criticism to which it has been exposed, viz. that "the episcopate was formed not out of the apostolic order by localization, but out of the presbyteral by elevation ".[2]   In regard to apostolical succession, there is truth in this, so long as we are speaking, with Irenæus, of the succession of witness to true doctrine, or of the performance of apostolic functions, such as discipline and teaching.   But when it is defined by Bishop Gore as "in each generation an authoritative stewardship of the grace and truth which came by Jesus Christ and a recognized power to transmit it, derived from above by apostolic descent ",[3] it is sufficient to let one bishop answer another, in the statement of Dr. Headlam: "So far as I am able to judge it was not held at all in the early Church.   I have, I think, read everything from the Fathers which is quoted in favour of Apostolic Succession, and I do not know any passage which speaks of succession by ordination in this sense."[4]   In fact, as Dr. Macgregor well puts it, the true successors of the Apostles as witnesses of Christ were not men, but the Four Gospels.[5]   He puts our alternatives clearly and forcibly when he asks: "Is the ministry of the word to be a dragging chain, with link holding simply by the next link, and thus, through saints and reformers and prophets and apostles, coming at last to the throne of God? or does it at every stage depend on God

---

[1] Headlam, *The Doctrine of the Church and Reunion*, p. x.   So also Hort in his *Christian Ecclesia*, p. 30, where he reminds us that the Lord's Supper was given to the Apostles alone, yet admittedly was meant for the whole Church: "The Twelve sat that evening as representatives of the Ecclesia at large ; they were disciples more than they were Apostles."

[2] Essay on "The Christian Ministry", p. 196 (in *St. Paul's Epistle to the Philippians*, ed. 1898).

[3] *Op. cit.*, p. 59.   [4] *Op. cit.*, p. 128.

[5] *Christian Freedom*, p. 186.

directly, on a Divine call and Divine instruction and Divine illumination by which alone the instructions can be understood? " [1]

In view, therefore, of the New Testament evidence, the Baptist feels amply justified in refusing to make any distinction between "clergy" and "laity" which implies a difference of status and privilege and not simply a function and service. In the wide sense of the New Testament, all Christians are called to minister, according to their "gift"; whatever they are able to do for the service of the community and of the world they are called to do. The ministry of "laymen" in this sense is fully maintained and jealously asserted amongst Baptists; there is nothing which a "minister" in the professional sense is called upon to do—preaching, administration of the ordinances of baptism and the Lord's Supper, the conduct of Church business, the performance of the marriage ceremony, the burial of the dead—which a "layman" as such is debarred from doing.[2] This clear principle, recognizing intrinsic gift instead of extrinsic office, is in no wise contradicted by the fact that Baptists have found it expedient to institute a more or less "professional" ministry, equipped by special qualities and training for the usual performance of these duties. But in the earlier Baptist generations there was no such professional ministry. As Dr. Whitley, writing of the period 1640-60, says:—

Baptists put in practice the priesthood of all believers, and had no paid ministry released from the discipline of ordinary life. In the country, the typical minister was a thatcher, a farmer, a maltster, a cheese-factor; in the town, the preacher had been during the week making shoes, pins, buttons, collars, hats, clothes, had been dyeing or upholstering or selling such wares; here and there might be found a scrivener, a writing-master, an apothecary, even a doctor. As the ministers rode to their Association meetings, like Canterbury pilgrims, the butcher and the baker were joined at least by a candle-maker and an iron-monger; they would change horses at a post kept by a Baptist post-master minister, and would be entertained by a brother shipwright or carpenter. The score of ex-clergy were lost in the multitude of common men who ministered to their fellows,

[1] *Op. cit.*, p. 194.
[2] There is a "Lay Preachers' Federation", but the use of lay preachers is not nearly so wide or so organized as amongst the Methodists.

speaking out of an experience they shared with those they addressed. The priesthood of all believers was illustrated on a new scale.—(*History of British Baptists,* pp. 96, 97.)

Such authority as these men naturally came to exercise in their office was derived from the community which (acting as it believed under the guidance of the Holy Spirit) called them to exercise it. The principle could not be better stated than as it is given at the very beginning by John Smyth:—

We maintain that the power of the Eldership (i.e. the ministry) is a leading, directing, and overseeing power, ministry, or service, in the Kingdom and Priesthood of the Church, and that the negative voice, the last definite determining sentence, is in the body of the Church whereto the Eldership is bound to yield, and that the Church may do any lawful act without the Elders, but the Elders can do nothing without the approbation of the body or contrary to the body."—(*Paralleles,* p. 440.)

Presumably the legal definition of a Baptist minister in the full sense at the present day would be one whose name appears in the current list of the *Baptist Handbook* as duly accredited. Behind this official recognition there are three stages, viz. (1) a credible vocation, the consciousness of a divine calling to this particular form of service ; (2) either a collegiate training in a recognized institution or a prescribed course of study tested by examination, together with some practical experience of the ministry during a probationary period ; (3) the external corroboration of the inner call by the invitation of a particular Church to become its minister. This has been formally expressed by the Assembly of the Baptist Union as follows:—

By the *Ministry* we mean an office within the Church of Christ (not a sacerdotal order) conferred through the call of the Holy Spirit and attested by a particular or local Church.
By *Ordination* we mean the act of the Church by which it delegates to a person ministerial functions which no man can properly take upon himself.[1]

There is no prescribed, or indeed very uniform, order for ordination, but there is an increasing desire amongst Baptists that it should be a solemn religious service, and not, as too often it has been, a public meeting devoted to personal

[1] Annual Assembly of April 24, 1923.

eulogies. The resolution just quoted wisely continues: " It is recommended that the ordination, or any subsequent induction service, should include the observance of the Lord's Supper." This is the more fitting, because the primary conception of the Supper amongst Baptists is that it expresses the fellowship of believers. It is within, not above, this fellowship that the minister is set apart for the service of all. His best work will be done through ordinary human intercourse with his fellows ; he must draw his motive for it from that high motive of constraining love which the Lord's Table sets forth ; he must live on that high level of spiritual life which is made possible alone by the nurture of the Holy Spirit, symbolized in the elements ; he must find his primary evangelical message in the Cross which the Table commemorates. In regard to the test of vocation, few tasks are more difficult and responsible than the selection of candidates for ministerial training. So many different qualities are required in a Baptist minister, and success depends on such a happy combination of these qualities, that no simple formula can be framed. Baptist individualism is carried into the ministry as into other realms of thought and action, with the result that a great deal is left to personal initiative and freedom. The student for the ministry is trained to think, but is encouraged in most of our colleges to think out his own system of truth ; he is trained to act, but in the spirit of Wellington's remark, " the secret of success consists in the application of good sense to the circumstances of the moment and at the moment ". The essential qualities are conviction, sympathy, and that rather mysterious forcefulness and distinctiveness which we call " personality ". Approval by a college selection committee is provisional, and does not guarantee admission into the Baptist ministry. A further test of vocation is found in the confirming call of the

---

[1] It has been my own practice, when conducting ordination services, to give an explanatory address to the ordinand and the Church on these lines, then to ask the ordinand to kneel at the Communion Table for the Ordination Prayer with the "laying on of hands " in which it is desirable for a representative of the Church and of the whole denomination to take part. The "laying on of hands" is a New Testament rite of identification, which does not imply (except for Simon Magus) any magical transference of power; cf. Acts vi. 6 and xiii. 3. But Baptists have largely forgotten its frequency in their earlier days, and are therefore often needlessly suspicious of the practice.

local Church and the approbation of the early years of work by the Association to which the Church belongs. In recent years the Assembly has found room on its too crowded programme for a brief service of recognition of ministers passing from the probationary to the fully accredited list ; this usefully reinforces the corporate relation, which has not been adequately recognized.[1]

[1] The Baptist minister is supported by the voluntary offerings of the particular Church which has invited him ; endowments are rare and small and do not seem to be without peril. On the other hand, from various funds, the whole denomination makes grants to poorer Churches, to enable them to bring up the normal stipend paid to the minister to a minimum of £250, with allowances for children (the minimum for an unmarried man is £208). A denominational Superannuation Scheme was adopted in 1928.

THE MISSIONARY SPIRIT OF THE BAPTISTS

THE great prophets of Israel transformed the idea of God by interpreting it in the light of moral conviction and social duty. In their ethical passion they either flung down the barriers of nationalism or left such gaps in them that they ceased to be barriers for all true successors of the prophets. The discovery of a duty is the salt of religion ; the implicit universalism of morality is certain to make itself explicit and to demand a corresponding universalism of religion, wherever there is room for true expansion. It is significant that a modern Jewish scholar should criticize Jesus for His ethical emphasis: "He both annulled *Judaism* as the *life-force* of the Jewish nation, and also the nation itself as a nation." [1] It is no accident that the foremost figure of the New Testament after Jesus should be not an ecclesiastic but a missionary, and that his chief difficulty should be with the nationalistic spirit of Judaism. The Christian faith is essentially a missionary faith, for it is faith in a God who deals with men in terms of their common humanity and leaves no room for the limits of nationalism or ecclesiasticism or sectarianism, save as these may minister to the more inclusive reality. Thus the missionary spirit is always a test of Christian conviction. It is true that we cannot reverse this, and say that where there is propagating zeal there is the Christian conviction of a world-gospel, because many other motives may lead men to become zealous proselytizers. But it is also true that no man can sincerely share the New Testament faith without desiring and seeking its expansion throughout the whole world. The measure of loyalty to the King is passion for the Kingdom.

We could not draw a faithful picture of Christian life in the New Testament times which ignored its essentially missionary character. The foreground is occupied by men who were first of all missionaries. In the Gospels Christ is the centre

---

[1] *Jesus of Nazareth*, by Joseph Klausner, p. 390.

of missionary activity ; we see Him sending His disciples to the cities and villages of Israel. The very name " apostle " is eloquent of this vocation of the first disciples ; they were men " sent off " to preach the Gospel. The Acts of the Apostles, the first of all Church histories, is really the record of the missionary labours of Peter and Paul in widening circles of appeal. The Epistles of Paul are the letters of a missionary to his converts, largely concerned with the practical problems of missionary work, but for which they would never have been written. The seer of the Apocalypse lifts his eyes from the Churches of Asia, creations and centres of missionary activity, to the unnumbered multitude out of every nation before the throne of God, and hears already that future song of praise to the Lamb repeated from the ends of the earth. But there is something to be seen which is even more impressive than the evangelistic energy of these protagonists of the faith. In the background of the picture we get frequent glimpses of unknown men and women, engaged in the ordinary occupations of life, yet not less earnest in their evangelism than their greater brethren. Their names for the most part are not enrolled in any book written on earth, yet to them, rather than to any apostle, the proud Church of Rome must ascribe its origin. A group of such names is found in the closing chapter of Paul's letter to the Romans, most of them being otherwise unknown to us. Yet it is clear that these unknown men and women were all of them living centres of personal evangelism, men and women who " laboured much in the Lord", men and women whose houses were often the homes of Churches. It is the spirit of personal evangelism which is the genuine missionary spirit, and all *forms* of missionary organization are subsidiary to this, whilst the usual appropriation of the adjective " missionary " to *foreign* missionary work is as much to be deplored as the parallel appropriation of " Christian worker " to a quasi-professional class of Christians.

A significant feature of this earliest evangelism was its naturalness and spontaneity. It moved along the lines of normal human contacts with an unstudied and untutored simplicity. Jesus Himself takes life as it comes, and uses the apparently casual opportunity—by the well, under the tree, on the cross. Paul sings hymns in prison or says grace on the reeling deck of a storm-tossed ship, and these are as much a part of his evangelism as the speech at Athens, and perhaps more influential. Aquila and Priscilla are eager propagandists, and their migrations from Rome to Corinth and from Corinth to Ephesus illustrate the trade relations and movements which had so great a part in the evangelization of the Empire. Trade followed the flag, or rather the Roman eagle, and Christianity followed trade, as a good map of the distribution of early Christianity will show. The movements of the centurion's party of soldiers guarding Paul remind us that a Christian soldier would naturally become a travelling missionary as his century or legion moved from place to place. We note Paul's hint about the possible influence of a Christian husband or wife on a heathen partner, and the letter to Philemon shows how the relation of master and slave could be evangelized. In fact, Celsus makes such personal evangelism the ground of bitter accusation : —

We see, indeed, in private houses workers in wool and leather and fullers, and persons of the most uninstructed and rustic character, not venturing to utter a word in the presence of their elders and wiser masters ; but when they get hold of the children privately, and certain women as ignorant as themselves, they pour forth wonderful statements (*Origen against Celsus,* iii, 55, trans. of A.N.C.L.).

The faith of the Baptists claims to be a return to the primitive simplicities of the New Testament, and in theory and practice has tended to repeat these features of the early days of Christianity. Their early ministers were laymen, as we have seen; their early missionaries and evangelists were themselves. It is instructive to take a typical case of such personal evangelism, which shows us how genuine conviction tends to propagate itself. Between 1790 and 1795 a youth named John Wheeler left his home on a Gloucestershire farm to make his way in the world. He found work in Northampton in a tallow-chandler's shop and attended All Saints' Church with his master's family. But when he was passing down College Lane one Sunday he was attracted by the singing in the Baptist chapel, went in, and was converted. He was baptized in the River Nene by Dr. Ryland in 1798, and soon began to do some village preaching. On a visit home his mother said to him: " John, they tell me thee hast become a meetinger. . . . Tell me all about it " ; and John told her to such effect that she came to share his faith. In 1805 John Wheeler

set up for himself as a tallow-chandler in the village of Bugbrooke, where he and five others from College Lane were
formed into a Baptist Church, to which he became the minister
for more than thirty years. Thomas Wheeler, his brother,
" thought he was religious enough " until he also came to
Northampton on the advice of John, and there came under the
same influences, but he was not baptized until he was at
Dunstable. Here he heard Robert Hall preach, and was so
deeply impressed that the next morning he gave his master
notice to leave, saying that he must sit under such a ministry.
He followed Robert Hall to Leicester, told him what he had
done, and asked for help in finding a situation there. Robert
Hall is reported to have drawn himself up to his full height
and to have said: " I never was so complimented in my life,
sir. I will go with you at once, sir, and see if I can find you
a situation "—which he did. Thomas became a deacon
eventually at the Harvey Lane Church. Meanwhile a third
son, Francis, had followed his brothers to Northampton, and
was baptized by the College Lane minister in 1812. The
Church sent him to the Bristol Baptist College to be trained
for the ministry, and he eventually became minister of the
Moulton Baptist Church (where Carey had been the minister)
and remained there for over thirty years. Whilst Francis
was an apprentice, he was the means of the conversion of a
fellow-apprentice who in later life is said to have turned the
mind of Park Street Church to the young man called Charles
Haddon Spurgeon. One of the converts of John Wheeler at
Bugbrooke was John Turland Brown, the future minister of
College Street, Northampton, and a future President of the
Baptist Union. An apprentice, Hail Marriott Mawby, who
married his master's daughter, rendered devoted service as a
deacon and Sunday-school worker at Long Buckby and at
College Street, Northampton.[1]

This homely narrative owes its value to its homeliness, for
it is typical of the propagation of the Baptist faith in what we
may call the middle period of its history. There was, however, some corporate as well as individual realization of mis-

[1] The account is taken from an unpublished manuscript by the late
Benjamin Wheeler, son of Francis Wheeler, written in 1881, of which
a copy is in my possession, made by H. M. Mawby. To the latter, as
it is only right to acknowledge in such a connection, I owe all my
opportunities for education.

sionary duty, even as when the Church at Antioch sent out Barnabas and Paul as its missionary representatives. Dr. Whitley, writing of the Baptist Churches in the seventeenth century, says: "The first distinctive feature was the recognition of the duty of evangelization and telling off special men for itinerant work.[1] . . . At first there was a separate commission for each journey ; soon they selected men who had peculiar aptitude for evangelization, told them off for it as their main work, and undertook to support them and their families. . . . Thus the Messenger came to be a regular officer, not of one Church, but of a group of Churches ; every such group came to realize its duty to support a missionary, every new Church was trained to realize its duty in this respect. This development went on in both groups of Baptists " (i.e. the Generals and the Particulars).[2]

In the eighteenth century the Baptist Churches shared in the general decline of religious fervour which preceded the Evangelical Revival. The "soft shell " of Arminianism was not a sufficient protection of the General Baptists against doctrinal decay, and (apart from the " New Connexion " of 1770) they cease to count. The " hard shell " of Calvinism protected the Particular Baptists from disintegration, but brought its own perils, which have been partly illustrated in the study of Ann Dutton (pp. 50 ff.). It would not be fair to make either the lack of the missionary spirit or moral " antinomianism " the necessary consequence of the Calvinistic doctrine of predestination, for Whitefield's Calvinism was joined to Wesley's Arminianism in the Evangelical Revival, and Arminianism as well as Calvinism has had to rebuke those who neglected the moral law on the ground of religious faith. But the experience of Andrew Fuller (1754-1815) as a young pastor will show how " hyper-Calvinism " could be made to

---

[1] The Fenstanton *Records*, pp. 72 ff. describe such a preaching tour by Henry Denne, duly appointed a Messenger by the Fenstanton Church.

[2] *History of British Baptists*, pp. 87, 88. Of the fifteen men who signed the Particular Baptist Confession of 1644, " every one who can be traced was an ardent evangelist " (p. 89). Cf. the resolution of the Kentish Association (1657): " Agreed that there be all possible care in propagateing the Gospel by Imploying the Messengers in the work of the Lord Jesus sending with each of them one young disciple . . . also that theire ffamilies be well provided for in their absence " (*op. cit.*, p. 68).

justify the lack of missionary zeal. He had been brought up in what he calls the " shackles " of such a distinction between the " elect " and the " reprobate " that the duty as well as the possibility of saving faith was confined to the former. It is evident that such a distinction so applied would inevitably fetter the preacher in his appeals to the unconverted, for whom nothing but the duty of obedience to the external law was obligatory. But by 1781 young Fuller had discovered that such a distinction was made neither by the Bible nor by such men as Eliott [1] and Brainerd in their preaching to American Indians. Fuller therefore worked out his freedom to preach to all the duty of faith, and the promise of forgiveness to every penitent sinner, without any abandonment of the doctrines of Calvinism proper (it was common ground that *saving* faith, could be experienced only by the elect). In 1785 he published his results in a book entitled *The Gospel of Christ worthy of all acceptation, or the obligations of men fully to credit and cordially to approve whatever God makes known.* This book had important consequences, not only for Baptists, but also for the world. " Fullerism ", as it was called, created a considerable controversy, but it offered an open door to those who were feeling the breath of the Evangelical Revival. Amongst these was a young Baptist minister who had to earn part of his living by keeping school and making shoes. William Carey (1761-1834) was in close personal touch with Andrew Fuller, of Kettering, and saw the application of his truth to a wider field of duty. At Moulton he had read Captain Cook's *Journal,* and had been kindled to missionary enthusiasm by its revelation of human need. At a ministers' meeting in 1786 he first raised the question " whether the command given to the Apostles to teach all nations was not obligatory on all succeeding ministers to the end of the world, seeing that the accompanying promise was of equal extent " ; but he was told by John Collett Ryland to sit down: " You're an enthusiast. When God pleases to convert the heathen, He'll do it without consulting you or me." [2] But in 1792 William Carey, then at Leicester, brought out a book of 87 pages, entitled, *An Enquiry into the Obligations of Christians, to use*

[1] Weitbrecht speaks of his work as " the first real Protestant missionary enterprise " (*Encyclopædia of Religion and Ethics,* viii, p. 729).
[2] *William Carey,* by S. Pearce Carey, 8th ed., p. 54.

H

means for the conversion of the heathens, in which the religious
state of the different nations of the world, the success of former
undertakings, and the practicability of further undertakings,
are considered.[1]   It is a great book, both in itself, in relation
to its author, and in its historical issues.   Already we may see
in its plain and scientific marshalling of facts, its absence of
rhetoric, its cogent insistence on a proved duty, those qualities
of mind and character which made Carey the great man he
was.   He first asks the question he had raised in 1786 and
had been persistently raising ever since—" whether the commission given by our Lord to His disciples be not still binding
on us ".   He reviews the history of missions through the
centuries in a way that shows his wide knowledge and reading.
He patiently tabulates the countries of the world, their populations and their religions, according to contemporary
knowledge.   He faces the practical difficulties in the way of
foreign missionary work, and disposes of them one by one.
Finally, he sets out the example and methods of a trading
company which has obtained a charter, and proposes the
formation of a missionary society on the same lines to undertake the practical work of evangelization abroad.   " We have
only to keep the end in view, and have our hearts thoroughly
engaged in the pursuit of it, and means will not be very
difficult."

His proposal was carried into effect in the autumn of 1792
at Kettering, after it had been enforced at Nottingham in the
spring by Carey's well-known sermon, " Expect great things
from God ; attempt great things for God ", and the new char-
tered company started with a subscribed capital of £13 2s. 6d.
Its first operation was to send out William Carey to Bengal as
colleague to John Thomas, a Baptist doctor who had already
done some missionary work there.[2]   Carey's intensely practical mind and general efficiency enabled him not only to
become self-supporting, but to earn large sums of money

---

[1] See photographic reproduction, Carey Press, 1934.
[2] Mr. F. D. Walker's discriminating study, *William Carey*, shows
his true place in the history of Protestant foreign missions.   "He was
not the 'Father of modern Missions' ; he was not ' the first Englishman to go out as a missionary to the heathen ' ; he was not ' the first
missionary to India '.   He was the founder of the Baptist Missionary
Society ; he was one of the first two Englishmen sent by a Missionary
Society as missionaries to the non-Christians of India " (p. 103).   The
faults of John Thomas have helped to hide his primacy.   "He was

which were unselfishly devoted to missionary work. His great powers as a linguist had already been shown in the acquisition of half a dozen languages whilst at home. In India he eventually became Professor of Sanscrit at Fort William College, and achieved an amazing amount of translation work in the missionary interest through his indefatigable industry and undaunted courage. His chief helpers were Joshua Marshman, first a weaver, then a schoolmaster, and from 1799 at work with Carey in Serampore, and William Ward, a printer and newspaper editor, whom the far-sighted Carey had earmarked before his departure from England. " The distinguishing characteristic of Carey's work was his adoption of the principle of concentration. It is true that he sent agents to distribute his translations of the Bible and to attempt to found mission-stations in places far distant from Serampore, but his life-work was the establishment of the training college at Serampore and of the group of schools in its neighbourhood. To a far greater extent than any of his predecessors he realized the comparative futility of diffused missions and the impossibility of converting India by means of European evangelists." [1] The Baptist Missionary Society is at present working in Bengal, Bihar and Orissa, [2] and North India, as well as in Ceylon (from 1812), the educational emphasis being specially prominent in its Indian work.

The missionary passion of the Society, sustained and led at home by the loyal devotion and remarkable energies of Andrew Fuller, sought an outlet in the West as well as in the East, and work in Jamaica was taken up in 1814, and for a considerable time received almost as much attention and support as that in India. Its outstanding feature of interest was the part taken by William Knibb (1803-45) in the abolition

the first Englishman set apart for definite missionary work in India, and the first to lead an Indian to the Saviour " (*op. cit.*, p. 228). There is a *Life* of him by C. B. Lewis (1873). But all this does not materially affect the universal recognition of Carey as the great pioneer in modern foreign missionary work. See K. S. Latourette, *A History of the Expansion of Christianity*, iv. p. 68: "He was the first Anglo-Saxon Protestant either in America or in Great Britain to propose that Christians take concrete steps to bring their Gospel to all the human race."

[1] *History of Christian Missions*, by C. H. Robinson, pp. 82, 83.
[2] The work in Orissa was carried on by the General Baptists from 1816 till 1891.

of slavery, to which reference will be made in the next chapter. The Jamaican Baptist Churches, counting over 30,000 members, were long self-supporting, though Calabar College was sustained from Britain.[1]   Another field of the Society's work was the Cameroons, on the West Coast of Africa (opposite to the island of Fernando Po, the scene of its first attempt), where flourished still the slave-trade that had so largely populated Jamaica.   " Soon after gaining his freedom, a man named Keith worked his passage from Jamaica, and proclaimed the Gospel on the very spot where he had been made a slave."[2]   The first Baptist mission-station on the continent of Africa was established in 1845 by Alfred Saker, who came to be known as " the Apostle of the Cameroons ".   It is significant that the first real impression on the Dualla natives was made by Saker's brickyard, for bricks could resist white ants.[3]   The African missionary has usually had to be ready to turn his hand to any and every occupation.   On the transference of the Cameroons to Germany in 1884 the Baptist work was handed over to German missionaries, but before this a new opening for African work was found on the newly discovered Congo River (of which the mouth is about as far south of the equator as the Cameroons are north of it).   In 1878 George Grenfell and Thomas Comber, who had been working with Saker, came to San Salvador, and began the most picturesque and romantic as well as the most arduous work of the Society.   It was inevitable that the pioneer missionary should be, like Livingstone, an explorer, and here George Grenfell won high distinction, fully recognized in the two fine volumes devoted to his work by Sir Harry Johnston.   With Grenfell's name is linked that of Holman Bentley,[4] who was the pioneer in linguistic work on Congo languages and dialects, of which

[1] See E. A. Payne, *Freedom in Jamaica*, 1933.   (It seems likely that in the years ahead renewed help from the Baptist Missionary Society may be desirable.   Work has also been done with permanent results elsewhere in the West Indies, e.g. Trinidad.)

[2] *The Centenary Volume of the B.M.S.*, p. 10.

[3] Sir Harry Johnston, *George Grenfell and the Congo*, vol. i, p. 35; see also *The Life of George Grenfell*, by George Hawker (1909).

[4] *W. Holman Bentley*, by H. M. Bentley (1907); see also his own *Pioneering on the Congo*, 1900. Vol. i, pp. 57 ff., refers to the generosity of Robert Arthington, of Leeds, in this connection.   He left a large bequest, used for expansion on many fields.

there are said to be two hundred. The most fully developed part of the mission is in the Congo language area, in the cataract stretch of the river between Matadi and Stanley Pool, but the stations of the Society extend over a thousand miles of the Congo River as far as Yakusu.[1] There is, moreover, extensive American Baptist missionary work in the Congo territory.

It is needless to say that in this new land the cost in human lives has been very heavy, from the time of the Combers onwards. But the greater physical peril and hardship bring a relatively greater visible return. It is a native Congo belief that the stars are the watch-fires of villages in the sky, for, as their primitive logic says, "the rain puts them out." In sober truth, the scattered stations of missionary work in the "Dark Continent" are centres of light and warmth, which none of the elemental forces will be able to extinguish.

The third great area of Baptist missionary work is in the provinces of Shantung, Shansi and Shensi, in Northern China, right, left and right of the great Yellow River, which, unlike the dense population of its shores, has cut so many new beds for itself in the course of the centuries.[2] Serious work began in 1870 with the arrival of Timothy Richard in Shantung, and his name remains the outstanding one in this field. He was prominent in the work of relief in the great famine of 1876-78, which was the occasion of the extension of missionary work from Shantung to the inland Shansi. Of this and other activities, including influential relations with high officials, a characteristically detailed account is given in Dr. Richard's valuable book, *Forty-Five Years in China*.[3] He laid special stress on the importance of Christian literature for missionary work in China, and was prominent in the work of the Christian Literature Society after 1891. He became Chancellor of the Shansi University, which was founded by the Chinese Government in 1901 out of the fine levied upon the province because of the Boxer outrages. There is also a

[1] See *Achievement*, by F. Townley Lord, 1942, an interesting popular account of the whole work of the Baptist Missionary Society, prepared for the ter-jubilee.   Missionary work was done in Italy from 1870 and in Brittany from 1843.

[2] Meredith Townsend, *Asia and Europe*, p. 279.   This appears to have been the original seat of the Chinese, no immigration being indicated (Moore, *History of Religions*, i, p. 1).

[3] There is a biography of him by W. E. Soothill (1923).

Christian University of Shantung, in which Baptists have an important share ; as in India, the educational side of evangelistic work receives increasing attention, together with a full recognition of the value of medical missions. The Boxer massacres of Shansi missionaries and Chinese Christians in 1900, springing from an intense anti-foreign propaganda, wrote a tragic page in the history of Baptist missions as well as of those of other Churches.   At Tai-yuan-fu, where a company of forty-six missionaries or their children were massacred, a considerable proportion were Baptists, and eight represented the Baptist Missionary Society ; from Sinchow another company of eight escaped into hiding in caves of the hills, only to be run down at last and massacred. The story of their sufferings [1] is like the acts of the martyrs in the early history of the Church, and, like all earnest missionary life, these common deaths preach the catholicity of truth, deeper than all denominational differences of judgment and conviction.

The missionary spirit is, of course, not the characteristic of any branch of the universal Church, but is found wherever there is vigorous Christian life and personal loyalty to the Head of the Church.   But it may fairly be claimed that the *emphasis* on the missionary duty and the response to that emphasis displayed since Carey's day do characterize Baptist Church life.   Its keenest interests and its chief form of corporate activity are found here.   Indeed, what the " Church " is to some other communions, the " Missionary Society " is to many Baptists.   As someone once remarked to the present writer, " It is in the missionary meeting that you may hear the beating of the Baptist heart ".   The work done on the foreign field since Carey's time will compare by no means unfavourably with that of other Churches, with greater resources of men and money, so far as Great Britain is concerned.   As we review it, even in so rapid an outline as that just given, certain features become apparent, significant for Baptists, as indeed for all Christians.

There is increasing recognition—indeed, general recognition to-day—that the future of missionary work must lie with native evangelists and the growth of native Churches.   This is not merely an inference from the magnitude of the work to

---

[1] See *The China Martyrs of* 1900, by R. C. Forsyth (1904).

be done ; it is discernment of the best way of doing it. Dr. Richard[1] remarks on the bringing in of fifty inquirers by one Chinese Bible-woman and of one hundred by another: " This proved for the hundredth time the fact that natives can best influence their fellow-countrymen to join the Christian Church ". The recognition of this fact will not mean a lightening of the missionary responsibility of the Church, for the training and oversight of these native leaders will need all the devotion of men and money the Church can bring ; but it will mean that the Christian faith will be interpreted by the native mind to the native mind, and that some of the results may not be those which would entirely agree with our Western interpretation. This line of thought has been forcibly presented most recently by Mr. Stanley Jones in his widely-read book, *The Christ of the Indian Road,* which is a plea for native liberty of interpretation, joined with a healthy confidence in the ultimate result. There should be less hesitation amongst Baptists as to this liberty than amongst those who are committed to a formal creed. The liberty that Baptists have claimed and won for themselves they must be prepared to give to others.

A further principle of modern missionary work is that it must erase some of the old lines drawn between " sacred " and " secular " activity, and be prepared to expand into all forms of usefulness that promote the extension of the Kingdom of God. This principle has not been easily reached, and we can see what it cost some of the greatest missionaries to convince those who were not face to face with the facts, like themselves. Even now many good people who support " missions " would be startled to realize that a missionary is not " preaching " the Gospel all the time, and that many things have to be done before it can be preached at all. But all these things belong to the Kingdom of God, if they do not belong to the Church as its nucleus and centre. When in 1801 Carey, Marshman, and Ward laid on the Communion Table the first Bengali New Testament—the result of seven and a half years of labour[2] they were consecrating Christian scholarship in the widest sense, and implicitly opening the door to all that educational work which Carey so valued, just as the baptism of the first Indian convert, Krishna Pal, was

[1] *Forty-Five Years in China*, p. 216.
[2] *William Carey*, by S. P. Carey, 8th ed., p. 211.

the consecration of the medical skill that had set his dislocated shoulder and won his loyalty to the Saviour John Thomas preached. No modern missionary has had a wider horizon in this respect than Dr. Timothy Richard, and we have seen that his work in famine relief opened up a new province to Baptist missions. The exploration of the Congo by Grenfell and Bentley was just as truly the work of the Gospel as the foundation of stations on its banks which their work made possible. All this is generally granted to-day, for it is in the line of our modern humanitarian emphasis. But Christians in general have not yet seen all the consequences of this new vision of the Christianization of all things by the purpose and the spirit in which they are done.

This leads directly to the question of the missionary motive. An illuminating summary by Canon Quick may be quoted: " Sometimes the motive has been the desire to save something more out of a wreck doomed to destruction by the forces of evil which are overwhelming it. Sometimes it has been the desire to herald and advance the reign of Christ upon the earth itself. Other-worldly Christianity has been inspired by the first motive, evolutionary Christianity by the second. Possibly the noblest motive of all is the passion to share and to serve the creative purpose of God, to make something on earth and out of earth, which is fit to be the eternal object of God's love ".[1]

This broader outlook, though it implies much greater sympathy with the large elements of truth in many non-Christian faiths, does not necessarily mean the perilous compromise with heathen customs. Baptist missionaries are often face to face with the same issue as the earliest preachers of the faith—how far is it expedient to baptize heathen customs as well as heathen converts? How far, for example, can the initiation rites of many tribes be permitted to continue in some modified form? How far is caste to be recognized? In general, it may be said that the Baptist missionaries have been unequivocal in demanding a clear cut from those practices that are bound up with superstition, and a clear sacrifice of the old standing and attitude in the name of the new faith. The value of believers' baptism by immersion is evident in this respect. Baptists seek genuine conversion and not merely

---

[1] *Catholic and Protestant Elements of Christianity*, p. 102.

a general uplift, and they recognize the peril of " Mass Movements ". Their success has been marked amongst people of the sturdy, independent type, e.g. the Lusnais.

When the Baptist Missionary Society began its work abroad in 1793, it was inevitable that it should be met with the criticism which, like economic poverty, we have always with us—that there were plenty of heathen at home.[1] They met this by undertaking itinerant preaching at home, and there was, for example, in 1796, a lengthy evangelistic tour by two appointed ministers in Cornwall. One of the two was William Steadman, who afterwards became the first President of the Northern Education Society (now Rawdon College), and made itinerancy a marked feature of the work of himself and his students. In 1797, however, a society to promote home evangelism was formed in London, and carried on a work that became very extensive at certain periods, a hundred whole-time agents being employed in 1835.[2] In 1879, however, the work of the Home Mission was taken over by the Baptist Union, which continued the previous development of policy in the direction of founding or supporting mission churches rather than itinerancy. Home mission work of this kind is now done rather through the Associations, with their more intimate knowledge of local conditions. Considerable progress has also been made in the organization of lay preachers.

No attempt can here be made to speak of the missionary spirit amongst American Baptists, from the time when Roger Williams, the first American Baptist, worked amongst the Indians (c. 1630) to the present day of the great American Baptist Societies for both home and foreign missionary work, which are proportionate to the magnitude of a leading denomination.[3] It is the less necessary to do so because we are not concerned with making a catalogue or writing a history, but with the missionary spirit of the denomination, which is illustrated as well in the smaller group in Great Britain as in the much larger group in the United States.

[1] Whitley, op. cit., p. 266.
[2] The Story of Baptist Home Missions, by C. Brown, p. 32 (1897).
[3] " It is significant that the call to engage in foreign mission work was the first thing that led to organization and unity among Baptists in the country " of America (Directory of the Baptist World Alliance, 1927, p. 46). This was in 1814.

The fact is that the Christian faith is imperialistic ; it cannot be content to be accepted as a useful institution, a beautiful if impracticable dream, one among many guesses at truth, or even as one religious truth amongst others. There is a noble as well as an ignoble intolerance—an intolerance of compromise which claims an imperial dominion with imperial confidence for an imperial truth, in the spirit in which the greatest missionary is seen standing in Rome uttering his last recorded message : " This salvation of God is sent unto the nations ; they will also hear."[1]

[1] Acts xxviii. 28.

VI

THE PASSION OF THE BAPTISTS FOR LIBERTY

IN the first paragraph of Milton's *Areopagitica*, that typically English defence of liberty, he speaks of the "passion" engendered by his subject and the occasion, the order of the Puritan Parliament forbidding the publication of any unlicensed book.[1] The passion of the Baptists for liberty is one of their most strongly marked characteristics, flowing directly from the spiritual individualism which is their primary emphasis. From the beginning of their history Baptists have been in the forefront of the battle for political and religious liberty, as their place in Cromwell's army shows. To them belongs the distinction of being the first to claim and the first to apply fearlessly the unfettered principle of freedom for religion,[2] which is the best tribute to its intrinsic worth. Their phenomenal growth in the United States of America must be partly due to this characteristic passion, so congenial to a constitution framed on the basis of political and religious equality and freedom.

[1] Milton held Baptist views, though of unorthodox variety. Cf. *A Treatise on Christian Doctrine*, p. 431 (ed. 1825): "Baptism, wherein the bodies of believers who engage themselves to pureness of life are immersed in running water, to signify their regeneration by the Holy Spirit, and their union with Christ in His death, burial and resurrection" (in the Latin ed., p. 317). On the other hand, his peculiar Christology (Arian rather than Socinian) separates him from Baptists in general, with whom he does not seem to have been in corporate communion. See Whitley, *A History of British Baptists*, Note C: "In what sense was Milton a Baptist?"

[2] Cf. W. F. Adeney (himself a Congregationalist) in the *Encyclopædia of Religion and Ethics*, ix. p. 382: "It should be observed that, while modern Nonconformists are opposed to any interference with religion by the State, and stand for complete religious liberty—Cavour's 'free Church in a free State'—this was by no means the case among the early Nonconformists, with the solitary exception of the Baptists." So also Skeats and Miall, *History of the Free Churches of England*, p. 19.

Already in John Smyth, the first Baptist, we find the explicit claim for full religious freedom : —

That the magistrate is not by vertue of his office to meddle with religion, or matters of conscience, to force and compell men to this or that form of religion, or doctrine : but to leaue Christian religion free, to euery mans conscience, and to handle onely ciuil transgressions Rom. 13. injuries and wronges of men against man, in murther, Adulterie, theft, etc. for Christ onelie is the king, and lawgiver of the church and conscience Jas 4. 12.—(*A Confession of Faith*, 1611, art. 84.)

But the first publication of such a claim is found in the black-letter 16mo called *A short declaration of the Mistery of Iniquity*, by Thomas Helwys, a foremost disciple of Smyth's.[1] In 1612 he felt it his duty to leave his master in Amsterdam and return to England, in order to testify openly to his Baptist faith. He had thus won the right to challenge his fellow-Separatists in Holland to " come and lay down their lives in their owne Countrie for Christ and His truth."[2] Thomas Helwys knew the risks he ran in publishing under his own name so direct an attack on authority as this. "Let none thinke that we are altogether ignorant, what building and what war fare we take in hand, and that we have not sitt downe and in some measure thoroughly considered what the cost and danger may be ". He was soon in prison and lost to our sight. The doctrine of full religious liberty, now so much a commonplace, then so perilous and fanatical an innovation, is definite and reiterated in this book, e.g. : —

Our lord the King is but an earthly King, and he hath no aucthority as a King but in earthly causes, and if the Kings people be obedient and true subjects, obeying all humane lawes made by the King, our lord the King can require no more : for mens religion to God is betwixt God and themselves ; the King shall not answere for it, neither may the King be iugd betwene God and man. Let them be heretikes, Turcks, Jewes or whatsoever, it apperteynes not to the earthly power to punish them in the least measure (p. 69).

This book has historic importance, as being the first published English assertion of this doctrine.[3] It was soon

[1] See the reproduction by Replika process issued by the Baptist Historical Society in 1935.
[2] *Op. cit.*, p. 112.
[3] So Whitley, *op. cit.*, p. 33.

followed by similar testimony from fellow-Baptists, such as Leonard Busher in *Religion's Peace* (1614) and John Murton in *Objections Answered* (1615) and *An Humble Supplication* (1620).[1] This last had a romantic origin and a historic issue, both deserving to be remembered. Of its origin we are told by Roger Williams, who in 1644 incorporated some of its argument in his book, *The Bloudy Tenent of Persecution*:—

The author of these arguments against persecution, as I have been informed, being committed by some then in power close prisoner to Newgate, for the witness of some truths of Jesus, and having not the use of pen and ink, wrote these arguments in milk, in sheets of paper brought to him by the woman, his keeper, from a friend in London as the stopples of his milk bottle. In such paper written with milk, nothing will appear ; but the way of reading it by fire being known to this friend who received the papers, he transcribed and kept together the papers, although the author himself could not correct, nor view what himself had written (*op. cit.*, p. 36 of 1848 ed.).

Roger Williams, who had emigrated to America in 1630, found as much intolerance of unorthodox opinions amongst the Puritans of New England as amongst the Anglicans of the old England, even though it was less violently expressed. He was banished from Massachusetts in 1635, and in the following year founded the settlement of Rhode Island, which had the distinction of being the first to grant full religious liberty. Roger Williams became a Baptist in 1639, and founded the first Baptist Church in America. His pioneer work in both civil rights and religious propaganda thus links itself with the book written in Newgate prison on the stopples of bottles in the milk they contained, and is inseparably interwoven with the world's history. " In subjection, in exile, in power, Baptists preached and practised religious liberty ; and from little Rhode Island the principle has been adopted as fundamental in the whole United States of America."[2]

The legal position of the first English Baptists was defined by the Elizabethan Act of 1593 directed against " seditious

[1] All these are given in the first volume published by the Hanserd Knollys Society, *Tracts on Liberty of Conscience* (1846). Copies of the very rare book by Helwys are to be found in the Bodleian, Trinity College, Dublin, and in the Angus Library, Regent's Park College. For the significance of Helwys and Murton see Burgess, *John Smith, etc.*, 1911.

[2] Whitley, *op. cit.*, p. 67.

sectaries and disloyal persons ".[1] Absence from the established worship for one month or presence at a " conventicle " caused liability to imprisonment ; non-submission within three months involved banishment from the realm. John Smyth and the other Puritan Separatists of Gainsborough and Scrooby were therefore simply anticipating the law when they voluntarily withdrew from England to Holland ; indeed, some of them did not escape imprisonment. When Thomas Helwys and his friends returned to London in 1612 the old law was still in operation, but they could now also be required to take the oath of allegiance, originally (in 1606) extracted from " Popish Recusants ". They had, of course, no personal difficulty in this, but the ecclesiastical authorities wished to debar them from its protection, as it was not intended to cover the case of Separatists.[3] Thus we find a Baptist petition of 1614, probably from Helwys and his friends in prison, which points out 'the injustice of this discrimination: " When wee fall under the handes of the Bishops wee can have no benefitt by the said oath, for they say it belongeth onely to Popish recuzantes, and not to others."[4] The civil power was more reasonable. It is worthy of notice that these petitioners expressly refuse the calumniating identification of themselves with the " Anabaptists ".

In spite of these legal disabilities and penalties, Baptist Churches contrived to maintain their corporate existence, even when the advent of Laud (Bishop of London, 1628 ; Archbishop of Canterbury, 1633) brought with it a more vigorous policy of persecution. For the period prior to 1640, when the assembling of the "Long" Parliament began a new era, we hear of six Baptist groups, two in London, the other four at Lincoln, Salisbury, Coventry, and Tiverton.[5] These were all of the "General" (i.e. Arminian) type. There is no

---

[1] Gee and Hardy, *Documents illustrative of the History of the English Church*, lxxxvi.

[2] Burgess, *op. cit.*, p. 94.

[3] Whitley, *op. cit.*, p. 38. He gives a clear summary of the two distinct sets of officials concerned in the administration of the law—the civil (sheriffs, magistrates, county judges, Star Chamber) and the ecclesiastical (archdeacons, bishops, archbishops, High Commission). See also Frere, *A History of the English Church in the Reigns of Elizabeth and James I*, pp. 350 ff.

[4] Burrage, *The Early English Dissenters*, ii, p. 215, where the whole petition is printed.

[5] Particulars will be found in Whitley, *op. cit.*, pp. 45-58.

evidence of any Churches of the other type (the "Particular"', i.e. Calvinistic) until the closing years of the period, though this (not without important modification) was destined to form the Baptist Church of the future. The subterranean continuance of Baptist life between 1620 and 1640 is shown by the gathered force of the current when the stream breaks into the open, and the rise of Puritanism into power gave Baptists their opportunity. It is an interesting coincidence that Oliver Cromwell first came into military prominence at Gainsborough in 1643, when he was successful in relieving the town, besieged by the Royalists.[1] Thus the place which saw John Smyth begin to express those convictions which issued in his becoming the first Baptist also saw the first notable victory of the Puritan leader, who was to draw so much of his military strength from Baptist ranks. We owe it to Dr. Whitley that the place of Baptists in Cromwell's army has been brought to light in its full extent.[2] The use of the term "Independent" to designate the religious texture of the army as distinct from the "Presbyterian" Parliament (1640-48) has obscured the fact that "the New Model Army" was largely recruited and officered from Baptists. A typical example has been given in the study of William Allen, adjutant-general (see Chapter II, §2). Other well-known names include those of Richard Deane, artillery general and subsequently admiral, associated with Blake and buried in Westminster Abbey ; Thomas Harrison, prominent throughout the whole period, who held chief command in Cromwell's absence (1650-51), impressive by his unshaken conviction and courage when executed in 1660.; Colonel Hutchinson, a Baptist of different mould, who escaped the penalty of regicide by submission, and has been made familiar to us by his wife's memoirs and by J. R. Green's illustrative use of him as a cultured Puritan ; Edmund Ludlow, prominent in connection with "Pride's Purge" in 1648, Commander-in-Chief in Ireland, 1659, who wrote his own memoirs in exile (twenty-five of his regimental officers were members of Baptist churches); Robert Lilburne, Commander-in-Chief in Scotland in 1654, and brother of John Lilburne, the Leveller leader, who also as a young man seems to have had Baptist contacts ;

---

[1] Carlyle, *Oliver Cromwell*, i, p. 138.
[2] *Op. cit.*, pp. 73-81.

William Gough, one of Cromwell's " Lords " and one of the four who were sent by the army to meet Monck.[1]

The place taken by these men and many others who could be named shows the passion of the Baptists for that religious liberty which had been so unjustly denied to them. Their political motives were distinctly subordinate to religious aims, as was true of Puritanism in general.[2] But it is seen more clearly in the Baptists than in others, because of their general opposition to Cromwell's political policy after the execution of Charles. This has been illustrated in the case of William Allen ; it could be illustrated also from most of those named above. They would not have " a ghost from the grave " of the Stuarts to tyrannize over them. The extreme form of this opposition was found in the " Fifth-Monarchy " movement, in which many Baptists were implicated.[3] The movement drew its name from " the kingdom of the saints " pictured in Daniel vii. as arising after the rule of the four beasts. They illustrated one of the many types of contemporary religious fanaticism. The movement culminated and collapsed in the armed rising of Thomas Venner in 1661, which naturally helped to discredit the Baptists, and drew from them many disavowals of it.[4]

The general position of the Baptists from 1640 to 1660 was naturally one of greater religious freedom, though with considerable variety of expression as the political movements of that kaleidoscopic time affected them. In the army, as we have just seen, and naturally where the army had control, they were protected—at least as soon as the army came into Cromwell's hands. He stood up for them and for others like

[1] Brief accounts of all these men will be found in the *Dictionary of National Biography*. There is an edition of the very interesting *Memoirs of Colonel Hutchinson*, with notes by C. H. Firth (1906). Ludlow's *Memoirs*, in three volumes, were first published in 1698-99 ; they are frequently cited by Carlyle, with the adjectives " solid " or " wooden " Ludlow. The well-known description of the ejection of the " Rump " will be found in ii, pp. 455 f. ; he derived it from Harrison.

[2] Trevelyan, *History of England*, pp. 375, 381. Cf. his remark on Laud's ecclesiastical policy: " It was indeed the chief cause of the Civil War, because it provoked the furious reaction of armed Puritanism in which Laud himself perished " (p. 393).

[3] See *Baptists and Fifth-Monarchy Men*, by L. F. Brown (1912). We may compare the relation of the Zealots to Pharisaism in the New Testament period.

[4] Whitley, *op. cit.*, p. 109.

them against the Presbyterian Puritans, who were as intolerant as Anglicans had been. " Honest men served you faithfully in this action. Sir, they are trusty ; I beseech you, in the name of God, not to discourage them. . . . He that ventures his life for the liberty of his country, I wish he trust God for the liberty of his conscience, and you for the liberty he fights for." [1]   Cromwell in his Protectorate gave expression to his ideas of comprehension and toleration. " While he preserved tithe and endowments, he put down persecution. The benefices of the Church were held by Presbyterians, Independents, or Baptists indifferently, while free congregations of a more fanciful kind multiplied outside. . . . The fatal flaw in his ecclesiastical policy was that he had not been able to give Anglicanism that share in the life of the Church which he had offered to grant it in the Heads of the Proposals." [2]

In the reaction from Puritan intolerance and political incapacity which characterized the Restoration of 1660, Baptists inevitably entered upon a period of severe persecution, lasting with intervals until the final settlement of the Revolution in 1689. They were not greatly concerned with the Act of Uniformity of 1662, which completed the expulsion of some 2,000 " Nonconformist " clergymen from the Established Church. Indeed, this expulsion indirectly benefited them, for it reinforced dissent with a number of able and cultured men, which it greatly needed. But the revengeful spirit of the " Cavalier Parliament ", which began in 1661 its seventeen-year-long tenure of power, found expression in the successive enactments of the so-called " Clarendon Code ". In its first year the Corporation Act required magistrates and other municipal officers to have " taken the Sacrament of the Lord's Supper, according to the rites of the Church of England "

[1] Letter of June 14, 1645 ; quoted in Carlyle's *Cromwell*, i, p. 192. How little the warning was heeded is seen in the fact that " the Long Parliament, with almost incredible folly, proceeded to pass measures for the lifelong imprisonment of Baptists, the prohibition of laymen from preaching in public, and the dismissal of all Independent officers from the New Model " (Trevelyan, *op. cit.*, p. 418).

[2] Trevelyan, *op. cit.*, pp. 430,431. The actual number of Baptists in the Established Church of this period was smaller than has been supposed. Whitley calculates that in 1659-60 " there were not more than thirty Baptists who were drawing public money for religious work ; of these about a dozen may have been clergy " (p. 160).

I

within the year previous to their election.[1] This exclusion of
Dissenters from municipal office affected only a small number
of Baptists, but its moral and indirect effect was far-reaching.
In 1664, however, they came under the ban of a temporary
Conventicle Act,[2] which inflicted heavy fines or imprisonment,
or ultimate transportation or death, on any person over sixteen
attending " any assembly, conventicle or meeting, under
colour or pretence of any exercise of religion, in other manner
than according to the liturgy and practice of the Church of
England ", if there were five present beyond those of the
same household. Prior to the passing of the Act, Baptists
were already suffering (from 1660) under the revival of the
old Elizabethan Act of Uniformity and Conventicle Act,
though the Star Chamber and High Commission Court were
not revived ; it was under the Elizabethan Conventicle Act
that the imprisonment of John Bunyan began in 1660, continuing until 1672. The fortunes of a Baptist Church from
1660 onwards can be followed in the story of the Broadmead
Church of Bristol.[3] As an example of the expedients to
which they were driven, a paragraph of 1670 may be
quoted : —

because we did not know which way they would begin upon us,
we shut our public meeting-house door when we understood they
were coming. Then they (the informers) fetched constables, and
broke open the door, came in, and took our names, for which
some of us were brought before the magistrates and convicted.
Then, against the next Lord's day, we broke a wall, up on high,
for a window, and put the speaker in the next house to stand
and preach, whereby we heard him as well as if in the room
with us. The bishop's informers come in again, take our names,
for which we were again brought before the mayor, and convicted.
So they did the third Lord's day. And the fourth Lord's day,
the mayor himself, with his officers and some aldermen, came
upon us, and turned us out ; but seeing they could not make us
refrain our meeting, they raised the train bands every last day
of the week, in the evening, one band to keep us out of our places,
and nailed up our doors, and put locks upon them; so they kept

[1] Gee and Hardy, *op. cit.*, cxvi.
[2] *Ibid.*, cxix, for the permanent Conventicle Act of 1670, which
inflicted fines only, and operated till 1813. Public opinion would not
tolerate the severity of the earlier form of the Act.
[3] *The Records of a Church of Christ Meeting in Broadmead, Bristol,*
1640-1687 (Hanserd Knollys Society, 1847).

us out by force and power, that we were fain to meet in the lanes and highways for several months (pp. 105, 106).

In 1665 the Five Mile Act was passed, directed against the Nonconformist clergy and other preachers, who had held official livings (of whom there were about thirty Baptists), requiring an oath of acceptance of the *status quo*, failing which such persons were forbidden to reside within five miles of the place of their ministry or to keep any school.[1] This was the last Act of the "Clarendon Code" proper, but in 1673 the Test Act was added, which extended the provisions of the Corporation Act by excluding consistent Nonconformists from all Government employment.[2]

In 1672 the unconstitutional claim of Charles to exercise dispensing power by a Declaration of Indulgence (which he had to withdraw) benefited some Baptists, including Bunyan. In 1687 James tried the same device in the interests of Roman Catholicism, but few Baptists welcomed it, for it was clear to most of them that relief would be purchased at too dear a price. Persecution had slackened after 1672, but had been renewed in 1683, when Charles found no sympathy with Roman Catholics amongst Dissenters.[3] The insurrection of Monmouth in 1685 brought terrible suffering on many Baptists of the west of England who were among his supporters. The execution of two grandsons of Kiffin (a leading Baptist of his time) has been described in detail by Macaulay, who quotes the remark of Judge Jeffreys, "You have a grandfather who deserves to be hanged as richly as you". Macaulay has made famous also the burning of another Baptist, Elizabeth Gaunt, who anticipated Howard by her visitation of prisoners in jails, her only offence being the sheltering of one of the rebels, who turned king's evidence against her.[4]

Baptists and other Nonconformists have to thank the pro-Romanist policy of James on the one hand, and the common fear of Roman Catholicism on the other, for their deliverance from the persecution of the Restoration period. "Crown and Church were bidding against each other for Nonconformist support. The Crown offered religious toleration and

[1] Gee and Hardy, *op. cit.*, cxviii.   [2] *Ibid.* cxx.
[3] Whitley, *op. cit.*, p. 145.
[4] *History of England*, I chap. v.

civic equality by illegal Declarations of Indulgence suspend-
ing the obnoxious statutes. The Church promised religious
toleration, secured by statute, as soon as a free Parliament
should meet.''[1] The latter won, and the outcome was the
Toleration Act of 1689.[2] Its principle was not the repeal of
any of the existent statutes against Dissenters, but exemption
from their operation provided prescribed oaths were taken.
concern for the abolition of slavery.[5] There were already
with certain exceptions. If there was conscientious objection
to the taking of an oath, a declaration of political loyalty and
of faith in the Holy Trinity, with an acknowledgment of the
inspiration of Scripture, might be substituted. Public worship
might be celebrated by Dissenters in any certified place, with
unlocked doors. This Act defined the legal position of Dissenters for the whole of the eighteenth century and the earliest
part of the nineteenth.   The Conventicle Act was not
repealed until 1813, the Test Act not until 1828.

However limited and grudging this recognition of the
rights of the individual conscience may seem to us to-day, it
was in the seventeenth century a great victory for the protagonists of liberty. It was the product of many factors, as all
great movements inevitably are. But the ultimately decisive
factor in history is not the folly of infatuated rulers, the
animosity of men smarting under a sense of past injustice, the
vested interests of a caste, but the way in which men individually face and ultimately control all these and many other
'' blind '' forces. Throughout the seventeenth century, as we
have seen, and from their earliest existence, Baptists had
demanded that liberty for religious worship which had to be
granted, for the whole nation's sake, before the century
closed. Baptists were the first in this country to make this
demand, and they had taken their full share of the battle,
both in the literal and in the figurative sense. Their claim
was now vindicated ; they had the legal right to exist, if not
much more. What would they make of their newly acquired
liberty? The answer of the greater part of the eighteenth
century is distinctly disappointing, for this was a period of
relative stagnation in the history of the Baptists. It might
seem, at first sight, as if they had nothing vital to live for,

[1] Trevelyan, op. cit., p. 470.
[2] Gee and Hardy, op. cit., cxxiii.

having won the right to exist, so that those would be justified who turn Burke's famous phrase about "the dissidence of dissent" [1] into a suggestion of dissent for the pleasure of dissenting, its *raison d'être* perishing with the occasion of the protest. But like many another equally superficial view, the real causes of the religious stagnation of the earlier eighteenth century lie deeper, and affect all the Churches alike. The decline in the passion of the Baptists for liberty, which left them content so long with a merely "tolerated" existence, [2] corresponds with, and is linked to, an equally marked decline in their evangelistic spirit. Deliverance was to come from other quarters, and even when the Evangelical Revival brought new religious life to the Churches, the Baptists were by no means the most responsive to it. But it is significant that English Baptist sympathies were with the colonists in the American War of Independence, [3] whilst American Baptist soldiers and chaplains took a share in it comparable with that taken by English Baptists in Cromwell's army. [4]

It was natural, indeed inevitable, that the revival of missionary interest amongst the Baptists in 1792, which introduces a new period in their history, should bring with it concern for the abolition of slavery. [5] There were already (from 1784) Baptist Churches amongst the negroes of Jamaica at the time when missionaries were first sent out by the Baptist Missionary Society to that island. Slavery still continued, though the slave trade had been abolished within the British dominions by Acts of 1807 and 1811, as a result of the movement initiated by Clarkson and Wilberforce. A further movement for the abolition of slavery itself was just beginning

---

[1] Speech on Conciliation with the Colonies, March 22, 1775.

[2] It ought to be said that Baptists were represented amongst the "Dissenting Deputies" of Churches in the London area, elected in 1732, for political action to repeal the Test and Corporation Acts, though they were unsuccessful for nearly a century. Subscription to the Anglican Articles was no longer required after 1779, but from 1757 till 1836 all marriages, except those of Quakers, had to be performed at the parish church.

[3] See the last paragraph of the study of J. C. Ryland (Chapter II, p. 72).

[4] Newman, *History of the Baptist Churches in the United States*, pp. 261, 279, etc. ; cf. Whitley, *op. cit.*, p. 234.

[5] The honour of being pioneers in this movement belongs to the Society of Friends ; cf. the impressive *Journal* of John Woolman (1720-72).

in parliamentary circles when Thomas Burchell and William Knibb were sent out (1823 and 1824) as missionaries to Jamaica.   Their advocacy of the interests of the slaves involved them in the bitter animosity of the planters, bringing with it the destruction of missionary property and even peril to the missionaries' lives in connection with an outbreak of slaves in 1831.   Knibb, returning to England in 1832, aroused keen indignation by his passionate denunciation of slavery, and led the Baptist contribution[1] to the public feeling which was expressed in the Act of 1833 ; under this Act slavery was terminated by a transitional period of apprenticeship which expired in 1838.

Throughout the nineteenth century Baptists took their full part along with the other Free Churches in the further attainment of political and religious liberty. The political differences of the two great parties corresponded with the religious difference of Churchmen and Dissenters. Some of the landmarks in the struggle, in addition to the repeal of the " Clarendon Code ", were the abolition of compulsory Church rates in 1868, the opening of parish churchyards in 1880, the opening of the Universities of Oxford and Cambridge to Dissenters in 1854-56, the abolition of theological tests for official posts at these Universities in 1871. A keen interest was taken by many Baptists in the movement for the disestablishment of the Anglican Church, promoted especially by the " Liberation " Society from 1844; the Irish Church was disestablished in 1868, and the Welsh in 1920. Whilst Baptists still feel that the " establishment " of one religious denomination above all others is an anomaly under present conditions, they are probably less disposed to-day to promote political action for its removal, and prefer to leave this, in the interests of religion, to the more or less inevitable course of events, within and without the Anglican Church. A great source of conflict has been the place of religion in elementary education from the time of its wide extension in 1870. The Act of 1902, which did so much to unify and improve secondary education, aroused great opposition amongst Free Churchmen generally because of the rate-aid given under it to Church " Voluntary " schools. In this, as in many other similar movements, the outstanding Free Churchman was a

---

[1] Knibb gave evidence before Parliamentary Committees for six days. (*A Memoir of William Knibb*, by J. J. Smith. p. 43.)

Baptist, John Clifford, who might be most fitly described as a soldier of liberty, religious and political. To him all things were moral,[1] and the distinction of sacred and profane changed its meaning into that between the good and the evil. Like Horace Bushnell and F. W. Robertson, he found his way to " a God of Right ",[2] and this emphasis explains his eager " political dissent " as well as his ardent religious evangelism. His passion for freedom led him to oppose the South African War of 1899, as it equally led him to support with all his great influence the war of 1914. No man had more fully earned the right to say " Freedom is the breath of a nation's life, and it is only as freedom is granted that it is possible for us to face our difficulties and master them, to understand our problems and find the true solution of them. And of all the liberties we should fight for there is no liberty so great and so absolutely essential as liberty of conscience ".[3]

Viscount Grey, in a lecture on " The National Genius of England ",[4] once said that the quality which had most helped the race in its development was the power of the passion for individual liberty, combined with a sense of the necessity of order. When we think of the religious and ecclesiastical expression of these outstanding qualities, we naturally think of the Anglican Church as the representative of *order* in this country ; we shall not be less true to historic facts in claiming that the Baptist Church has consistently and from the beginning been the representative of the passion for individual *liberty*, and in this has been a pioneer to the other Free Churches of England.

The Baptist tabernacle is not always a graceful structure, but at least we may say this of it, that the twin pillars at its door are evangelism and liberty. This has been its attraction to the men and women of low degree from whom its worshippers have been chiefly drawn. They have found within its walls a living message of the love of God in Christ that has lightened the darkness of their world ; the very crudity with which that message has often been stated has made it the more understandable to them. They have also found there a warm sympathy with the toilers of the earth, more difficult

---

[1] *Life,* by Marchant, p. 193.
[2] *Op. cit.,* p. 24.
[3] *Op. cit.,* p. 226.
[4] As reported in *The Times* of December 13, 1926.

to find, perhaps, within buildings that belong to a higher culture and wider opportunities. The human need for the Gospel, combined with the human instinct for freedom— these have built the Baptist tabernacle.

A fellow-Baptist of wide experience once said to me, " Spurgeon and Clifford together sum up the Baptist denomination ". The justice of that remark is most apparent when we consider the outstanding qualities of these two great men, the evangelistic ardour of the " Particular " Baptist, Spurgeon, and the democratic passion of the " General " Baptist, Clifford. Both men aroused strong feelings of dis- like in those who differed from their views or lacked sympathy with their " style " ; both men were capable of arousing the most devoted personal attachment in those admitted to their intimacy. The " Down-grade Controversy " of 1887-88 showed them characteristically defending their dominant interests, evangelical orthodoxy on the one hand and the rights of Christian freedom on the other.[1] The two men and what they stood for are complementary in any adequate view of the Baptist faith. True evangelism and true liberty are but different applications of the same truth, which is at once eternal life and the maker of all freedom.

A charge sometimes brought against Nonconformity is that it is negative, and therefore has no future. So far as such a charge is sincere, and not a mere trick of debate, catching at a name, it rests on an inadequate knowledge of the history of the last three centuries. Baptists and others opposed the official religion of the State and fought with sword and pen against abuse and tyranny, but they did this for the sake of a positive faith—a faith as definite and as urgent as any for which the Catholic Church has ever stood. Their passion for liberty was ultimately inspired by the supreme positive prin- ciple, which stands in contrast with all kinds of emphasis on the external expression of religion—the *intrinsic* authority of the Gospel, which witnesses to itself by its own nature.[2]

The achievement of the liberty for which Baptists and other

---

[1] Accounts of the controversy, from naturally different standpoints, are given in Fullerton's *C. H. Spurgeon*, pp. 310-16, and Marchant's *Dr. John Clifford*, pp. 155-67.

[2] See Chapter IV, 4 ; also my essay on " The Validity of Christian Experience " in the volume called *The Future of Christianity* (ed. Marchant).

Free Churchmen have contended has brought with it perils of its own. They are now free to enter many doors which once were closed to them ; this means that they are the more exposed to the influences of that " worldliness " which their ancestors in the faith denounced. It is a much more difficult thing to maintain the high ideals of the Baptist faith when the Baptist life is no longer more or less secluded. " It is easy in the world to live after the world's opinion ; it is easy in solitude to live after our own ; but the great man is he who in the midst of the crowd keeps with perfect sweetness the independence of solitude."[1] This truth is often ignored by those whose social environment unconsciously shapes their Christian ethics.

On the other hand, the fact that the external rights of liberty in religious faith and worship have been already won may obscure the vision of those even greater issues which are never fully won. Liberty within is a more difficult attainment than liberty without. Prejudices which we nurture within our own hearts are more subtle and dangerous than those whose folly and injustice we can see plainly when they belong to others. Baptists need to remember, perhaps more than most, that if there is an externalism of Church authority which has worked mischief in religion, there is also an externalism of the appeal to Scripture, not less alien to the living truth of Christ. There are conventions and traditions in the religious life of Baptists which need constant scrutiny by the highest and most spiritual standards lest that which once helped becomes a hindrance to the faith. It is easy to pass resolutions for the amendment of others which nobody will ever take seriously ; it is hard to resolve to amend oneself, at the cost, perhaps, of effort and pain. If Baptist life and faith are threatened by a multitude of attractive interests which tend to the loss of earnest simplicity and devotion, we must not forget the tendency of those who still stand in the old ways to misjudge their brethren and to become hardened in the Gospel. There are enemies of the truth as it is in Jesus more subtle than ecclesiastical courts and more stubborn than the most ancient vested interests. There are prejudices and errors of knowledge and judgment within every community which can be overcome only by a struggle as protracted and

[1] Emerson, essay on " Self-Reliance '

patient as that of the past for denominational existence. There is, in fact, an unachieved liberty *within* faith as well as *for* faith, and its best safeguard is found in the dominating principle of that book which this chapter began by quoting, Milton's *Areopagitica*: " Give me the liberty to know, to utter, and to argue freely according to conscience, above all liberties."

VII

THE STRENGTH AND THE WEAKNESS OF THE BAPTISTS

THE great majority of religious men are what they are ecclesiastically because they have grown up in it. This is as it should be, since nothing atones for the absence of those memories of childhood and youth which are progressively hallowed by the faith of the grown man, and gain a richer interpretation by the experience of life. The familiar walls of the church, the familiar phrases of prayer and praise, even the familiar tones of voice of him who first opened to us the way of the Spirit, gain a sacramental quality, so as to be inseparable in memory from the experience they mediated. They have helped to bring us into a living tradition that we might discover " how great a thing it is to live at the end of so many ages, heirs to the thoughts of the wise, the labours of the good, the prayers of the devout ".[1]

Yet it is also true that each of us enters this living stream with his own unique life, his own capacities for emotion ready to be stirred, his own thoughts striving to become articulate, his own will claiming its free exercise. The truth —at least, the truth for *me*—lies in, and is tested by, a personal reaction to this tradition. " Tradition and conscience are the two wings given to the human soul to reach to truth. . . . Where you find the general permanent voice of humanity agreeing with the voice of your conscience, be sure that you hold in your grasp something with absolute truth— gained and for ever yours."[2] This, of course, implies the right and the duty of each to criticize the religious tradition in and through which he lives. Such criticism is the essential condition not only of progress, individual and corporate, but even of clear conviction and intelligent faith. This is true

[1] Martineau, *Home Prayers*, p. 6.
[2] Mazzini, quoted by Bolton King, *Mazzini*, pp. 240, 244.

for all religion ; it ought to be especially true for those forms of it which emphasize voluntary choice and personal faith as primary duties.

We may often gain much help in the process of examining our own religious faith and practice by learning how it looks to one who stands outside our own communion, provided he be sympathetic, well-informed, and able to give expression to his thinking. Some years before this book was planned, I asked three such competent observers to give me their frank opinions on '' The Strength and the Weakness of the Baptists.'' I summarize their answers, for the sake of brevity. The Congregationalist answered: '' Your strength is your correspondence with the original practice of the New Testament and the fact that you make the moral meaning of baptism unmistakable. Your weakness is that all matters of ceremony are secondary to the truths of the Gospel, that your special emphasis is a bar to Christian reunion, and that you lay stress on one side only of the meaning of baptism, i.e. individual faith, whereas it also symbolizes divine grace.'' The Wesleyan answered: '' Your strength is your devotion to evangelical truth, and rich Christian experience, and your willingness to bear criticism about baptism. Your weakness is theological narrowness and excessive individualism, the lack of a connexional system, so that the ministers of smaller Churches suffer, and too little use is made of lay preachers, and the undue emphasis implied in the name ' Baptist ', for which, of course, you are not to blame.'' The Quaker said: '' Your strength is your evangelical emphasis, your open and public confession of faith, with definite and dramatic entrance into the Church, the stress on personal decision, and the stand for supremacy of conscience. Your weakness is your theological narrowness, your Scriptural literalism, the making baptism essential to Church membership, the want of a circuit system which would bring in more lay ministry, and the lack of sufficiently definite Christian teaching to young people.'' The general justice of these criticisms would be admitted by many Baptists, and the practical agreement is significant. The strength of Baptists lies in their Scriptural individualism, their weakness chiefly in the defects of their quality. We cannot emphasize one word in a sentence without running the risk of slurring over other words ; we cannot emphasize one truth without the risk of inadequate attention to other truths, as history has repeatedly taught.

The direct appeal to the authority of Scripture is common to all the Protestant Churches, but there is a special motive for the Baptist use of it. Baptists are continually thrown back on the Bible to justify what seems to many a strange and arbitrary idiosyncrasy. But intelligent use of the Bible to justify the baptism of believers trains men in the intelligent use of the Bible for other purposes, teaches them to look up things for themselves, and to trust no reports at second-hand —a habit which is always one mark of a good student. Such direct use of the Bible serves to bring men into touch with the experience it records, and often into that intuitive experience in which God and man are face to face. The value of such Bible-reading is great; there can be hardly any more serious feature of the religious life of to-day than the very marked decline in it—a decline which, unfortunately, Baptists also exhibit.

On the other hand, the very simplicity and directness of this use of Scripture brings its own perils. The individual believer is encouraged to interpret it for himself, but he often lacks the most elementary training for this. The prejudice of ignorance borrows the strength of genuine religious conviction, and sometimes issues in a papal dogmatism. Baptists as a whole are often wanting in any sense of history, whether the history of the thousand years in which the experience behind the Bible slowly deposited itself in the literary record, or those intervening centuries of the history of the Church which have added so much to the interpretation of the Bible. It may be admitted that this is a defect in some degree common to many Churches, but other Churches have silent correctives of overweening confidence which Baptists lack— such as the respect for education amongst the Presbyterians, or the long and rich perspective of the parish church and 'the Prayer Book amongst the Anglicans. Whilst "Fundamentalism" as a belligerent movement has relatively little hold amongst Baptists of this country, there is still a good deal of suspicion of even the moderate amount of Biblical scholarship which has been more or less assimilated by most other Churches. Yet Baptists, of all people, ought to welcome that criticism which takes men back beyond the letter to the living spirit, and unbares the experience which was first creative of the literature. Fortunately, the Baptist love of liberty comes in to correct the tendencies of assertive literalism and eschatological vagary, and heresy-hunters are not popular with a Baptist Union Assembly.

The real strength of the emphasis on individual experience (see Chapter III) has already been exhibited, and need not be further developed, except to say that it brings men face to face with God in Christ. This makes the intrinsic nature of His Gospel, as known in experience, the ultimate authority— indeed, the only authority in the real sense, for " God is love " and the Gospel of His love is the revelation of His nature, and what further testimonial does God ever need? But the connected weakness found alongside of this strength amongst Baptists needs careful thought, for it affects the whole conception of the Church and the life of the Church. It does not seem to me too much to say that Baptists as Churchmen are still largely dominated by an eighteenth-century philosophy of society, disguised under their traditional interpretation of Scripture. That pronounced individualist, Jean-Jacques Rousseau, discussed the social forms of life as if they were the arbitrary and voluntary creation of a number of unitary individuals, instead of being the cradle in which the individual life is nurtured and the breast at which it sucks. Similarly, it is possible to talk of conversion and the work of the Holy Spirit as if it occurred in a social vacuum, in order that a number of unitary products might subsequently be brought together to form a Church. But this ignores the fact that in personality there are the two elements of individuality and sociality growing side by side from the very beginning, and not less in religious than in biological and cultural and moral developments. The family is already a social environment, and without it there could be no individual life, yet it is possible for a Baptist to write, " fatherhood and sonship are relations expressive of individual and not of corporate experiences ".[1]

How can there be a father before there is a son, or a son before there is a father? The truth is rather that the social relation implied in fatherhood and sonship is just as much a capacity of personality as the individual consciousness. If it were not for such relationship as the family and the clan

---

[1] Mullins, *The Axioms of Religion*, p. 39.

and the State imply there could be no development of the individual consciousness at all. These things are, of course, the commonplaces of sociology to-day, but they are singularly ignored in many discussions of the "separated" Church. The only difference is that the application in this case is to man's highest interests. The Church is not an arbitrary "extra", a sort of religious club he may choose to join ; it is the crowning religious expression of that sociality which is part of his very constitution. Because it is that, it becomes the temple of the Holy Spirit in larger ways that the individual temple of a single life can offer. It is unreasonable to contrast the work of the Holy Spirit in the individual life and in the social group as if there could be any rivalry ; these realms are complementary and, closely—indeed inseparably—interwoven. Baptists must and will continue to stand for the truth of a regenerated Church membership expressed in believers' baptism ; but they will never make that testimony as effective as it ought to be till they have added to it a nobler Church-consciousness, and a profounder sense of the whole group, as well as of the individual life, as the arena of the Spirit's activity.[1] It belonged to them in the earlier days, when the Church was identified with the narrow group of "true" believers, and the world lay without ; it has gradually grown dim—except for a few old-fashioned Churches— through the increasing relation of the "believer" with that outside world, and his recognition that the old distinction of "saved" and "lost" is no longer possible—at any rate, in its old sense and scope. A nobler Church-consciousness can come only through a new conception of the Church—such a conception, for example, as that which runs through the Epistle to the Ephesians. At the risk of saying something that may be misunderstood by those within and those without, I would say quite deliberately that Baptists need an "Oxford Movement" of *their own order,* so as to give their truth of an individual relation to God its complementary truth of a social relation to Him. Such a movement would doubtless bring some changes in worship and in polity, not those changes which are like new patches on an old garment,

---

[1] This must not be taken to ignore the fine achievements of Baptists in voluntary giving, for work at home and abroad, to which reference is made elsewhere—the more remarkable because this has been done in the absence of any "connexional" system.

but those true changes of a living development in which the unity is not lost.[1]

The third point in which both the strength and the weakness of the Baptists may be discerned relates to believers' baptism itself, and brings to a focus what has just been said about the relation to the Bible and to the Church. The first and foremost contribution of Baptists to the Church Catholic is like that of the Hebrew prophets—the essential and primary place of the moral within the religious. The moral change wrought in genuine conversion, the personal repentance and faith which are the religious features of that conversion, the open confession which commits the life to a new purpose—these great truths are admirably and forcibly expressed in believers' baptism by immersion, and expressed as no other Church expresses them. All this is New Testament faith and practice. But it is not the whole faith of the New Testament.

Does not baptism express much more than a personal act? Is it not, *by virtue of being that,* the New Testament door of entrance into a life of supernatural energies, the surrender to that "Law of the Spirit" which the Apostle set in strongest contrast to the common life of men? Let any Baptist, with an open mind, set himself to study the New Testament references to baptism, and he will perhaps be surprised to find how closely it is related to the gift of the Holy Spirit. The baptism of John expressed a moral decision; the baptism of Christ is sharply contrasted with this, as a baptism with or in the Holy Spirit. There is the same contrast in the conversation of Christ with Nicodemus, when entrance into the Kingdom is made conditional of being "born of water and the Spirit". That Paul closely related water-baptism and that which it symbolized is evident, for "in one Spirit were we all baptized into one body . . . and were all made to drink of one Spirit ". If the descent into the waters of baptism meant death and burial with Christ, in that mystical union with Him which carries with it death unto sin, not less did it mean to Paul the ascent into new life, defined by him as newness of "Spirit". The Colossians are reminded not only that they were buried with Christ in their baptism, but that they were raised with Christ in the same baptism, the

---

[1] Something has already been said in Chapter I on the difficulty, yet discipline, of the practical reconciliation of individual conviction and social tradition within the Church. See also p. 85.

power of the new life working through their faith. It is not without significance that when Paul speaks of the one Body and the one Spirit, he should straightway pass on to speak of the one baptism expressing the one faith which unites to the one Lord, "The Lord the Spirit", as he elsewhere says. Thus, to be baptized into Christ is to put on Christ, i.e. to enter that realm of the Spirit over which Christ is Lord.

It needs to be said, of course, that the connection between water-baptism and the baptism of the Spirit is of no mechanical kind, such as quasi-magical ideas of the ceremony would suggest. The Spirit-baptism of Cornelius and his friends preceded their water-baptism; in fact, the water-baptism was administered to these Gentiles (without precedent) on the ground that they had already received the gift which it expressed. The group of disciples at Ephesus who had not received the Holy Spirit at the time of their "Johannine" baptism were baptized again into the name of the Lord Jesus, and after Paul had laid his hands upon them, the gift hitherto withheld was given. But these are mentioned as exceptional cases. The recipient of baptism in the New Testament times normally expected to be the recipient of the spiritual powers of the new life which he entered by his baptism. There could be no risk of encouraging the idea of "baptismal regeneration" (in the modern sense), because *all who were baptized were already believers,* i.e. the moral and spiritual conditions of their personal faith became the real channel of the Spirit's highest energies. Indeed, it was the very divorce of baptism from personal faith which has made "sacramentarianism" possible.

Let us try to enter into the experience of a believer baptized in those first days, using the interpretative reconstruction of a scholar who stands outside the present issue:—

In baptism (of course, adult) something happened. Faith had been there before, receptiveness toward the good news of Christ. The Divine Spirit had been already present, taking of the things of Christ and showing them to the believer. But now, once for all, the convert made his own the movings of the Divine love in his heart. And thus there would come to him in his baptism a wonderful spiritual quickening, a new enhancing of the power and grasp of faith, a fresh realization of communion with the once crucified and now risen Lord. Hence, there is good ground for the statement of von Dobschütz that "according to the early

Christian view we may speak of real effects of baptism in the sense that here the person does not give himself something by his activity, but God gives him what he has only to receive." [1]

Baptists have been reluctant to recognize this " baptismal grace ", just because, in their judgment, it is utterly misrepresented and distorted when ascribed to unconscious infants. The reaction from a false doctrine of divine grace in baptism has made them suspicious even of the genuine sacramentalism of the New Testament. We have been saying *believers'* baptism so emphatically that we have failed, or at least are failing now, to say with anything like equal emphasis, believers' *baptism*, i.e. the entrance of believers into a life of supernatural powers.

Here, then, is the present Baptist opportunity, and it is a great one. No other Church has been loyal to the New Testament connection of baptism with personal faith. No other Church, therefore, could give so forcible a testimony to the work of the Spirit on the believer, which is not less emphatically linked with baptism in the New Testament. If any Baptist reader is afraid that this may mean a sacramentalism of the lower kind, with consecrated water rather than the evangelical truth in the heart of the believer as the primary medium of the Spirit, let it be said quite distinctly that I am pleading for the connection of water-baptism with the Spirit in exactly the sense in which all Baptists plead for its connection with personal faith. If the New Testament teaches the latter, it assuredly also teaches the former, and Baptists are really committed to both. If appeal be made to such a word as the Apostle's " Received ye the Spirit by the works of the law, or by the hearing of faith? ", the answer is that undoubtedly personal faith is the realm of the Spirit's activity, but the confession of that faith in believers' baptism brought a new opportunity for divine grace, because it was itself an act of personal faith.

Though this book is not a history of the Baptists, enough has been said of the different types of life within the three centuries to show the great changes that have taken place. Doubtless other changes equally great will mark our further development, and no man can foresee them. But at the present time, and in this country, the Baptist future seems to depend on the relation to the distinctive feature of believers'

[1] H. A. A. Kennedy, *St. Paul and the Mystery Religions*, p. 249.

baptism. Baptists must make either more or less of it. If they make less of it, they will be absorbed into Congregationalism, and their distinctive testimony and consciousness will be lost—a result I should greatly deplore. If they make more of it, it must be along the line indicated of a greater spiritual content, and not simply of a literalistic appeal to the Bible. Believers will not be deterred from baptism by immersion if they are taught the rich and full meaning given to it by the New Testament.

Apart from this characteristic feature (and all it implies) the future of the Baptists is bound up with the future of the evangelical faith. The presentation of that faith, in order to be successful, has always to be in terms of contemporary thought and life. This is true even when the presentation is antithetical, or perhaps we should say that its especial truth is then seen. Thus, at the present time, the fundamental need is for a clear assertion of the reality of religion over against the modern challenge that religion is a subjective illusion. Here the primary Baptist emphasis should be on the appeal to experience, that experience of obedience to the will of God which brings the proof of the teaching that it is of God. The central truth of the evangelical faith is the sacrificial love of God realized in the grace of Christ. Over against the idea of a passive or absent God, or a God fettered by the " laws " of His universe, we have to teach that God is active, present, redeeming, and that man, by His grace, may have a direct relation of fellowship with Him. All revivals of religion are in essence due to the realization that God is much nearer than we thought. Further, the Baptist emphasis on conversion asserts moral responsibility and human freedom over against the naturalism and determinism of the past generation (themselves profoundly shaken by the new physics). Most of all there is needed a new and clear teaching of the doctrine of the Holy Spirit, as against the rationalism that rejects all mystery, and the externalism which materializes mystery into manageable forms. The true emphasis is that of the New Testament—on personal faith as the human condition of divine activity, which is the truth supremely expressed in believers' baptism.[1]

[1] See A. C. Underwood, *Conversion: Christian and Non-Christian*, for an excellent account of baptism as " The Dramatic Representation of Regeneration " (chap. ix).

APPENDIX I

THE FINAL AUTHORITY[1]

A Baptist minister[2], after more than a quarter of a century's pastoral work in Baptist Churches, tells us that all through this period his mind was disturbed by the haunting question, "By what authority doest thou these things?" Finally, he settled his doubts and difficulties by accepting the authority of the Church of Rome:—

"The externals of the Church, if the expression may be allowed, never appealed to me. What did appeal, and over-whelmingly appeal, was its historic descent, its firm and authoritative foundation, and the reality of its presence in the world as the 'Body,' the very Voice, of the Living Christ . . . . the only foundation and pillar of the truth, the only interpreter of the 'revelation', the only guardian of the Faith once delivered to the Saints."

This is not the place to enter on any criticism of this appeal to history. History is a two-edged tool, and it can destroy that which it is taken up to defend. It is sufficient for our present purpose, which is positive and constructive, to note this as a clear and actual example of the transference of loyalties from the individual authority of personal conviction to the social authority of a community, from the Bible as interpreted by the individual, to the Bible as finally and authoritatively interpreted by the Church. Of course, the challenging question has a far wider application than to ministerial status and of service in any one denomination. It ought to be put by every Christian to himself, whatever his particular vocation, and whatever be the Church to which he belongs. Some answer to it is essential to any intelligent response of faith, and to any adequate

---

[1] As stated in the preface to this new addition, Dr. Robinson proposed to add a new chapter with this title. The draft here printed was the last piece of work he accomplished. He put it into my hands when he had to be moved to a Nursing Home, but as he was unable to go through it, even in typescript, it has been included here as an appendix.—E.A.P.

[2] J. F. Makepeace, whose *All I could never be* (Blackwell, 1924) describes this development (1872-1912). The passage cited occurs pp. 111-112.

acceptance of revelation. In fact, the answer must affect our whole conception of what revelation is, both in content and method. Our very philosophy of revelation is often a more or less rationalized form of our individual contact with the Beyond. It is natural enough that we should emphasize the particular media which have been the " means of grace " to ourselves. They become our most individualised sacrament, however trivial their occasion and origin. In them the temporal form acquires an eternal content. But, in putting the question to ourselves, we must not be content to answer it simply by a choice between the Bible and the Church. That is far too superficial an answer, however popular it may be. The truth lies deeper, and like all historical data, is much more complex. Both individual conviction and the authority of a community are involved in any and every religious decision, whilst in every profession, Protestant or Roman Catholic, both Bible and Church are involved, and essentially involved. The difference is in the ultimate emphasis, and a difference of emphasis can easily become a difference of kind. (In fact, most of the differences of human life could be explained as differences of emphasis.)

In the Baptist life and faith, as has been described in this book, the emphasis clearly falls on the side of the individual conviction. The rite of baptism is, as in the New Testament, administered only to those who take the initiative in making a personal profession of faith. The Church is avowedly constituted of believers who have been individually convinced of the truth of that which they profess. The most essential aspect of the ministerial vocation is not any prescribed rite or ceremony, but individual vocation. The gifts and fruit of the Holy Spirit are far oftener conceived in their individual relations to the believer than as corporately conditioned. It would, however, be quite wrong to ignore the influence of a corporate tradition running through all this. Most of those who " spontaneously " avow the Baptist form of faith on the basis of individual conviction have, in fact, grown up in a Baptist environment. Consciously or unconsciously, they have been subjected to Baptist influences from their earliest days. Those influences are a particular form of the common evangelical tradition. This claims, and rightly claims, to set forth and employ important elements of Biblical truth. But, not less than any other form of tradition, though in different ways, " it depends chiefly for its active propagation on the continuity of a community in and by which it is cherished. Baptist life and faith may indeed be, as we have seen (Chapter VII), criticised for not making enough of the factors of community, and no purely individualistic reply to this kind of criticism would be adequate. But the community-factors are there, and inevitably there."

Similar things hold true of the Roman Catholic tradition, though the other way round, and in much more systematized fashion. The child, already received into the Church by its baptism, normally grows through and into a tradition which is transformed into a habit, and becomes "second nature." The social side of human personality thus receives fullest recognition from the very outset of life. The element or factor of personal conviction, however, is not ignored, but remains more or less latent until individual responsibility can exert itself. Then, the tradition made familiar by long habit is consciously accepted and continued, or there may be a deliberate rejection or neglect of it, and a man goes out into the wilderness of the unfamiliar. In a "conversion" to Roman Catholicism, the emphasis falls yet more clearly on personal decision (made under the guidance of the Holy Spirit)[1].

In all this, the place assigned to the Church is manifest, and it becomes explicit in the decrees of the Council of Trent. But the warning already given must be remembered. The decrees do not set the Church in direct antithesis to the Bible. All that is claimed (and it is a sufficiently comprehensive "all") is that the Church has been divinely authorised to interpret the Bible. Such a claim fully endows the tradition with all that it needs to make it *de jure* as well as *de facto*. This authority to interpret belongs to the divine purpose, and the Church, in effect at least, becomes the final authority. The initial question is answered—by the transference of responsibility to other people.

It is plain, then, that acceptance of the authority of revelation does not resolve itself into a simple choice between the conviction of the believer and that of the religious community. There is a new product[2] and since both factors are involved, a place must be found for both in our philosophy of revelation. This is a far-reaching subject, and I can do little more here than refer to the larger book in which I have tried to deal with it.[3] The path of understanding takes us from any thought of the individual and the community in isolation to the fuller recognition of their unity in the hands of God, and in the operation of His providence. As, indeed, in all the normal

[1] A classical expression of this is known to all in Newman's "Lead, kindly Light."

[2] We may illustrate by the most familiar examples in nature, viz. oxygen and hydrogen continuing to give water as their product. At a higher level we have the union of soul and body, spirit and matter, in personality.

[3] *Redemption and Revelation* (1942).

developments of life; and not only in those attaching to religion, the community is essential for the training and preparation of the individual, and the individual to the constant renewal of the community. At some point, the conscious contact of the two will raise the question as to which should be uppermost in authority ; the answer decides a man's ecclesiastical choice. But he will never wholly escape from the factor which he subordinates, since he is characterized by both individuality and sociality. In their divinely wrought unity they exert their dual authority, and the Bible stands out from history as the unique record of man's converse with God, and of God's converse with man. As such the Bible will exert its proper authority, and on sufficient grounds it rules to its own degree intrinsically, simply by being what it is.

One confirmation that we are on the right path in thus thinking of the authority of revelation is that the whole development becomes a training in moral responsibility. All along the individual learns to make decisions, and not the least in the culminating one. God uses in revelation the methods familiar to us in all true education, the aim being the evocation of personality. But these methods are those of the invitation or pressure of the community, which becomes the great and necessary corrective of individual wilfulness or ignorance.

The final authority must always be God, but He has many media, and supreme amongst them all is the life, death and resurrection of His Son, Jesus Christ, proclaimed by the Church, and within the fellowship of the Holy Spirit, to which the witness of the Spirit within the believer testifies.

H. W. R.

APPENDIX II

SELECTED BIBLIOGRAPHY

The earliest Baptist historians were Crosby (1738-40), Ivimey (1811-30) and Taylor (1818). Evans (1862-64) and Cramp (1875) produced useful studies, but their work must now be supplemented by the extensive documentary material made available of recent decades both by the secular and the ecclesiastical historians. The standard modern history is W. T. Whitley, *A History of British Baptists* (1923, second edition 1932). For Scotland and America add *A History of the Baptists in Scotland* (ed. by Geo. Yuille, 1926) and A. H. Newman, *A History of the Baptist Churches in the United States* (sixth edition, 1915). *The Baptist Quarterly* and *The Chronicle* (published quarterly by the American Baptist Historical Society) continue to make important contributions to the study of Baptist history. There is also value in the briefer general accounts of H. C. Vedder, *A Short Baptist History* (1897), J. T. Christian, *A History of the Baptists* (Nashville, 1922), G. O. Griffith, *A Pocket History of the Baptist Movement* (1929) and A. C. Underwood, *A History of the English Baptists* (1946).

The Baptist movement on the Continent of Europe may be studied in J. H. Rushbrooke, *The Baptist Movement on the Continent of Europe* (1923) and *Some Chapters of European Baptist History* (1929). H. Gieselbusch (ed.), *Um die Gemeinde Ausgewählte-Schriften von Julius Köbner*, (Berlin, 1927), R. Baresel, *Julius Köbner* (Kassel, 1930) and Hans Luckey, *Johann Gerhard Oncken und die Anfänge des deutschen Baptismus* (Kassel, 1934) represent the beginnings of the scientific study of German Baptist origins.

A number of important Reports have been issued of recent years defining the Baptist attitude to modern ecclesiastical issues. Particular attention may be called to " The Baptist Reply to the Lambeth Appeal " (1926), " The Report of the Special Committee appointed by the Baptist Union Council on the question of union between Baptists, Congregationalists and Presbyterians " (1937), and to two Reports submitted to the Atlanta World Congress in 1939: " The Baptist Contribution to Christian Unity " and " The Reports and Findings of the Oxford and Edinburgh Conferences." The full Reports of the Baptist World Congresses contain important material dealing with varied aspects of Baptist life and thought.

McGlothlin, *Baptist Confessions of Faith* (1910) opens up an important field of study. Baptist theories of the Church, Ministry and Sacraments are treated in H. Wheeler Robinson, *Baptist Principles* (1925), A. Dakin, *The Baptist View of the Church and Ministry* (1944), E. A. Payne *The Fellowship of Believers: Baptist Thought and Practice Yesterday and To-day* (1945) and R. C. Walton, *The Gathered Community* (1946). Two other books by the last named set the Baptist contribution in the larger framework of modern Church (1944) and *The Church Awakes: the Story of the Modern Missionary Movement* (1942).

Other books on special topics that deserve notice are H. S. Burrage, *Baptist Hymnwriters and Their Hymns* (1888), Carey Bonner, *Some Baptist Hymnists* (1937), J. H. Shakespeare, *Baptist and Congregational Pioneers* (1905), L. F. Brown, *Baptists and the Fifth Monarchy Movement* (1912), as well as a number of important studies of local Baptist history.

E. A. P.

APPENDIX III

SUMMARY OF BAPTIST STATISTICS

Taken from the *Summary of Statistics,* 1940
published by the Baptist World Alliance.

CONTINENT	Churches	Pastors and Missionaries	Members	Sunday Scholars
EUROPE (1) ...	5,357	3,930	660,881	508,633
ASIA	4,786	1,939	479,174	210,635
AFRICA ...	1,952	535	118,330	46,540
AMERICA :				
North	58,156	43,293	10,931,936	7,155,960
Central and West Indies...	752	564	74,099	66,312
South	733	497	62,978	58,015
AUSTRALIA and NEW ZEALAND	527	460	40,716	47,789
Totals (1)	72,263	51,218	12,368,114	(2)8,093,884

NOTES.

(1) This excludes the U.S.S.R., where two strong groups, the " All-Union of Baptists " and the " All-Union of Evangelical Christians," merged into a single Union in 1944. Both are uncomprisingly Baptist, and more than twenty years earlier (both being already members of the Baptist World Alliance) had accepted a common declaration of faith and order. Precise and certified reports of their membership are not yet available; they themselves in a published statement (1942) asserted that they number four millions, but it is uncertain whether this figure represents community strength or church membership. In any case their inclusion would very substantially increase the total.

(2) Owing to the impossibility of obtaining complete figures during war-time, the Alliance has issued no statistical statement since 1940. Sufficient reports, however, have reached its office to indicate that the total membership—with the U.S.S.R. still omitted—is in 1945 well over thirteen millions.

Baptists are now the largest Free Church communion in the world. The Methodists, who report, according to Dr. Newton Flew in *A Christian Year Book,* 1945 (p. 50), 11,666,646 communicant members, are nearest to them in numbers.

J. H. R.

INDEX

I.—PERSONS

II.—SUBJECTS

The Fellowship of Believers

Baptist Thought and Practice
Yesterday and Today

BY

ERNEST A. PAYNE

Senior Tutor, Regent's Park College, Oxford

With a Foreword by
Dr. H. WHEELER ROBINSON, M.A.

THE KINGSGATE PRESS
4, Southampton Row, London, W.C.1
1944

AUTHOR'S NOTE

This book was undertaken at the request of the Publication Committee of the Baptist Union. I am under particular and deep obligation to Dr. Wheeler Robinson for counsel and encouragement in its preparation, for his reading of the typescript, and for his foreword. My indebtedness to him in respect of the matters here treated, as of much else, began, however, twenty-two years ago when I entered Regent's Park College as a student, and it is of an extent and character that is beyond any adequate verbal acknowledgment. The typescript of these chapters has also been read by the present Principal of Regent's Park College, the Rev. R. L. Child, and to him also I owe a debt of gratitude for many valuable suggestions. Much of the material was given at a Summer School for Baptist Ministers of Northamptonshire and Huntingdonshire held in Oxford in July, 1944. To them, therefore, I dedicate these pages, which may have as motto some words of Kierkegaard: "Life can only be understood backwards, but it must be lived forwards."

E. A. P.

Oxford.

CONTENTS

FOREWORD

W HAT is the Church? Every form of it is compelled to give some sort of answer to that question, whether in theory or in practice, and that compulsion is felt to-day more than ever before. But you cannot answer the question, or even understand fully the answers given by others, unless you know two things. The first is what the Church *gives*. That means the inside knowledge of one who really shares in the intimate life of a community. To speak or write about the Church without ever knowing at first hand what it gives is like writing the geography of a land or the sociology of a people unvisited by the author. The Church creates a particular kind of life, for it is essentially the fellowship of men and women stirred to new life by a common faith. We must live in it and of it, in order to know what it is. The knowledge possessed in this way by many a quite ordinary man or woman with no gift of expression is worth far more than the opinion of some well-known journalist who shares the belief of Anatole France that the Church is like an old woman—alive, but only just!

The other essential for a worth-while answer to the question, What is the Church? is the ability to answer another question, What *was* the Church? History, true history, is not mere antiquarianism. It is the record of that life of yesterday which has made the life of to-day what it is. The present is always building on the past, and incorporating much more of it than we are apt to realize. If we are to plan and build wisely, we must know what those before us have done. What was the secret of those ancestors of ours which enabled them to pass on an inheritance to us? How often will the student of the past discover that what is acclaimed as the newly-found truth of to-day was already there through a succession of yesterdays!

This is one of the things in which Mr. Payne's little book is opportune and practical. He can teach his Baptist readers, for example, that their forerunners were in much closer association as Churches than they often are to-day. In some matters, the independence of the local Church is a valuable safeguard of Christian liberties. But it can easily become a form of selfishness alien to the Spirit of the Body of Christ, and far from the teaching and example of the New Testament. The early Separatists, from whom we Baptists emerged, were protesting against the parish as the basis of Church fellowship, because it included many who were not believers. But is there any reason why a particular group of *believers*, who happen to live in a particular geographical area, should necessarily be self-contained and self-sufficient, equipped with all the ministries and resources of the Church? In practice, we recognize that they are not, and we appoint area-superintendents and committees and many other institutions to supplement the deficiencies of the local group. But it may well be that Baptists are now compelled to go deeper and to ask how far they are pledged to the policy of " Congregationalism." Is there any test of methods of organization and government save that they should be the best to promote the faith and service of the Gospel?

H. WHEELER ROBINSON.

Chapter One

THE SUBJECT AND THE SOURCES

I

" Let the Church be the Church." The slogan was coined in 1937 in connection with the Oxford Conference on Church, Community and State—one of the series of great Christian gatherings which future historians will note as taking place with increasing frequency in decades following the Edinburgh Missionary Conference of 1910. " Let the Church be the Church." The slogan has been echoed again and again during the past few years in many different parts of the world. But what is the Church, and where is it to be found? These questions have forced themselves forward with increasing frequency and insistence.

A variety of causes—chief among them a deepening realisation of the vastness of the task facing Christians in their attempt to evangelise the heathen world, a loss of confidence and power in Europe and North America, and a more vivid sense of the essentials of New Testament religion—has of recent decades brought closer together the different Christian groups into which the one Church split in the generations following the Reformation. Deeper unity and fellowship, closer co-operation and collaboration, have been sought in many parts of the world, and with no inconsiderable measure of success. In certain areas, as for example Canada and Scotland, and among certain groups springing not too distantly from a common source, such as the Methodists, important mergings and re-unitings have taken place. But as the main non-Roman Christian traditions have conferred together, they have with increasing frequency found themselves held up by awkward questions as to the Christian ministry and the sacraments of Baptism and the Lord's Supper, questions about which their procedure differs, questions which involve deeper issues regarding the nature of both the Gospel itself and the Church. Again one asks, What is the Church, and what is its relation to the Gospel?

The secular conflicts of the past decade have made the question sound out still more insistently. On the Continent of Europe and in the Far East the followers of Jesus Christ have found themselves facing demands by the State which they were unwilling to concede. At first the totalitarian and authoritarian powers merely restricted the activities of Christians both within and without their territories. Then more exacting demands were made. There was dictation as to who should or should not be within the Christian fellowship and as to how particular racial groups should be treated. In spite of growing danger, many Christian communities, Catholic, Orthodox and Protestant, with mounting confidence, said No to these demands. The stage seemed set for a renewed struggle between Church and State, but one on a vaster scale than ever before. This was indeed the background of the Oxford Conference of 1937, from which came the cry " Let the Church be the Church." The World War which began in 1939 broke in upon a situation already tense and confused in many lands. There is sufficient evidence that in Germany many courageous Christian leaders have continued to refuse unquestioning obedience to the dictates of the State. In occupied lands like Poland, Holland, Norway, Greece and even France, it is clear that the Church was the last stronghold of national resistance. The same may perhaps be found to be true in the areas of South-East Asia and the Pacific seized by the Japanese. When then is this body or institution so unexpectedly strong and resilient? A few years ago—as on a number of previous occasions—its early disappearance as an anachronism was confidently predicted. But there is clearly life still within it. What then is its nature and function?

The same question may be found agitating Christians concerned with the internal problems of their own particular fellowships. The Orthodox Church as a result of its experiences during the early years of the Russian Revolution, no less than the Lutheran and Reformed Churches in Germany, has had to busy itself with this fundamental issue. The Anglican Church, the Church of Scotland and the various Free Churches are all occupied with it. Problems of ecclesiastical adjustment and reorganisation all lead back to deeper questions about the Church itself. " There is great need to-day for laying fresh emphasis upon the doctrine of the Church." So declares the important report on *God's Will in Our Time*, presented to the General Assembly of the Church of Scotland in 1942 (p. 16). For seven years an influential group of Baptist ministers and laymen gave careful attention to practical matters connected with Baptist polity. At the last they were constrained to say: " As our work has proceeded we have reached the conclusion that the time has come for a fresh enquiry into the Baptist doctrine of the Church. Not a few of our difficulties arise from an inadequate perception of the nature of the Church as the Body of Christ " (*Polity Report*, p. 5). Conclusions very similar have been reached by those in other Christian communions.

" Let the Church be the Church." Yes, but what is the Church, and what is its relation to the purpose of God? What is the right order for a Gospel Church? What place in its life have the sacraments? Are ministers or officers essential to its nature or well-being? What is the relation to one another of different Christian communions and of local Christian communities?

II

These are big questions. That they are being so widely asked after nearly two thousand years of Christian history suggests that there is no easy answer to them. Clearly, however, they are fundamental questions and those who busy themselves with them may hope for a reward.

To be again face to face with these issues represents a striking change from the situation a generation ago when many were ready to dissociate the idea of the Church from that of the Gospel and to reject the former as something added and unnecessary, indeed something that distorted the essential message of Jesus of Nazareth. Lecturing in Berlin in 1899, Harnack declared of Jesus: " He Himself founded no community in the sense of an organised union for divine worship " (*What is Christianity?* p. 152). In the same year Fairbairn announced: " There is no evidence that Jesus ever created, or thought of creating, an organised society. There is no idea He so little emphasises as the idea of the Church " (*Catholicism, Roman and Anglican*, p. 176). It is only fair to note that both these scholars were really protesting against particular types of Church and the theories and pretensions on which they were based. Nevertheless, their words may serve to remind us (1) that any enquiry about the nature of the Church has to be carried back to the New Testament itself, and (2) that we are moving out from a period of negation into one of renewed affirmation. The popular understanding, or misunderstanding, of what the scholars of a previous generation said has undoubtedly contributed to a carelessness in regard to the Church, both practical and theoretical. How far even Free Church scholars have moved from the days of Harnack and Fairbairn may be seen most conveniently in Dr. Newton Flew's *Jesus and His Church* (1938; 2nd edition, 1943) which argues that the idea of a new community, *ecclesia* or Church was fundamental to the teaching and intention of Jesus.[1]

In the chapters that follow we shall be concerned in

---

[1] Cf. N. Micklem in *The Christian Faith*, 1944 edition, p. 111: " If we eliminate the Church from the thought of our Lord, we throw away the one clue which interprets all He was and said and did." The whole chapter is a defence of this position.

particular with Baptist thought and practice regarding the Church, its ministry and its sacraments. Baptists already have a long and honourable history in many parts of the world. The name by which they are known fastens upon their attitude to one of the two Gospel sacraments. Like many other nicknames, it may distract attention both within and without the ranks of the Baptists from more important matters.[1] It has indeed been seriously claimed for Baptists by their most distinguished modern historian that " their distinctive feature is the doctrine of the Church " (Whitley, *A History of British Baptists*, p. 4). If this is so, then they are likely to have an important contribution to make to the modern debate, and it is very desirable that their views be clearly set forth. Their own house has to be set in order. Baptists have probably suffered as much as any Christian community of recent years from the general slackness, casualness and confusion regarding the doctrine of the Church, and have departed as widely as any from the traditions of their fathers. If they are to make their contribution to the modern discussion of these questions and to meet the challenge of the modern situation, one of their first tasks is to rediscover what have been the essential and characteristic notes of their witness.

This is not as easy as might be expected. Baptists have produced no very learned array of theologians, and those who have been outstanding among them have not given a great deal of attention to the doctrine of the Church. The materials for a study of Baptist thought and practice—and it is with the English tradition that we shall be mainly concerned—have been by no means exhaustively worked over. They may be conveniently divided into five categories: (1) certain pronouncements issued in recent years by the Council of the Baptist Union of Great Britain and Ireland (and by one or two other organised Baptist bodies), mainly in reply to questions

[1] Note that in its original form, " Anabaptist," it was repudiated by the seventeenth century pioneers. See p. 61 below.

or proposals from the Conferences on Faith and Order held at Lausanne in 1927 and Edinburgh in 1937; (2) the small number of treatises directly devoted to questions of the Church by Baptist writers, the most notable of which seem to be Daniel Turner's *Compendium of Social Religion* (1758: 2nd edition, 1778), the relevant sections of John Gill's *Body of Practical Divinity* (1770), Charles Stovel's *Hints on the Regulation of Christian Churches* (1835), Joseph Angus's prize essays *The Voluntary System* (1839) and *Christian Churches* (1862), and, of recent days, the provocative but not very happily named booklet by Dr. Dakin, *The Baptist View of the Church and Ministry* (1944);[1] (3) the Circular Letters of the various Baptist Associations, particularly those of the closing decades of the eighteenth century—which usually dealt with theological and ecclesiastical topics and therefore form a most important, but so far largely unregarded, field for the study of Baptist life and faith; (4) the reports on Baptist procedure which may be found in Church and Association Minute Books, Rippon's *Baptist Register* (1790-1802), and the Baptist magazines and periodicals which have succeeded it; and (5) the early Baptist Confessions, mainly from the seventeenth century—a convenient though not wholly adequate collection of which may be found in W. J. McGlothlin's *Baptist Confessions of Faith* (1910).

The first of these categories—obviously the most easily accessible—is unfortunately disappointing. When the Methodists realised how much the issues raised by recent ecumenical conferences and the " reunion movement " generally must circle round the nature of the Church, they set up, as long ago as 1935, a very strong Commission to study the question from the standpoint of their own special tradition and experience, and produced a report which has been a most useful document in recent years. The Baptist reply to the (Lambeth) Appeal to all Chris-

[1] To these should perhaps be added John Smyth's *Principles and Inferences Concerning the Visible Church*, 1607, and *The Differences of the Churches of the Separation*, 1608, but both these important pamphlets were written before he had come to " Baptist " views.

tian People, adopted by the Annual Assembly at Leeds in 1926, is a very valuable statement,[1] including important sections dealing with the Church, Ministry and Sacraments, but it is brief and does not seem to have been based on a great deal of historical study. Nor does it deal with many of the questions that are now seen to be important from the standpoint of Baptist polity as well as that of our relations with other groups of Christians. The comments passed by the Baptist Union Council in 1930 on the official report of the Lausanne Conference (at which, unfortunately, Baptists were not officially represented) were in the main scrappy and negative. They will be found, together with a number of general Free Church statements, in the drawing up of which individual Baptists had a share, in the two volumes of *Documents on Christian Unity* edited by Bishop G. K. A. Bell (O.U.P., 1924 and 1930). The Theological Commission appointed by the Lausanne Conference to carry further the discussion of certain of the issues raised brought together a number of important papers in the volume *The Ministry and the Sacraments* (ed. by Dunkerley, 1937). There are two brief Baptist contributions, the one by Professor I. G. Matthews, of Crozer Seminary, U.S.A., which adopts a largely " Zwinglian " view of the sacraments, and one by Dr. A. C. Underwood, of Rawdon College, protesting against the inadequacy of this view and stating his readiness to accept Dr. J. S. Whale's exposition of the Congregationalist position, save as regards the subject of baptism. In 1932 the Baptist Union Council set up a special committee on the question of union between Baptists, Congregationalists and Presbyterians. Its report, issued in 1937, is an important document, but it concentrates almost exclusively upon baptism and has little to say directly about the nature of the Church, or its organization and ministry. The same must be said of the report of a Commission on " The Baptist Contribution to Christian Unity," appointed by the Baptist World

[1] See Appendix B.

Alliance, which was considered at the Baptist World Congress in Atlanta in 1939.

It would appear, therefore, that the fresh enquiry into the Baptist doctrine of the Church for which the Polity Commission asks is from every point of view overdue and that it is likely to be a substantial task demanding a knowledge of Baptist history and a grasp of essential Baptist principles and inevitably leading back to the New Testament itself. The pages that follow are intended as no more than a preliminary submission of some of the historical evidence that has to be considered and some suggestions as to its bearing on modern issues. Theology and doctrine, particularly Christian theology and doctrine, must never be divorced from history, and, as has been well said, " history should be studied always as a process; not as a picture."

III

There are one or two further preliminary considerations which must be kept constantly in mind. Firstly, Baptists come of Reformation stock. Their teaching and practice cannot be separated from that of other Reformation bodies. In some cases Baptists have given little direct attention to questions of Church and Ministry, because they have been quite content to accept what others have had to say on these matters. A book like John Owen's *The True Nature of a Gospel Church* (1689) undoubtedly exercised a wide influence on many Baptists, though, as we shall suggest later, it does not adequately represent the position of many of them on certain important matters.

Secondly, Baptists come of no one Reformation stream exclusively. Many of them have been very strongly Calvinistic in their theology. It would even be urged by some to-day that no other Christian body remains so loyally Calvinistic in essential belief as does the Baptist.

Nevertheless, those who know their Baptist history are never likely to echo the cry that has been heard within Congregationalism of recent years: " We are of Geneva." Baptists have never looked exclusively to one city, even to Geneva, for the inspiration of their thought and practice. The possible connection between the early English Baptists and the Continental Anabaptists is an intricate and thorny historical problem.[1] Now that the term " Anabaptist " is seen to have been as wildly hurled about and to have had as little definite content as the modern " Bolshevik ",[2] when used as a general term of abuse, there is less reason for indignantly repudiating it than there was. The Anabaptist movement was one of the most significant and vital religious movements of the Reformation epoch and those who think of it solely or mainly in terms of the unfortunate and disgraceful happenings during the siege of Münster are sadly astray. Some Anabaptist influence, direct and indirect, almost certainly went to the making of the earliest Baptist communities in this country and there is every reason to be proud of it. Mennonite influence there certainly was during the years when Baptist thought and practice was in its embryonic stage among Separatist exiles in Holland. The earliest " General " Baptists are perhaps better described as pre-Calvinist rather than anti-Calvinist in their theology. Their practice in Church matters, as we shall see, was markedly different from that of the earliest Separatists and Congregationalists. From the beginning of the seventeenth century to the end of the nineteenth, Baptist life ran in two distinct streams—that of the General Baptists and that of the Particular or Calvinistic Baptists. There were differences between them of practice as well as doctrine. This is one of the reasons why it is

[1] See, e.g. *Baptist Quarterly,* II, pp. 24f., papers by W. T. Whitley and A. J. D. Farrer; *Transactions of the Congregational Historical Society,* XII and XIII, articles by Duncan B. Heriot.

[2] This is admitted by the distinguished Roman Catholic historian, Maximin Piette. See *John Wesley in the Evolution of Protestantism,* 1938, p. 36.

difficult as well as dangerous to generalise or dogmatise about Baptist beliefs. There has been variety in our life, and sometimes tension. Things stressed in one generation have sometimes fallen into the background in the next, only to be revived again later on. It is a rich and diverse tradition to which we are able to appeal. For this inheritance Baptists may well be grateful, though the more they have made it their own, the more they will realise how careful they must be not to use the adjective " Baptist " in any narrow or exclusive sense.

Thirdly, Baptists come of the lineage of John Smyth, who in 1606 drew up the historic covenant of the Separatist church in and around Gainsborough. "As the Lord's free people," said William Bradford, who was one of the company, and who later went with the Pilgrim Fathers to America " (they) joined themselves by a covenant of the Lord into a church estate, in the fellowship of the Gospel, to walk in all His ways, made known, or to be made known unto them, according to their best endeavours, whatsoever it should cost them, the Lord assisting them." The temper and outlook of these words were no doubt the inspiration of the better known dictum of John Robinson, a slightly younger man, deeply influenced by Smyth: " The Lord has more Truth yet to break forth out of His Word." Smyth set his friends and associates upon a quest and a pilgrimage. Theirs was, by its very nature, a progressive covenant. With the New Testament in their hands, they were to promise to conform to what should be made known to them by the Spirit. Loyalty to this led in Smyth's own case to his becoming convinced that admission into the true Church should be by baptism in the scriptural manner. Later, doubting the rightness of the self-baptism with which he had begun the reconstitution of his church, he joined himself with many of his followers to the Mennonites, among whom, he felt, the truly scriptural usage had been maintained; though this action meant that the partnership between himself and his friend, Helwys, was broken. When, in 1612, in the last months of his life, Smyth wrote his *Retraction and Confirmation*, he had moved a stage farther and had come to feel that " matters of the outward Church and Ceremonies " were of secondary importance to Christian charity. " Difference in Judgment for matter of circumstance," he declared, " as are all things of the outward church, shall not cause me to refuse the brotherhood of any penitent and faithful Christian whatsoever " (*Works*, ed. by Whitley, II, p. 755).

The principle of the Gainsborough covenant is of fundamental importance for an understanding of Baptist life at its best. Baptists have claimed freedom from the authority of any sacerdotal hierarchy, freedom from the State, freedom of conscience, freedom of private judgment. They have been, on the whole consistently, suspicious of creeds and verbal statements. Hence, in large measure, the difficulty of tying them down at any point to belief in this or that theory. They have claimed the guidance of the living Spirit of Christ present within His Church, a guidance inspired, confirmed and held in check by appeal to the Scriptures and, in particular, to those of the New Testament. The final court of appeal has been neither to church pronouncements, nor to history and tradition as such, but to the conscience of the church inspired by the Spirit of God as a result of the study of the Bible. " The deepest impulse of Baptist life has been the upholding of the sole and exclusive authority of Jesus Christ against all possible encroachment," said Dr. John Clifford at the Baptist World Congress of 1911. That has implied the Lordship of Christ within the Church— the Lordship of the living Christ still guiding and directing His people.

These things should be kept carefully in mind in considering the evidence as to Baptist belief and practice which will be set forth.

2

THE VISIBLE CHURCH

I

BAPTISTS are among the children of the Reformation. They came of that mighty movement which sought to restore the purity of the Church. The corruptions of medieval Catholicism had become so great that over wide areas of Europe there was swift response to the trumpet call of Luther and his associates. With enthusiasm and zeal men set about sweeping away a system which had come to hinder rather than help their approach to God. The original Lutheran movement was primarily religious. Its emphasis was upon personal justification by faith and the right of private judgment in matters of religion. The word uttered by Luther was of epoch-making significance, a rediscovery of vast resources of spiritual power, which had revolutionary consequences for every side of European life. It is well, however, to remember that " it had never been Luther's aim either to found a new Church, or even within the historically existing Church to carry out any elaborately pre-arranged form of reorganisation " (H. E. Jacobs, *E.R.E.*, VIII, p. 202). He was himself never quite at ease in the discussions regarding the form of Church order which was to follow from the principles which he had enunciated. Only slowly did the full consequence of his appeal to Scripture become apparent. The varied views which were soon to be found among the Reformers showed the complexity of the issues involved. Zwinglians, Anabaptists, Calvinists were before long busy with the task of trying to erect a Church order which should be in accordance with that portrayed in the New Testament. That they differed on many matters is not surprising when one considers the newness of the quest upon which they were engaged, the confused political situation of the time, the verbal authority they ascribed to the text of Scripture and the nature of the evidence with which they had to deal.

The new ideas were soon at work like a ferment in England. Henry VIII, the great Tudor sovereign, was at first a vigorous and honoured champion of the old Catholicism against the subversive views of Luther. Later, personal and political considerations led him to break with Rome, and he found certain of the principles enunciated by the Reformers not inconvenient to him. The English Reformation was, however, essentially a compromise, an attempt to go so far but no farther, an effort to set up a National Church with the supreme authority firmly in the hands of the sovereign and the bishops instead of those of the Pope. There was soon a strong Puritan party convinced that the reform of the English Church ought to be more radical, far more like that which had been carried through on the Continent, particularly in those areas which had adopted the views of Calvin.

From among the Puritans came the Separatists. Those who despaired of any adequate reform of the ecclesiastical abuses in this country and those who, in their study of Scripture, found themselves led to reject altogether a State-established Church and a Church governed from above by an episcopally ordained hierarchy, or even by synods of presbyters, formed " Separatist " Churches, local communities of believers in the Gospel starting *de novo* to model their life and worship on the New Testament. Persecution by the civil and religious authorities drove many of the Separatists abroad, first to Holland, later to the American Colonies. From among the Separatists came the Baptists. A New Testament Church, they said, must surely observe the New Testament rites in a New Testament manner. They were but one among many groups who in the opening decades of the seventeenth century earnestly sought to discover the pattern of Gospel churchmanship. Underlying the bitter theological controversies and the political upheavals of Stuart and Commonwealth England there was a wistful searching for the true Church. We who, three centuries later, are vexed with many of the same problems, should have a new sympathy with our spiritual ancestors.

Certain fairly clear convictions emerged during the course of the Reformation movement which has been cursorily surveyed in the preceding paragraphs. They are part of the religious heritage of those whose beliefs about the Church we shall examine more closely. The Continental Reformers—Lutheran, Anabaptist and Calvinist—the Puritans, the Separatists and their seventeenth century descendants all held firmly to the principle that salvation is by faith, that is, by direct individual response to the grace offered by God in Christ. Neither priest nor Church stands between God and the believer. Secondly, all alike made an appeal to Scripture and regarded it as authoritative both for faith and practice. It was perhaps almost inevitable that, thirdly, in reaction from the idea of the Church as a great visible institution centralised and authoritarian, not a few should stress the idea of the Church invisible, the company of the elect whose names are known only to God, and that they should place their emphasis—so far as the Church visible is concerned—on the local company of believers, who come together deliberately because of their common faith to carry out the ordinances of the Gospel and who can rely on the word of Jesus recorded in Matthew xviii. 20: " Where two or three are gathered in My name, there am I in the midst of them." These three ideas—worked out in varied fashion —are the foundation of the tradition in which Baptists stand. They form the background of the seventeenth century creeds and confessions to which we now turn. They have remained basic to our life and witness down to the present time. There is, however, a fourth determining principle, of equal importance, to which we have already called attention, viz. a belief in the presence of the Spirit of the living Christ with His people, leading them on to ever fuller apprehension of truth and to an ever holier way of life. The Separatists and their descendants were avowed " seekers." They recognised themselves as voyaging on largely uncharted seas. They were sure, however, that, if they were faithful, the way would be revealed to them.

II

With these things in mind we may turn to some of the early Baptist statements regarding the Church and to a consideration of the church polity which they set forth. We may well begin with some sentences from the final Confession of the company to whom John Smyth ministered in Holland. Smyth is generally regarded as the father of the General Baptists, that is, the earlier of the two main streams of Baptist witness. The opening articles of the Confession set out at length, in the language of Scripture, a theological compendium, leading up to an emphatic declaration of the necessity of personal repentance and faith. It continues :

" 64. That the outward church visible consists of penitent persons only, and of such as believing in Christ bring forth fruits worthy amendment of life.

" 65. That the visible church is a mystical figure outwardly, of the true, spiritual invisible church; which consisteth of the spirits of just and perfect men only, that is, of the regenerate. . . .

" 69. That all penitent and faithful Christians are brethren in the communion of the outward church, wheresoever they live, by what name soever they are known, which in truth and zeal, follow repentance and faith, though compassed with never so many ignorances and infirmities; and we salute them all

with a holy kiss, being heartily grieved that we
which follow after one faith, and one spirit, one Lord,
and one God, one body, and one baptism, should be
rent into so many sects and schisms: and that only
for matters of less moment " (McGlothlin, *op. cit.*,
pp. 78-9).[1]

A noble spirit breathes through this last clause and the
words deserve to be far better known than they are. They
show a breadth and charity which, while they have not
always been universally echoed among Baptists, have yet
happily never been without witnesses in their midst. It is
only after this clause, which has important implications for
the doctrine of the visible church, that Smyth goes on to
define the baptism of penitent and faithful persons, the
Lord's Supper, the ministry of the church, Christian discipline, freedom of conscience, Christian ethics and finally
the Christian hope, as he and his friends viewed these
things.

The Confession of the group who followed Thomas
Helwys and returned to London with him in 1612, there
establishing the first Baptist church in England, is shorter
than that of Smyth but more explicit regarding the church.

" 10. That the Church of Christ is a company of
faithful people, separated from the world by the word
and Spirit of God, being knit unto the Lord, and
one unto another, by baptism, upon their own confession of the faith and sins.

" 11. That though, in respect of Christ, the
Church be one, yet it consisteth of divers particular
congregations, even so many as there shall be in the
world, every of which congregation, though they be

---

[1] Of the hundred clauses of the Confession only three are without
Scripture references. This is one of the three. But Whitley, *The
Works of John Smyth*, 1915, I, p. lxxi, seems hardly to do Smyth
justice when he says: " The question never became important to
Smyth how one church was related to another, so he never raised it,
much less examined Scripture to answer it. He neither affirmed nor
denied Independency."

but two or three, have Christ given them, with all the means of their salvation, are the Body of Christ, and a whole Church. And therefore may, and ought, when they are come together to pray, prophesy and break bread, and administer in all the holy ordinances, although as yet they have no officers, or that their officers should be in prison, sick, or by any other means hindered from the church.

" 12. That as one congregation hath Christ, so hath all, and that the Word of God cometh not out from any one, neither to any one congregation in particular, but unto every particular church, as it doth unto all the world, and therefore no church ought to challenge any prerogative over any other. . . .

" 16. That the members of every church or congregation ought to know one another, that so they may perform all the duties of love one towards another both to soul and body. . . . " (McGlothlin, pp. 88-90, spelling modernised and Scripture references omitted).

Here the spiritual autonomy of each local company of believers is asserted, their right to appoint their own officers claimed, and their numbers limited to a group who can have " particular knowledge one of another."

In practice it was some time before Baptists established very large churches. In the case of the General Baptists these usually covered a considerable geographical area, divided for convenience into a number of worshipping centres. Only occasionally could the members all meet together for the Lord's Supper or for church business. The scattered community was held together by its officers, some of whom had to travel long distances. At the end of the seventeenth century there was, for example, a London church functioning as one unit for the election of elders and deacons which had at least seven sections in different parts of the metropolis.[1] Similarly, at Slapton in Northamptonshire might be found a church with mem-

1 See *Baptist Quarterly*, VII, pp. 321f.

bers in nine or ten different villages and a presiding elder living fifteen miles away in Northampton.[1]

These early Baptists jealously guarded the right of the local church to appoint its own officers, and specifically rejected any suggestion that one church could have authority over another. They suffered persecution in their resistance to the attempts of the magistrates and the bishops of the Established Church to control them. They were never, however, so foolish as to believe that a particular church did not need the fellowship of other churches. Representatives of thirty congregations in Leicestershire, Lincolnshire and adjoining counties met in 1651 and drew up a common Confession to which they invited the adherence of other churches " in England, Wales, Army, or elsewhere." Nine years later, representatives of General Baptist churches all over the kingdom met in London and drew up what is usually called " the Standard Confession of 1660."

Eighteen years later, in what is known as the " Orthodox Creed " of 1678, drawn up by General Baptists from Buckinghamshire, Oxfordshire and adjoining counties, " General Councils, or Assemblies " were thus provided for and described :

" XXXIX. General councils, or assemblies, consisting of Bishops, Elders, and Brethren, of the several churches of Christ, and being legally convened, and met together out of all the churches, and the churches appearing there by their representatives, make but one church, and have lawful right, and suffrage in this general meeting, or assembly, to act in the name of Christ; it being of divine authority, and is the best means under heaven to preserve unity, to prevent heresy, and superintendency among or in any congregation whatsoever within its own limits, or jurisdiction. And to such a meeting, or assembly, appeals ought to be made, in case any injustice be

[1] See Anderson, *The Baptist Churches at Weston by Weedon, etc.*, 1930.

done, or heresy, and schism countenanced, in any particular congregation of Christ, and the decisive voice in such general assemblies is the major part, and such general assemblies have lawful power to hear, and determine, as also to excommunicate " (McGlothlin, p. 154).

The words " make but one church " are particularly significant. The General Baptists were clearly not Independents in the commonly accepted use of the term. It is worth noting, moreover, that the Confession is supported at this point by references to the Council at Jerusalem recorded in Acts xv, to Matthew xviii. 18-20, and to I Corinthians v. 4-6.

Similarly, the Particular Baptists, a Calvinistic group who came out of Separatism and Congregationalism on the issue of believers' baptism, and who spread rapidly during the Commonwealth period, established " Associations " of churches which drew up common confessions. A Confession first produced by seven London congregations in 1644, and several times re-issued with larger numbers adhering to it, has been described by McGlothlin as " perhaps the most independent of the Baptist Confessions and . . . one of the noblest productions ever put forth by them " (*op. cit.*, p. 170). He claims that it probably still represents the views of the Baptists of the world more nearly than any other single Confession. In it there occurs this article:

" XLVII. And although the particular Congregations be distinct and severall Bodies, every one a compact and knit Citie in it selfe; yet are they all to walk by one and the same Rule, and by all meanes convenient to have the counsell and help one of another in all needfull affaires of the Church, as members of one body in the common faith under Christ their onely head " (*op. cit.*, p. 186-7).

Almost all subsequent Particular Baptist Confessions show the strong influence of the historic Confession laid before Parliament by the Westminster divines in 1646 and generally accepted as a classic exposition of Calvinism.[1] Save in regard to the spiritual autonomy of the local congregation in the appointment of its own officers and on the matter of believers' baptism, the Baptist variations are mainly verbal.

All these documents are inspired by what may rightly be described as High Churchmanship. A particular group of believers is conceived as drawn together into fellowship and by the selection of officers, the proper observance of the sacraments and the disciplining of its members may be assured of the presence of Christ and may claim to be truly part of the visible Church. But it must be in communion with other local churches. That is an essential part of its churchmanship. The individual groups are regarded as " separate hearts of one whole "—to borrow the language of a modern poet.[2] The 1677 Particular Baptist Confession (reaffirmed in 1689 after the accession of William and Mary by the representatives of one hundred and seven churches in England and Wales, and subsequently issued in many different editions)[3] makes this quite explicit.

> " Chap. XXVI. 14. As each Church and all the members of it are bound to pray continually for the good and prosperity of all the Churches of Christ, in all places; and upon all occasions to further it (every one within the bounds of their places and callings in the exercise of their gifts and graces) so the Churches

[1] It was issued in 1648 in English and Latin by Parliamentary authority and was until the Restoration the Confessional Standard of the United Kingdom.

[2] Laurence Housman, *The Continuing City.* Cf. P. T. Forsyth's metaphor of the local church as an " outcrop " of the total and continuous church, one everywhere (see *The Church and the Sacraments,* 1917). Cf. also A. G. Hebert, *The Form of the Church,* 1944, p. 64, on " the partial truth of the Congregationalist conception of the Church, in which it has been truly seen that the whole mystery of the Church is present in each local part."

[3] McGlothlin, p. 219, describes it as "the most influential and important of all Baptist Confessions." The sections bearing on the matters discussed in this book will be found in Appendix A.

(when planted by the providence of God so as they may enjoy opportunity and advantage for it) ought to hold communion amongst themselves for their peace, increase of love and mutual edification " (McGlothlin, p. 267-8).

Questions of doctrine and administration, and even of the internal peace of individual churches, should be submitted to the representatives of churches meeting in assembly. Their conclusions cannot be imposed upon the particular churches, or their officers. An assembly had not for the Particular Baptists what is called " churchpower." The acceptance of decisions must be voluntary. Nevertheless, in practice the spiritual authority of such assemblies was very great, and they were an essential part of the churchmanship of the early Baptists.

III

This matter is of considerable importance. Associations, Synods, Unions and Assemblies of churches are not to be regarded as optional and secondary. They are the necessary expression of Christian fellowship, a necessary manifestation of the Church visible. The local congregation is not truly a church if it lives an entirely separate life. We have already referred to the influence of John Owen's *True Nature of a Gospel Church* in Baptist circles. The great Independent divine there sets out, in language which Baptists often borrowed, the principles of Congregationalism. It is right that Baptists as well as Congregationalists should have their attention called to the important part which Owen assigned to fellowship and communion between churches.[1]

Churches, said Owen, once they have been properly constituted, " are obliged unto mutual Communion among themselves, which is their consent, endeavour and

[1] For the discussion of this issue by Congregationalists see D. T. Jenkins, *The Nature of Catholicity*, 1942, and N. Micklem, *Congregationalism and the Church Catholic*, 1943.

conjunction in and for the promotion of the Edification of
the Catholick Church, and therein their own, as they are
Parts and Members of it " (*op. cit.*, 1689 edition, p. 234).
He urged the widest possible co-operation and fellowship
between Christians who have all " one and the same God
and Father, one Lord Jesus Christ, one Faith and one
Doctrine of Faith, one hope of their calling or the promised Inheritance, one Regeneration, one Baptism, one
Bread and Wine; united unto God and Christ in one
Spirit, through the bond of Faith and Love " (p. 242).
He defined their communion with one another as " their
joint actings in the same Gospel Duties towards God in
Christ, with their mutual actings towards each other, with
respect unto the end of their Institution and Being, which
is the Glory of Christ in the Edification of the whole
Catholick Church " (p. 244). " No Church therefore is
so Independent, as that it can always, and in all Cases,
observe the Duties it owes unto the Lord Christ and the
Church Catholick, by all those Powers which it is able to
act in itself distinctly, without conjunction with others.
And the Church that confines its Duty unto the Acts of
its own Assemblies, cuts itself off from the external Communion of the Church Catholick; nor will it be safe for
any Man to commit the Conduct of his Soul to such a
Church " (p. 251).

These are searching and weighty words, strikingly
relevant to our modern situation. What follows is even
more pointed. " That particular Church which extends
not its Duty beyond its own Assemblies and Members, is
fallen off from the principal end of its Institution. And
every Principle, Opinion, or Persuasion, that inclines any
Church to confine its Care and Duty unto its own Edification only; yea, or of those only which agree with it in
some peculiar practice, making it neglective of all due
means of the Edification of the Church Catholick, is
Schismatical " (p. 251).

Owen believed that it was by means of synods and
councils that the churches should express their fellowship

in the Church Catholic. These synods should consider questions of faith and order, questions of peace and unity, questions of discipline (i.e. Christian ethics), questions of worship. They have the duty and responsibility of positive action on these matters and have not to wait until specifically appealed to. Owen expressly provided, however, that even an individual, being " not only a Member of (a) particular Church, but by virtue thereof of the Catholick Church also " (p. 252), had the right of appeal to a synod. He ascribed to synods a three-fold power: (1) declarative, (2) constitutive, and (3) executive—the last in cases of jurisdiction submitted to it.

In these concluding and largely neglected pages of Owen's treatise is to be found a comprehensive justification, on Congregationalist principles, of the movement towards co-operation and union among those of different Christian traditions which has occupied so much of the energy of Christian leaders during the past thirty years. There is also to be found the theological and biblical rationale of unions and associations of churches sharing a common practice and organisation.

IV

Whilst they have often shown themselves somewhat shy of the wider implications of Owen's contentions, Baptists have been notable from the earliest times for the vigour of their Association life. We have already noted the explicit provision for this in the seventeenth century Confessions. It has continued a vital part of Baptist church life. Several Associations were formed—or in a few cases reconstituted—in the eighteenth century. Still more came into existence in the nineteenth century, and it is the twenty-seven Baptist Associations which form the basis of the Baptist Union. This is worthy of emphasis, for it is sometimes suggested that the Union simply links together individual churches,[1] while certain modern developments, like that of personal membership, have

[1] See, e.g. Dakin, *op. cit.*, p. 19.

tended, probably unfortunately, to obscure what should be its real nature and function. Even now, however, half the membership of the Council which conducts the business of the Baptist Union consists of representatives of the affiliated Associations.

How Associations of Churches have been regarded in Baptist circles may be judged by two or three quotations. The Circular Letter of the Eastern Association for 1777 undertakes a formal exposition of their nature and purpose, daringly setting them on a level with ordinances of the Church such as baptism and the Lord's Supper. Baptist churches aim, it is urged, at " the revival of primitive Christianity." " What we wish at present more particularly to recommend to you is this branch of primitive discipline *Associating*, which, we think, although it hath been degraded from its pristine dignity, and corrupted into an engine of the most savage inhumanity, is yet as capable of restitution as baptism, or the Lord's Supper, or any other primitive institute " (p. 6). Reference is made to the value of the guidance of the first Christian churches by the apostles and to the importance of the Council of Jerusalem (Acts xv.). Mosheim, the eighteenth century church historian, is quoted for the view that synods and councils were common in the second century A.D.; rather, argues the letter, they were a part of church life from the very beginning, but unfortunately they became corrupted, first, by assuming a coercive power and authority which should have been alien to them, and, secondly, by confining their membership to ministers or clergy. It is pointed out that " as soon as ever liberty of conscience was granted," that is, in 1689, Baptists came together in a general assembly, and at the time of writing nearly a century later they are organised in a number of convenient Associations, each of ten or fifteen churches. What is needed is a union of these provincial associations with an annual, or perhaps, triennial, assembly of delegates chosen therefrom. This, it may be noted, would result in an organisation rather more presby-

terian or synodal than our present Baptist Union, which
was first formed in 1813, reconstituted in 1831 and further
reorganised in 1863. The 1777 Letter goes on to plead for a
more general assembly of all the Nonconformist denominations. Fifty years earlier the London ministers of the
Presbyterian, Congregationalist and Baptist denominations had formed an organisation, and in 1732 the Committee of the Dissenting Deputies (which included laymen)
began its work in the metropolis. But these were only
London organisations. The bold project of the Eastern
Baptist Association had to wait for fulfilment till the
formation of the National Free Church Council in 1892.

That this Circular Letter of 1777 represented the general
standpoint of those responsible for the revival of the life
of the Baptist Associations in the closing decades of the
eighteenth century is confirmed by the fact that in 1779
it was substantially reproduced and elaborated in the
Circular Letter of the Kent and Sussex Association.
Almost equally significant is the fact that John Rippon
in 1790 opened his *Baptist Register*—the earliest of Baptist magazines—with a lengthy poem on " The Association " by Benjamin Francis. This may not be great
poetry but it is clear indication of the large place which
the Associations and their annual gatherings had in the
Baptist consciousness.

> " No worldly motive, and no base design
> But love of truth and purity divine,
> With pious zeal for the Redeemer's cause,
> That first conven'd thee and ordain'd thy laws,
> While Christian friendship joined her aid apace,
> To give thee strength, stability and grace. . . .
>
> So, yearly, meet, from parts remote, in Thee,
> When summer smiles on every herb and tree,
> Th'associate brethren, pastors, deacons, friends,
> And the full crowd that in thy train attends. . . .
> O blest assembly ! . . . . "

One may further note how much space was given in the
Register to the Letters and Breviates of the Associations,

and those not only of this country, but of America, where also from the beginning they were an essential part of Baptist life.

Only one nineteenth century witness need be called. So doughty a Baptist as Charles Stovel, writing in 1835, declared: " One great, and most important object in these days, is to give an effective character to the different associations." And that he intended the adjective "effective " to have real content is shown by the fact that he recommended the special study of the Epistles to Timothy and Titus, " for each of these individuals were entrusted with that kind of superintendence which is now held by the whole association " (*Hints on the Regulation of Christian Churches*, p. 163).

To sum up: these various citations make clear that from the seventeenth century Baptists have regarded the visible Church as finding expression in local communities of believers who constitute themselves churches by the election of officers, the observance of baptism and the Lord's Supper, and Christian discipline, and who find an extension and expression of their life in free association, first, with other churches of their own faith and order, but also with all other groups of Christians loyal to the central truths of the apostolic Gospel. This, in outline, is the Baptist doctrine of the Church as visible. It is something very different from the exaggerated independence, self-sufficiency and atomism which have sometimes been favoured of recent days. It is high churchmanship in its emphasis on the faith which is presupposed by the local covenant and by the rite of baptism, which since the days of Smyth has often taken the place of the latter. It is high churchmanship in its assertion of the Lordship of Christ and the " Crown Rights of the Redeemer." It is high churchmanship in its loyalty to " the ordinances of the Gospel "— ministry, sacraments and discipline. It is high churchmanship in its inner urge towards communion, fellowship and unity with all those other Christians who together make up the Church Catholic.

Chapter Three

THE MINISTRY OF THE CHURCH

I

THE Annual Baptist Assembly at Liverpool in 1930, on the motion of the Baptist Union Council, adopted a reply to the Reports of the World Conference on Faith and Order held at Lausanne in 1927. In the course of it the following sentences occur: "We cannot agree that the ministry, as commonly understood, is essential to the existence of a true Christian Church, though we believe a ministry is necessary for its highest effectiveness. We think of the function of the ministry in terms of leadership rather than of government and discipline. We believe that, while we should frankly discuss our differences, at this time it may be a gain to emphasise our agreement on the permanent and essential marks of the Church." (*Report of the Council*, 1930, pp. 38-39; *Convictions*, ed. by L. Hodgson, 1934, p. 62).

A reference to the Lausanne Reports will show that this comment had reference to the section in which it is declared:

> "The Church on earth possesses certain characteristics whereby it can be known of men. These have been, since the days of the Apostles, at least the following:
> (1) The possession and acknowledgment of the Word of God as given in Holy Scripture and interpreted by the Holy Spirit to the Church and to the individual.
> (2) The profession of faith in God as He is incarnate and revealed in Christ.
> (3) The acceptance of Christ's commission to preach the Gospel to every creature.

(4) The observance of the Sacraments.
(5) A ministry for the pastoral office, the preaching of the Word, and the administration of the Sacraments.
(6) A fellowship in prayer, in worship, in all the means of grace, in the pursuit of holiness, and in the service of man " (*Faith and Order*, 1927, edited by H. N. Bate, p. 464. Cf. E. S. Woods, *Lausanne*, 1927, p. 68-9).

The Baptist Union Council apparently accepted the first four marks of the Church and the sixth, but expressly denied the fifth. This was perhaps the result of a traditional and healthy reaction from the view implied by the phrase " No bishop, no church "; but it was surely a very strange exception to make, and can hardly be excused by the phrase in the reply qualifying the word ministry—" as commonly understood." Report No. III from Lausanne has in it no more about the ministry than the sentence quoted above. On Report No. V, which deals explicitly with the ministry, the Council said little more than that Baptists " do not confine the administration of Sacraments to ordained ministers, nor stipulate for the laying on of hands."

One of the aims of this chapter will be to show that whatever is the view of present-day Baptists, their predecessors of the seventeenth and eighteenth centuries would have accepted wholeheartedly the Lausanne declaration regarding the ministry as essential to the church, that they would have reserved to the ministry—" as commonly understood"—presidency at the Lord's Table, and that in ordination services the laying-on of hands was general among them. Further, evidence will be submitted to show (1) that the presence of other ordained ministers at ordination services was one of the ways in which the larger aspects of Christian fellowship were recognised and safeguarded, and (2) that the ministry among Baptists was not, as has recently been alleged by Dr. Dakin (*op.*

cit., pp. 44f) confined to the pastoral office. Incidentally, it will be made clear that when Baptists found a place in the ranks of their ministers for those still engaged, part-time at least, in so-called secular callings, they were not intending thereby to lower the standards of entry into the ministry or to alter its status.

II

The seventeenth century Confessions make it clear that no company of believers would have been regarded as properly constituted as a church or in a full church-state until officers or ministers had been chosen. Here Baptists of both the Arminian and Calvinistic theological traditions were at one. Where they differed was as to the orders of ministry as set out in the New Testament. Smyth's last Confession asserts:

" 75. That the preaching of the word, and the ministry of the sacraments, representeth the ministry of Christ in the spirit; who teacheth, baptiseth, and feedeth the regenerate, by the Holy Spirit inwardly and invisibly.

" 76. That Christ hath set in His outward church two sorts of ministers: viz., some who are called pastors, teachers or elders, who administer in the word and sacraments, and others who are called deacons, men and women: whose ministry is, to serve tables and wash the saints' feet " (McGlothlin, *op. cit.*, p. 80).

Three things are to be noted here: first, the character assigned to the ministry as representing Christ, secondly, the inclusion within it of deacons as well as pastors, teachers and elders, and thirdly, the admission of women to the diaconate. The liberal attitude of the early Baptists to the ministry of women is specially notable. Though this is not provided for here, there were in England in the seventeenth century not a few women preachers among the Baptists. Dr. Rufus Jones has drawn particular attention to their work (see *Studies in Mystical Religion*, p. 419).

Helwys's Confession follows much the same lines as Smyth's, with two interesting and important additions. There is, first, a clause regarding the election of church-officers which is to be " with fasting, prayer and laying-on of hands." Secondly, it is asserted that " the officers of every church or congregation are tied by office only to that particular congregation whereof they are chosen; and therefore they cannot challenge by office any authority in any other congregation whatsoever except they would have an Apostleship " (McGlothlin, *op. cit.*, p. 91). Here there seems to be the germ of the later General Baptist office of " Bishop, or Messenger," as distinct from those of Pastor and Deacon. The Confession of the thirty congregations which joined together in 1651 stresses the fact that those who are chosen ministers should be adequately supported by the free-will gifts of the churches, but that they should in turn be ready on occasion to work with their hands. " Fasting and prayer," it is said, " ought to be used, and laying on of hands, for the ordaining of servants or officers to attend about the service of God " (McGlothlin, *op. cit.*, pp. 105, 108). " The Standard Confession of 1660 " asserts that those are owned as " Ministers of the Gospel " who are deliberately chosen and ordained " to exercise their gifts not only in the Church but also (as occasion serves) to preach to the World " (*ibid*, p. 113).

It is in the so-called "Orthodox Creed" of 1678, drawn up at a time of great suffering for all Dissenters, when it was desired to emphasise points of agreement rather than difference, that there is to be found the most fully articulated General Baptist statement regarding the officers of the church. They are, it is said, of three kinds: (1) Bishops, or Messengers, (2) Elders, or Pastors, and (3) Deacons, or Overseers of the poor. " Bishops " are to be chosen '' by the common suffrage of the church, and solemly

set apart by fasting and prayer, with imposition of hands, by the bishops of the same function, ordinarily, and those bishops so ordained have the government of those churches that had suffrage in their election, and no other ordinarily; as also to preach the word, or gospel, to the world, or unbelievers. And the particular pastor, or elder, in. like manner is to be chosen by the common suffrage of the particular congregation and ordained by the bishop or messenger God hath placed in the church he hath charge of; and the elder, so ordained, is to watch over that particular church; and he may not ministerially act in any other Church before he be sent, neither ought his power, or office, any way to infringe the liberty, or due power, or office of his bishop. . . . The deacons are in like manner to be chosen by election and ordination, and are in their particular congregations, to receive the charity and free benevolence of the people '' (McGlothlin, *op. cit.*, pp. 146-7).

Bishops and elders are entitled to proper maintenance. It is they who baptise and preside at the Lord's Table. It is in their hands that '' the discipline and government of the Church '' rests. Clearly, the bishops, or messengers, of whose work some details may be found in the pages of Dr. Whitley's *History*, exercised functions analogous to those entrusted of recent years to the General Superintendents appointed by the Baptist Union.

The Particular Baptists, instead of a three-fold order of ministry, favoured in general a two-fold one, that of Elders or Pastors (occasionally using the title Bishops) and Deacons. Their polity, as we have already seen, was more like that of the Independents, with stress upon the local church, each with its own officers, yet all the members sharing in matters of discipline. Nevertheless, they explicitly asserted the right and duty of calling out from the local church persons " to prophesie . . . and so teach publickly the Word of God " (1644 Confession. McGloth-lin, *op. cit.*, p. 186), and also " to send forth such breth-ren as are fitly gifted and qualified through the Spirit of Christ to preach the Gospel to the World" (1656 Somerset Confession. McGlothlin, p. 211-12). These preachers were not tied to any one church, but exercised a wide and successful evangelistic ministry, as is clear from the growth of the Baptist movement during the middle decades of the seventeenth century. Among the Particular Baptists appointment both to the pastoral office and to the dia-conate was marked " with imposition of hands of the Eldership of the Church, if there be any before constituted therein " (1689 Confession. McGlothlin, *op. cit.*, p. 266). It seems always to have been customary for as many neighbouring pastors as possible to gather to join in ordination services.[1] The records in old Minute Books and later in the *Baptist Register* and the early issues of the *Baptist Magazine* show that both pastors and deacons were " ordained " with " the laying on of hands " at least until the early years of the nineteenth century.

III

The principles involved in the statements of their Con-fessions long determined Baptist theory and practice. The attitude to the ministry and the manner of entry into it in the eighteenth century are made clear from a number of sources. Only a few illustrations can here be given.

[1] Cf. Fuller, " On Ordination," *Theological and Biblical Magazine,* 1804-5. For Congregationalist theory and practice see Doddridge, Appendix to Ordination Sermons dated 18 September, 1745, and also J. S. Whale, *The Ministry and the Sacraments,* 1937, p. 214 : " Ordi-nation to the ministry is a spiritual act of the whole Church, and though entirely within the competence of the local Church, it invari-ably takes place in the presence of and with the assistance of repre-sentatives of other gathered Churches." Cf. Lindsay, *Church and Ministry in the Early Centuries,* p. 330.

One of the most interesting cases is that of Andrew Fuller. He first spoke at one of the services in his native Soham in 1771. The church was then pastorless, one of the deacons leading the worship each Sunday. Two years later " the work of opening the Word on Lord's days was wholly committed to Bro. Fuller, though not yet publicly sent into the ministry." In January, 1774, following a request that he should preach a funeral sermon, he was " called to the ministry " (the phrase is his own) and from then onwards did his preaching from the pulpit. Another seven months passed before " the church requested Bro. Fuller to take the pastoral care of them ", and he was not " ordained pastor " till May, 1775. The " ordination " (again the word is his own) was conducted by Robert Hall, of Arnesby. A number of other ministers were there. It included the laying-on of hands.

Clearly there is here implied a wider conception of the ministry than the solely pastoral, and ordination is held to involve the presence of ministers, or pastors, from other churches. Even more significant is what occurred a few years later when the church at Kettering began to desire Fuller as its pastor. The first soundings were made in 1779 and the discussions relating to the matter occupied three years. It never occurred to Fuller that this was a matter simply between himself and Kettering, or between Kettering and Soham. It concerned the Baptist churches in the neighbourhood, and the matter was repeatedly submitted to the leading ministers of the Association. At one point the whole question was referred to Robert Robinson, of Cambridge.

Similarly, in the case of William Carey. The Church Book at Olney, under date August 10, 1786, states : " This evening our Brother William Carey was called to the work of the Ministry, and sent out by the Church to preach the Gospel, wherever God in His providence might call him." Three months later, the Moulton Church book has this entry : " Agreed universally to call our Minister Mr. Carey to the office of Pastor, which was accordingly done—and Consented to on his Part." That is to say, the term " minister " was used in a wider sense than that of " pastor." This is confirmed by the striking passage on the work and character of " a Christian minister " which occurs in Carey's *Enquiry* (p. 72). " He engages," says Carey, " to go where God pleases, and to do, or endure what He sees fit to command, or call him to, in the exercise of his function."

Precisely similar is the case of Samuel Ruston, of Hamsterley, Durham, whose call to the ministry is described in the *Baptist Register*, II, p. 483. First, he was called " to exercise his talents before the church alone on the Lord's day evenings." Next, " the whole church unanimously agreed to call him to the work of the ministry," and at a special service " the church's call of him to the ministry, to preach the word and baptise those who were proper subjects, under the direction of the church, and as eligible to the pastoral office, when called to it, was announced."

How Baptists themselves described the authority and work of the minister may be seen from Hercules Collins's *The Temple Repair'd or An Essay to revive the long-neglected Ordinances, of exercising the spiritual Gift of Prophecy for the Edification of the Churches, and of ordaining Ministers duly qualified*, issued in 1702; from Daniel Turner's *Compendium of Social Religion*, which first appeared in 1758 and of which a second enlarged edition was issued in 1778; and from the relevant sections of Dr. John Gill's *Body of Practical Divinity*. Hercules Collins was a well-known London Baptist minister of Restoration times who suffered imprisonment in Newgate gaol. Daniel Turner was minister in Abingdon from 1748 till his death in 1798. He was the friend of Isaac Watts, and later of Robert Robinson and John Rippon, and exercised a very wide influence throughout the Midland counties. The memorial tablet in the Abingdon chapel describes him as " the scholar, the poet, the Christian." John Gill was a learned commentator and expositor whose work was very highly regarded in Baptist circles and beyond. He stood for a high, even hyper, Calvinism.

"There are necessary ordinances to be administered in the Church of Christ till the end of the World, therefore Ministers are necessary," wrote Collins. "The word of Reconciliation is committed to them, the Administration of Baptism and the Lord's Supper. All these are necessary in the Church, and therefore all Churches ought to imitate the Apostles, who took a special care for a standing Ministry in the Church" (*op. cit.*, p. 51). Collins was ready to speak of ordination as "a gospel-ordinance." "Ever retain," he said, "and never part with that Rite and Ceremony in Ordination of Imposition of Hands, with Prayer, on the Person ordained" (pp. 58, 59).

Half a century later, in language that sounds very modern, Turner claimed that each particular local church is a part of "the universal Church." He pleads for the keeping open of the Lord's Table to all "who appear to love our Lord Jesus Christ in sincerity" (*op. cit.*, p. 174) and for regular joint Communion Services between different branches of the Church; he asserts that "every regular member and minister of the word, in any particular church, is in fact a member and minister of the Church universal: and though under special obligations to that particular church, yet hath a right to commune with, or minister to any other upon all proper occasions, as parts of the same whole" (*ibid*, pp. 9-10). He regards the union of particular churches for the promotion of their common interests and the maintenance of their "purity" as "oftentimes necessary, or at least prudent," though such unions must not "assume arbitrary jurisdiction over the local church" (*ibid*, pp. 46-7). "That there be some," he says, "one or more in every particular church, invested with official power, is necessary, and of divine appointment, for the due administration of the word and sacraments; the maintaining due order in the church, and due execution of the laws of Christ" (*ibid*, pp. 49-50). "It is to be wished," he continues, in words

which have been unconsciously echoed in the recent Polity
Report, " that those churches, who allow themselves to
continue long without a settled ministry amongst them,
would seriously consider, how clearly the scriptures . . .
not only point out its utility and importance, but prove
it a divine institution, with which it must be very wrong
and dangerous to trifle. For though they may have occasional supplies, yet they have no right to expect the like
measure of the divine presence and blessing from them,
as from a settled ministry; nor indeed any blessing at all,
if they use the former to the sinful neglect of the latter "
(*ibid*, pp. 51-2). The ordinary officers of the church are
"(at least) bishops (sometimes called pastors and elders)
and deacons " (*ibid*, p. 55). "They are to be ordained, or
solemnly set apart and appointed to their work (usually)
by the assistance of other officers of chief power and
authority in the churches " (*ibid*, p. 67). " As to the
imposition of hands in ordination, it seems to be at least
a very convenient and proper rite upon such occasions;
and as far as I can find constantly used in the primitive
church " (*ibid*., p. 70).

Gill deals with the Church and its officers in Volume III
of his *Body of Practical Divinity*, which appeared in 1770,
not long before his death. He begins with an exposition
of the idea of a gathered church not essentially different
from that which John Owen, the Independent, had put
out a century earlier. The primitive church, he urges,
had as officers (1) apostles, prophets and evangelists—but
these offices are now extinct, and (2) pastors and deacons
—offices which continue. For a man to come to the
pastoral office there must be a call, both inward and
outward. He must be a member of the church to which
he is to be ordained as pastor. " To the public instating
of him into his office, it is necessary there should be a
recognition and repetition both of the church's choice and
call of him, and of his acceptance of it, for the confirmation thereof, and for the satisfaction of ministers and
churches in communion; who meet to see their order, and

to assist, especially the former, by prayer for them, and by giving a word of exhortation to them, if desired " (III, p. 265).   Ordination is to office in the particular church alone, however, and Gill favours " a stretching out of the hands " as signifying choice or election, rather than " an imposition of hands," that is, χειροτονία rather than χειροθεσία.   The latter, he thinks, was limited to the apostles and was used by them only on certain special occasions, as, for example, at the appointment of the first deacons.

Gill answers with a negative certain questions which clearly agitated the churches of his time.   (1) A pastor may *not* officiate as such in another church or administer the Lord's Supper.   " A man can never act as a pastor, where he is not so much as a member . . . and, in consequence, cannot administer the Lord's Supper in it, which is an act of office-power " (pp. 276-277).   (2) A church may *not* depute a private member to administer the ordinance of the Lord's Supper.   "As Dr. Owen observes, it would render the ministry only *convenient*, and not absolutely *necessary* to the church, which is contrary to the institution of it " (p. 279).[1]   (3) A pastor may *not* remove from one congregation to another if it is for worldly advantage.   He may only do so " when it appears to be for the good of the interest of religion, and of the Church of Christ in general; but this should not be without the consent of the church of which he is pastor : nor without the advice of other churches and ministers " (p. 280).   The principal work of the pastor, in Dr. Gill's view, is the feeding of the Church of God committed to his care.   He is *not* to feed " dogs that worry the flock . . . nor swine . . . nor the world's goats " (*op. cit.*, III, 271).   Here comes out the hyper-Calvinism of the eighteenth century, the attitude of mind which made old John Ryland say to Carey, " Sit down, young man !   When God wants to

---

[1] See, e.g. *The True Nature of a Gospel Church*, 1689, pp. 92f, 137, etc.   Cf. Savoy Declaration, 1658, XXXVIII, iv, and Thomas Goodwin, *Works*, XI, p. 416.

convert the heathen, He'll do it without your help or mine." Dr. Gill expressly excludes deacons from preaching and the administering of the ordinances. They are to prepare business for church-meetings. They are to "serve tables "—" the Lord's table," " the minister's table," " the poor's table " (*op. cit.*, p. 291).

Turner and Gill are clearly not in agreement on all points, but both have a high doctrine of the ministry and regard it, as did Collins, as an essential part of the order of a true church.

Throughout the eighteenth century it continued necessary for many a man exercising ministerial functions, whether as a " messenger " or as a " pastor," to obtain part of his support from some " secular " calling. Dr. Whitley, writing of the preceding century, says that " the great majority of Baptist ministers earned their own living " (*History of British Baptists*, p. 152). Perhaps this was still true. Baptists were not a very numerous or wealthy people, and could not raise large sums for ministerial support. Dissenters generally still suffered many civil and social disabilities and handicaps. But enough has already been said to show that office in the church was most solemnly regarded. The calling out of men to be pastors or evangelists was no light thing. When Nathaniel Overbury, the woolstapler, was made Baptist pastor in Tetbury in 1721, or when Carey, the shoemaker, was ordained at Moulton sixty years later, it was not because the office was carelessly regarded or because the churches wanted ministers on the cheap. Overbury and Carey were, of those in their midst, the most fitted spiritually for office within the church. Had their congregations been able fully to support them they would probably have done so. When Robert Robinson, of Cambridge, became a farmer, when Elisha Smith, of Blockley, entered the silk trade, or when Ash, of Pershore, Ryland, of Northampton, Sutcliff, of Olney, and Gray, of Chipping Norton, opened schools, it was the better to support themselves and so to fulfil their ministry, and it was done

—in most of these cases—with real reluctance. The ministerial records of these men will stand comparison with those of any of their contemporaries, and not least those of the clergy of the Established Church.[1]

IV

Many important developments in Baptist practice followed upon the founding of the Baptist Missionary Society in 1792. Its leaders were treading uncharted paths at home as well as abroad, but they were men of common sense and they believed in the guidance of the Holy Spirit.

Carey was valedicted from Leicester in the spring of 1793, and it was certainly not felt that he forfeited his ministerial status, though he demitted office as pastor of the Baptist church there. In 1795 Grigg and Rodway were set aside for a mission to Sierra Leone with prayers and the laying-on of hands, in conscious imitation of Acts xiii. 1-3. Thereafter they were spoken of as " ministers " (see, e.g. *Periodical Accounts*, II, p. 19). Both had been trained at Bristol College. Fountain was sent out to India in 1796 without training and is spoken of as being accepted " as a missionary." In 1799 Marshman and Grant were solemnly designated at Bristol for missionary work and Ward and Brunsdon at Olney. There was later a further valedictory service in London, and on Monday evening, May 13th, just as the party was about to set out, the four new missionaries, together with Fuller and Sutcliff, went into an upper chamber " to pray together and to commemorate our Saviour's death " (Taylor, *Biographies*, No. XV, p. 12). This was an historic night for Baptists. It is doubtful whether, according to previous practice, this observance of the Lord's Supper was allowable.[2] It is important, however, as showing a group of men, led by the Spirit of God under the stress

[1] Cf. the present-day attitude of the Disciples of Christ as described by Dr. William Robinson in *The Ministry and the Sacraments*, 1937, pp. 267-8.

[2] See e.g. Thomas Goodwin, *Works*, XI, p. 417.

of new challenges and spiritual needs, refusing to be
bound by older ecclesiastical practice. Just as the Society
quickly came to speak of its missionaries as ministers—
and here the seventeenth century Baptist Confessions and
Carey's own words already quoted pointed the way—so
it came to feel that the Lord's Supper might be observed
by a company which was not in the strict sense a gathered
church. As the number of recruits increased, so the custom
developed of both ordaining and valedicting men for
service abroad. At Oxford in 1806, for example, Chater
and Robinson were ordained with the laying-on of hands
by Ryland, Fuller and Sutcliff. In the nineteenth century,
when the title " Reverend " came to be used by Baptist
pastors in this country, it was also taken by missionaries
serving overseas. Both came to be known as " Baptist
ministers." Charles Stovel, in his *Hints on the Regulation of Christian Churches* (1835), explicitly includes in
his description of the ministry two categories : first, pastors, and secondly, evangelists at home and abroad.

It was the growing work of the Baptist Missionary
Society that first presented Baptists with a further challenge necessitating departure from previous practice.
When Fuller died in 1815, he was succeeded as secretary
by Ryland and Hinton, the one pastor and College President in Bristol, the other pastor in Oxford. Hinton soon
resigned and his place was taken by Dyer, of Reading. In
a few months it was clear that a full-time secretary was
necessary, and Dyer gave up his pastoral service to devote
his whole time to the Society. Since 1818, the Society has
always had at least one, and latterly several, fully trained
"ministers" at its headquarters. It was not felt that Dyer,
or Angus, or Trestrail, or Bailhache, or John Brown
Myers ceased to be " Baptist ministers " while they were
serving the B.M.S. They always retained the title "Reverend ". Similarly with those called to give their whole time
to the training of ministerial candidates. In the same way,
when the work of the Baptist Union grew so much that
it required a full-time secretary, the Baptist community,

with a due sense of responsibility, believing itself to be under the guidance of the Spirit of God, came to feel that one of its number, duly trained as a " minister of the Word," should be set aside for this particular task. Of recent years, at least one other " minister " besides the Secretary has been on the headquarters staff of the Baptist Union, while from time to time others have been seconded from the pastorate for special work such as evangelistic campaigns, chaplaincies, and certain interdenominational undertakings.

Moreover, the steady movement of events has been towards the linking of each individual minister with the Baptist Union as representing the whole Baptist community. Speaking on " The Christian Ministry and the Baptist Churches " at the meetings of the Baptist Union in Bradford in 1908, Dr. Charles Brown pleaded for " a vital connection between each minister and the Baptist Union from the first to the last; that his membership in it should be worth something, and that it should assume some measure of responsibility for him." " I would like to see some men freed from pastoral cares and responsibilities and set apart for the service of the whole body," he declared (*Baptist Times*, October 2, 1908). This has come to pass increasingly. Recognition regulations and Sustentation and Superannuation Funds are but the material expression of new spiritual relationships. To see in the Baptist Union rules, as Dr. Dakin seems to do, no more than " natural obligations related to palpable benefits " (*op. cit.*, p. 57), is to miss their real significance.

These developments imply an enlarged churchmanship, but not one in any essential matter out of accord with the principles enunciated in the earliest Confessions. When Baptists realised their obligations to the heathen world they entrusted this service to the B.M.S., which thus became the expression and channel of an essential part of their churchmanship. Later on, when the Union was formed, the local churches entrusted it with certain matters vital to " the true nature of a gospel church." For a century or more, therefore, Baptist churches have fulfilled their churchmanship not only through their local worship and service, but through the B.M.S. and B.U. And this has inevitably involved new applications of the doctrine of the ministry. The pastor, the missionary, the College Principal, the secretary, the chaplain, have each a place in the ministry of the Church. Due recognition of special gifts and special functions has always been an essential part of true churchmanship. Those who, like the Baptists, seek to base the foundations of their polity on the New Testament, can appeal to the great Pauline passages, 1 Corinthians xii. 28-31, Romans xii. 5-8, and Ephesians iv. 11-12, with their lists of the varied gifts bestowed by the Spirit for the leadership, discipline and service of the Church. Apostles, prophets, evangelists, pastors, teachers—all are required " for the equipment of the saints, for the business of the ministry, for the up-building of the Body of Christ " (Moffatt, Eph. iv. 12).

Chapter Four

THE LORD'S TABLE

I

CHURCH officers, duly chosen and commissioned, were regarded as necessary to the proper functioning of the church. Of that there can be no doubt after a study of Baptist records. One of the chief tasks of the ministers of the church has always been reckoned to be the due observance of the Lord's Supper. The coming together of the members for that service has been regarded as one of the marks of true churchmanship. The Lord's Supper long had in the life of the local church a central position corresponding to that which the table itself occupied in the older meeting-houses. The Minute Books of the seventeenth and eighteenth centuries contain many cases which show how exercised were the church members when one of their number failed to " fill up his place at the Lord's Table." Beddome's *Scriptural Exposition of the Baptist Catechism* (1752) places great stress on proper preparation for Communion. Baptists, no less than Christians of other traditions, have regarded this as a specially sacred place and occasion. Baptists were not represented officially at the Conference on Faith and Order at Lausanne in 1927. Had they been, it is likely that their spokesmen would have accepted the declaration that " the Sacrament of the Lord's Supper is the Church's most sacred act of worship in which the Lord's atoning death is commemorated and proclaimed, and that it is a sacrifice of praise and thanksgiving and an act of solemn self-oblation " (see Bell, *Documents on Christian Unity*, II,

p. 15), though they might have hesitated a little at accept-ing the word " sacrament," for some of their number have always been shy of the term.

The earliest Baptist Confessions, in the sections dealing with the Lord's Supper, stand naturally close to the teach-ing of the great Reformers. Roman Catholic doctrine concerning the transubstantiation of the bread and wine is expressly repudiated. Here, as elsewhere, Reformers, Puritans and Separatists were seeking to recover the New Testament faith and practice. Only slowly, and not with-out disagreement on certain matters, was any new theory worked out. The three main types of interpretation have been characterised by three almost self-explanatory Ger-man words—the " wunderhaft," the " historisch " and the " mystisch." They are associated with Luther, Zwingli and Calvin respectively. The great German Re-former, though he rejected Roman teaching, was still much under the influence of medieval thought and vigorously asserted the real physical presence of Christ in the consecrated elements; his theory is usually described as one of " consubstantiation." Zwingli, the Swiss, was most eager to return to the simplicities of the New Testa-ment, and though it is often argued that he was not really a " Zwinglian " in the sense in which that term is now usually employed, yet he began a tradition that insisted on the primarily memorial character of the Lord's Supper and its significance as a means of uniting a congregation of believers in a common attestation of loyalty to their Lord. Calvin, the Frenchman, may be said to stand between Luther and Zwingli in this matter. " By his contemporary admirers his teaching was rightly regarded both as a spiritualising of Luther's and as a deepening of Zwingli's " (Hugh Watt, *E.R.E.*, V, p. 567). Calvin defined a sacrament as " an external sign, by which the Lord seals on our consciences His promises of goodwill towards us, in order to sustain the weakness of our faith, and we in turn testify our piety towards Him both before Himself and before angels as well as men " (*Institutes*,

IV, xiv, 1). At the Table by faith the believer and his Lord are united. Sacraments are for Calvin Sacraments of the Word and must be accompanied by the proclamation of the Word.

The influence of both Zwinglian and Calvinistic views has been strong on Baptist thought and practice. A few years ago Dr. Wheeler Robinson wrote: " The interpretation of the Lord's Supper most common amongst Baptists would be technically described as ' Zwinglian '— though it must be remembered that there was a recognition of mystical union with Christ in Zwingli's teaching which did not find full expression in his controversies. There is also a growing minority of Baptists whose interpretation of the Lord's Supper is Calvinistic rather than Zwinglian, and a growing consciousness that this rite has not taken the place amongst us which belongs to it, and that it should be celebrated with greater reverence " (*Life and Faith of the Baptists*, 1927, p. 118n). Ten years later Dr. A. C. Underwood affirmed that " Baptists stand for a *via media*, rejecting, on the one hand, all *ex opere operato* theories of the sacraments, and, on the other hand, all theories which reduce them to *nuda signa* " (*The Ministry and the Sacraments*, 1937, p. 225). More recently Dr. Dakin has committed himself to the generalisation that " Baptists repudiate altogether the notion that the service is one of memorial only " (*The Baptist View of the Church and Ministry*, 1944, p. 32). The evidence to be reviewed in this chapter suggests that all these statements require some modification. On this matter, as on many others, the diversity of the Baptist inheritance is plain. From the beginnings of Baptist witness in the seventeenth century, there have been many Baptists who have been staunch Calvinists in their interpretation of the Supper, but there have been many others who have favoured Zwinglian views. It is doubtful if either one or the other can claim to be the dominant tradition, and it is interesting to discover that it has frequently been among the Particular Baptists, that is,

those Calvinistic in their attitude to questions of election,
that Zwinglian views of the Lord's Supper have been
most trenchantly advocated.

II

John Smyth had no scruples regarding the use of the
term "Sacrament." It was applied by him both to
baptism and to the Lord's Supper. His last Confession,
drawn up about 1610, appeared first in somewhat imper-
fect Dutch and two or three years later in English. The
phrases used are of considerable interest. Smyth shows
here, as on other matters, considerable independence of
mind.

"72. That in the outward supper which only baptised persons must partake, there is presented and
figured[1] before the eyes of the penitent and faithful,
that spiritual supper, which Christ maketh of His
flesh and blood which is crucified and shed for the
remission of sins (as the bread is broken and the
wine poured forth), and which is eaten and drunken
(as is the bread and wine bodily) only by those which
are flesh of His flesh, and bone of His bone: in the
communion of the same spirit.

"73. That the outward baptism and supper do
not confer and convey grace and regeneration to the
participants or communicants: but as the word is
preached, they serve only to support and stir up the
repentance and faith of the communicants till Christ
come, till the day dawn, and the day-star arise in
their hearts.

"74. That the sacraments have the same use that
the word hath: that they are a visible word, and that
they teach to the eye of them that understand as the
word teacheth the ears of them that have ears to hear,
and therefore as the word pertaineth not to infants,
no more do the sacraments.

"75. That the preaching of the word, and ministry of the sacraments, representeth[1] the ministry of
Christ in the Spirit; who teacheth, baptiseth, and
feedeth the regenerate, by the Holy Spirit inwardly
and invisibly " (McGlothlin, *op. cit.*, pp. 79-80).

It is to be noted that only baptised persons were allowed
to the Table and that the close linking of the Word and
Sacraments, after the manner of Calvin, confirmed Smyth
in excluding infants.

The later seventeenth century Confessions, both those
of the General Baptists (e.g. the so-called " Orthodox
Creed " of 1678), and those of the Particular Baptists
(e.g. the 1677 Confession) were closely modelled on the
Westminster Confession. They are indeed, in the main,
revisions of that great Calvinistic Confession in the light
of the special Baptist testimony regarding baptism. Following Smyth, the General Baptists continued to use the
term " sacrament ". Quite early, the Particular Baptists
replaced it by the term " ordinance," and where the
Westminster Confession had " commemoration " used
the word " memorial ". This verbal change does not
seem to have represented any substantial move towards
Zwinglianism.[2]

An interesting and independent line of teaching comes
from Bunyan. As we shall see in the next chapter, he
refused to make differences of view regarding the subject
or mode of baptism a barrier to Christian fellowship, and
his approach to the Lord's Supper was very similar. In
his *Confession of My Faith and a Reason of My Practice*,
written at the end of his long imprisonment, he declared :

" I desire you . . . to take notice; That touching
shadowish, or figurative ordinances, I believe that
Christ hath ordained but two in his Church, viz.

---

[1] These words are probably conscious echoes of Tertullian's use of
repraesentat and *figura* in *Adv. Marcionem*, I, 14 and IV, 40.

[2] Note that the 1658 Savoy Declaration of the Independents uses
the term " sacrament," but speaks of the Supper as a " memorial " of
the sacrifice of Christ.

Water baptism and the supper of the Lord : both which are of excellent use to the church in this world; they being to us representations of the death and resurrection of Christ; and are, as God shall make them, helps to our faith therein. But I count them not the fundamentals of our Christianity, nor grounds or rule to communion with saints; servants they are, and our mystical ministers, to teach and instruct us in the most weighty matters of the Kingdom of God; I therefore here declare my reverent esteem of them; yet dare not remove them, as some do, from the place and end where by God they are set and appointed; nor ascribe unto them more than they were ordered to have in their first and primitive institution. It is possible to commit idolatry even with God's own appointments " (*Works of Bunyan*, Offor's edition, II, p. 604).

Here Bunyan shows a characteristically sane and yet reverent attitude to the sacraments, an attitude which became widely influential in Baptist circles, particularly in the southern midlands. It was not accepted without controversy. William Kiffin, merchant, Commonwealth Member of Parliament and Baptist preacher, strenuously protested against Bunyan's readiness to sit at the Lord's Table with those who took different sides in the " baptismal controversy," that is, with Paedobaptists as well as Baptists. A century later Abraham Booth argued with Robert Robinson and the Rylands over the same issue. In the following generation the question of the right " terms of communion " flared up again, with Joseph Kinghorn, of Norwich, taking the more rigid side and Robert Hall championing a wider Christian fellowship. To certain aspects of this controversy we must return in the next chapter. It has here to be noted that it has occupied far more attention in Baptist circles than have theological questions regarding the meaning and significance of the Lord's Supper itself.

III

During the eighteenth century Zwinglian views seem to have become somewhat more general among Baptists. The temper of the age with its suspicion of the mysterious and inexplicable may perhaps have contributed to this.[1]

Daniel Turner, of Abingdon, whose views of the nature of the church and its ministry have already been referred to, emphasised the Lord's Supper as a bond of fellowship. The Table, in his opinion, should be open to all " who appear to love our Lord Jesus Christ in sincerity " as " a standing, visible, external pledge and means, of that divine union and fellowship all true Christians have with Christ and one another in one body, as morally distinguished and separated from the world " (*op. cit.*, pp. 173-4). In strikingly modern language, Turner argues that Christians of different views ought to be ready to meet one another at the Lord's Table, and that this would not only have " a particular and powerful tendency to subdue our mutual prejudices . . . but also more clearly evince the divine original of the church" (*ibid*, pp. 198-9). As we have seen, Abraham Booth did not agree with the opening of the Table in this manner. He was, in most matters, a rather high Calvinist. Nevertheless, in 1778, the year in which the second edition of Turner's *Compendium* appeared, Booth used strongly Zwinglian language of the Supper. " The design of the Great Institutor was that it should be a memorial of God's *love to us* and of Immanuel's *death for us*. . . . Yes, the love of God, in giving his dear, only Son; and the death of Christ, as our divine substitute and propitiatory sacrifice, are the grand objects we are called to contemplate at the Lord's Table " (*Works*, II, p. 350).

In the Circular Letters of the influential Northamptonshire Association there do not seem to have been many discussions or exhortations regarding the Lord's Supper.

[1] Cf. F. J. Powicke in *Evangelical Christianity* (ed. by W. B. Selbie), 1911, pp. 106f, for the view that it was in the eighteenth century that Congregational churches " lapsed " into Zwinglianism.

This probably implies that it was not the subject of any special controversy. It certainly does not mean that it was lightly regarded. The Minute Books of the local churches prove that. Moreover, in the 1777 Circular Letter, John Ryland, senior, treats of " The Beauty of Social Religion," basing himself on Daniel Turner and John Gill, and incidentally quoting with approval Daniel Waterland; baptism and the Lord's Supper are " the two positive institutions of the New Testament " and " appear to be of unspeakable importance to the glory of God and the very being of the true Church of Christ on earth " (pp. 9-10). A quarter of a century later John Sutcliff, of Olney, wrote a Letter on " The Ordinance of the Lord's Supper considered." Though he was one of the leaders of the revival and expansion of Particular Baptist churches in the midlands, his views are more definitely Zwinglian than any we have so far noted.

> " It is a standing memorial of Christ. When you see the table spread and are about to partake of the bread and wine, think you hear Christ saying, ' Remember me.' Remember who he is. . . . Again: Remember what he has done. . . . Once more: Remember where he is and what he is doing. . . . As the great high priest over the house of God, he represents the persons of all his people, and presents their services, perfumed with much incense. . . . Especially in this ordinance there is a representation of the death of Christ."

Much of Sutcliff's letter is taken up with insistence on the cardinal importance of regular attendance at the Table in obedience to the command of Christ.

It was left to Robert Hall, a younger contemporary of Sutcliff, the greatest preacher of his age and the champion against Kinghorn of a Table open to others besides those immersed on profession of faith, to protest against a merely memorial view of the Lord's Supper. It is " appointed to be a memorial of the greatest instance of love that was ever exhibited, as well as the principal pledge

of Christian fraternity " (*Works*, III, p. 10). Nevertheless:

> " To consider the Lord's Supper as a mere com-
> memoration . . . is to entertain a very inadequate view
> of it. If we credit St. Paul it is also a *federal rite* in
> which, in token of our reconciliation with God, we eat
> and drink in his presence: it is a feast upon a sacri-
> fice, by which we become partakers at the altar, not
> less really, though in a manner more elevated and
> spiritual, than those who under the ancient economy
> presented their offerings in the temple. In this ordi-
> nance, the cup is a spiritual participation of the
> blood, the bread of the body of the crucified Saviour"
> (*ibid*, p. 45).

> " It is first a feast upon a sacrifice, in which we are
> actual partakers by faith of the body and blood of
> the Redeemer offered upon the Cross. Considered in
> this view it is a *federal rite*, in which we receive the
> pledge of reconciliation, while we avouch the Lord
> to be our God, and surround his table as a part of his
> family. In its secondary import, it is intended as a
> solemn recognition of each other as members of
> Christ, and consequently in the language of St. Paul,
> ' as one body and one bread ' " (*ibid*, pp. 61-2).

This is high sacramental language, almost more
Lutheran than Calvinist.

IV

Baptists were probably the first among English Protestants to have a special collection of hymns for use at
the Lord's Table. In 1697 there appeared Joseph Stennett's *Hymns in Commemoration of the Sufferings of our
blessed Saviour, Jesus Christ, composed for the celebra-
tion of his Holy Supper.* Stennett, who was born in 1663
and who died in 1713. was a Baptist minister of considerable literary gifts, widely respected for his learning and

character. Many fruitless attempts were made during the reign of Anne to get him to conform to the Church of England. None of the fifty hymns would make much appeal to-day, but they are important evidence of the attitude to the sacrament at the beginning of the eighteenth century. Two of Joseph Stennett's communion hymns had a place in Rippon's *Selection*, the first edition of which appeared in 1787. Rippon included nineteen communion hymns, making use of some by Watts and Wesley, but drawing chiefly on Baptist writers—Daniel Turner, Benjamin Beddome, Anne Steele, and Joseph Stennett, as well as the latter's son and grandson, Dr. Joseph Stennett and Dr. Samuel Stennett. The *New Selection* of 1829 has only thirteen communion hymns, but four of the contributors were Baptists. Out of the twenty-eight communion hymns in *Psalms and Hymns*, which was first issued in 1862, only one was by a Baptist. In neither of the editions of the *Baptist Church Hymnal* (1900 and 1933) is there any hymn by a Baptist in the communion section. That may mean no more than that Baptists have not proved themselves effective hymn-writers and that the field of choice has been widened. It may, however, indicate that during the last century the service has ceased to have so central a place in the life of the churches.

That there was change of sentiment in the nineteenth century, in this as in other matters, is clear. The German Baptist Confession of Faith, drawn up in 1847, was predominantly Calvinistic in theology, but American Baptists are said to be mainly, and sometimes rather aggressively, Zwinglian. In America, and in Britain, men and women, other than ministers or church officers, are to be found presiding on occasion at the Lord's Table. In many churches the service has become a brief appendix to one of the main diets of worship, attended by only a small proportion of the membership. In a volume of sermons which appeared in 1884, Alexander McLaren, the great Baptist expositor, declared, in striking contrast to Robert Hall : " All our theories about the meaning and value of this Communion Service must be found within the four corners of that word . . . a memorial rite, and as far as I know, nothing more whatsoever " (*A Year's Ministry*, First Series, p. 101). When the Baptist Union replied to the Lambeth Appeal of 1920, the section on the Lord's Supper was brief and untheological, chiefly concerned to insist that the effectiveness of the " rite," as it was called, could not depend upon the " episcopal ordination " of " a celebrant."[1] In the years subsequent to the Lausanne Conference of 1927, a Theological Commission set up by the Faith and Order Movement collected a number of important papers dealing with the interpretation of the Christian ministry and sacraments by the different Christian traditions. Dr. Underwood did not feel it necessary to offer any independent treatment of the Lord's Supper on behalf of Baptists. He was ready to accept the thoroughgoing Calvinistic contribution submitted by Dr. J. S. Whale on behalf of the Congregationalists. How little serious attention has been given by Baptists of recent decades to the meaning and place of the sacrament in the life of the church may be judged by the fact that neither in the *Transactions of the Baptist Historical Society*, which first appeared in 1908, nor in its successor the *Baptist Quarterly*, issued regularly since 1922, does there seem ever to have been an article dealing either historically or theologically with the Lord's Supper.

Yet are not the words of Benjamin Beddome in his Catechism still true: " What are the outward Means whereby Christ communicateth to us the Benefits of Redemption? The outward and ordinary Means whereby Christ communicateth to us the Benefits of Redemption are his Ordinances, especially the Word, Sacraments and Prayer, all which are made effectual to the Elect for Salvation " (*op. cit.*, Quest. XCIII)? And is not the Lord's Supper still rightly described as one of the " effectual Means of Salvation "?

[1] See Appendix B.

Chapter Five

BAPTISM

I

BAPTISTS are known by a nickname referring to their practice in regard to the second New Testament ordinance or sacrament, that of baptism. Like the term "Christian", as first coined in Antioch, and many another nickname, it is an honourable designation of which no one need be ashamed. It is, however, not nearly as apt as " Christian ". It tends to distract attention from the great reaches of Christian faith and practice common to Baptists and all those of the Protestant and Free Church traditions, and is therefore frequently a source of misunderstanding. Moreover, baptism is observed by all the great Christian traditions (save those which reject all outward rites and symbols) and in not a few receives even greater emphasis, both in theory and practice, than it does among those styled Baptists. In origin the name is a shortened form of " Anabaptist ", which at any rate in the sixteenth and seventeenth centuries had the virtue of accurately describing those to whom it was given. They were "rebaptisers" They repudiated the so-called baptism of infants, holding that it was not true baptism, and by encouraging men and women to submit to the rite as a sign of conscious personal faith in Christ, could fitly be described by their opponents as those who baptised a second time. After the Münster episode of 1533-5, however, the name Anabaptist had a sinister sound. It was a term of abuse, almost the ugliest that could be used throughout the following century. Those who drew up the earliest of the Confessions to which we have been referring were eager to avoid and repudiate the name. That of Smyth is on behalf of " certain English people living at Amsterdam ". The 1651 Confession deals with " the faith and practice of thirty congregations gathered according to the primitive pattern". What we now describe as the Particular Baptist Confession of 1644 and the standard General Baptist Confession of 1660 are in the name of " churches which are commonly (though falsely) called Anabaptists". Those who drew up the 1677 Confession[1] speak of themselves as " Christians baptised upon profession of their faith ". But a nickname once given sticks. Some kind of popular label is inevitable. For several generations the longer form " Anabaptist " continued to be used by their opponents.[2] The prefix gradually came to have less point, and at length all parties acquiesced in the shorter form.

These matters are important for the gaining of a true perspective. The pioneers of the modern Baptist movement were seeking to recover the purity and strength of the primitive church. Many of them had come by way of a long pilgrimage from the Anglican or even the Roman Church. They had been in company with other Reformers, Puritans and Separatists, until in their search for truth and their study of Scripture they became convinced that New Testament baptism was of believers only and that the root of many an abuse and corruption lay in departure therefrom. As has already been suggested, it is mere affectation to try completely to dissociate Smyth and Helwys from those on the Continent who had in the sixteenth century already come to reject the sprinkling (or, as it came later to be called, the rantism) of infants.

[1] See Appendix A.

[2] Cf., e.g., John Wesley, *Journal*, 28 October, 1743, and 13 January, 1746, 4 August, 1766, and 18 May, 1788.

The Englishmen were certainly in direct touch in Holland with Mennonites, and they read Calvin as well as the New Testament. There are few better introductions to the beginnings of modern Baptist witness than Calvin's apology for paedobaptism in the definitive 1559 edition of the *Institutes* (IV, xvi). In it may clearly be seen both the excited and irrational prejudice against those who rejected infant-baptism and the involved and laboured explanations necessary to defend it. Infant-baptism had been repudiated by Michael Servetus, and the violence of Calvin's language is no doubt in part due to unhappy memories of his controversies with Servetus and the burning of the latter in Geneva in 1553. Calvin writes of those who reject infant-baptism as " furious madmen," " frenzied," " malignant spirits." His defence of the practice turns almost entirely on the equation of baptism and circumcision,[1] and he can give no clear answer to the question why if faith be admitted to be necessary in those coming to the Lord's Table, it must not also be present in those submitting to the other gospel sacrament. His language is much too violent for one really sure of his ground. And had he not himself defined a sacrament as " an external sign, by which the Lord seals on our consciences his promises of good-will toward us, in order to sustain the weakness of our faith, and we in our turn testify our piety towards Him, both before Himself, and before angels as well as men " (*Institutes*, IV, xiv, 1)?

When John Robinson valedicted those of his church setting out for distant America, he is said to have addressed them in these words: "I cannot sufficiently bewail the condition of the Reformed Churches, who are come to a Period in Religion and will go at present no further than the instruments of their Reformation. The Lutheran can't be drawn to go beyond what Luther saw; whatever part

[1] Smyth's explicit repudiation of this will be found in his *The Character of the Beast, or The False Constitution of the Church*, 1609 (*Works*, ed. by Whitley, pp. 563f). Cf. Beddome, *Scriptural Exposition, etc.*, 1752, Quest. XCIX: " Doth not Baptism come in the Room of Circumcision? No."

of His will our God has revealed to Calvin, they will rather die than embrace it; and the Calvinists, you see, stick fast where they were left by that great man of God, who yet saw not all things. . . . I beseech you remember, it is an article of your church-covenant, that you be ready to receive whatever truth shall be made known to you from the written Word of God " (Neal, *History of the Puritans*, Pt. II, ch. ii). It was in this spirit that Smyth, Helwys and the other early Baptist pioneers approached questions as to the nature of the church, its ministry and its sacraments, and not least the sacrament of baptism.

II

We do not find here, any more than on other matters, complete unanimity of view. Divergences as to the nature and meaning of sacraments in general inevitably affect thought and practice in regard to baptism as well as the Lord's Supper. Smyth in his last Confession was clear that " the outward baptism of water " should be administered only to " penitent and faithful persons " and that " the outward supper " should be partaken of only by those so baptised. Just as the Supper " presented and figured " Christ's spiritual feeding of His true disciples, so in baptism there is "presented and figured the spiritual baptism of Christ, that is, the baptism of the Holy Ghost and fire, the baptism into the death and resurrection of Christ " (McGlothlin, *op. cit.*, p. 79). Helwys's Confession asserts that " every church is to receive in all their members by baptism upon the confession of their faith and sins wrought by the preaching of the Gospel, according to the primitive institution and practice, and therefore churches constituted after any other manner, or of any other persons are not according to Christ's testament " (*ibid*, p. 89). Both Smyth and Helwys clearly have Romans vi. in mind in their interpretation of the rite.

The General Baptist Confession of 1651 emphasises the fact that New Testament baptism was by immersion and that those so baptised were "at the same time or day . . . of the visible Church of God" (*ibid*, p. 103). The 1660 Confession appears to insert other stages into the process of church-membership. First there must be teaching and preaching, then the baptism or immersion of those professing repentance and faith, next prayer and laying-on of hands that the Holy Spirit may be received;[1] then, and only then, is the believer a member of a properly constituted church (*ibid*, pp. 115-116). The Orthodox Confession of 1678, keeping as close as its authors could to the Westminster Confession, describes the two sacraments of baptism and the Lord's Supper as " ordinances of positive, sovereign and holy institution, appointed by the Lord Jesus Christ, the only law-giver, to be continued in His church, to the end of the world : and to be administered by those only who are rightly qualified, and thereunto called, according to the command of Christ " (*ibid*, p. 144). Baptism is described as a sign of entrance into the covenant of grace and into the church, a sign of the remission of sin, and a sign of fellowship with Christ in His death and resurrection; but it must be administered only to those who really profess repentance and faith.

The Particular Baptist Confession of 1644 asserts that " the things signified " by baptism are : "first, the washing the whole soul in the blood of Christ; secondly, that interest the saints have in the death, burial and resurrection; thirdly, together with a confirmation of our faith, that as certainly as the body is buried under water, and riseth again, so certainly shall the bodies of the saints be raised by the power of Christ, in the day of the resurrection, to reign with Christ " (*ibid*, p. 185). A new note is struck by the assertion that baptism is not

---

[1] This matter was later the subject of some controversy in certain Baptist circles. The church-covenant of Slapton (Northants) inserted in a book bearing the date 1681 provides for differences of opinion on the question of laying-on of hands. See W. G. Anderson, *The Baptist Churches at Weston-by-Weedon and Sulgrave*, 1930, pp. 4-5.

tied to a particular church or a particular church-officer, but may be administered by any disciple engaged in preaching. This practice, and the view underlying it, later exercised considerable influence in certain Baptist circles. The 1677 Confession[1] accepts the more common tradition which had been clearly enunciated by Calvin (*Institutes*, IV, xv, 20), that both the sacraments should be administered only by the duly appointed officers of the church.

These seventeenth century Confessions give clear expression to the convictions of the early Baptists. It soon became evident, however, that many of those who shared their views on the nature of the Gospel and church-polity generally were not ready to follow them on the matter of baptism. Inevitably the question presented itself whether difference of opinion on this one matter should be a ground of separation from church-fellowship and, in particular, from the Lord's Table. In many places, during the troubled periods both of the Commonwealth and the Restoration, those who separated themselves from the Anglican Church were few in numbers and subject to violent persecution and abuse. To many it seemed that this was a matter for the individual conscience and that it would be not only folly but iniquity to divide on the issue of baptism those whose interpretation of the main articles of faith and practice was one. Moreover, many scrupled to re-baptise, even if they agreed that the earlier baptism had not been true to New Testament practice.

The most famous exponent of this view was John Bunyan. His words on "shadowish, or figurative ordinances" have already been quoted. He returned to the subject in 1673 in his lengthy and vigorous pamphlet, *Differences in Judgment about Water Baptism no Bar to Communion.* " The Church of Christ ", he claimed, " hath not warrant to keep out of their communion the Christian that is discovered to be a visible saint by the word, the Christian

---

[1] See Appendix A. Cf. J. H. Bacoats at the Atlanta Congress : " Nearly all Baptists regard the proper administrator to be one who has received authority from the church to baptise " (*Report*, p. 177).

that walketh according to his light with God " (Offor's edition, II, p. 617). Faith, not any outward ceremony, must be held the means of entry into the visible church. " I find not," says Bunyan, " that baptism is a sign to any but the person that is baptised " (*ibid.*, p. 619). He pleaded earnestly for a wide Christian charity. His views were quite unacceptable to William Kiffin and many other Baptist leaders, but there grew up throughout Bedfordshire and the neighbouring counties a very large number of churches which admitted to membership both Paedobaptists and Baptists. During the century following Bunyan probably the majority of the churches in the midlands and the south of England were of this type. Hence it is that in not a few towns the modern Congregationalist and Baptist churches have a common origin with the year of foundation claimed by both denominations.

This tradition of "mixed, or free communion" churches is so important that a few illustrations may be given. In the Church Book of College Street, Northampton, the following note was annexed to the Church Covenant in November, 1700, and continued to be read at the reception of new members at least until the close of the nineteenth century :

" And whereas we differ in our judgment about water-baptism, we do now solemnly declare, That we that are for infant-baptism do not hereby, nor will not impose on the others or any of our brethren or sisters that are among us who are for baptism upon profession of faith. And on the other hand, we that are for Believers Baptism do not, nor will not impose upon the consciences of any of our brethren or sisters that are amongst us, that are for Infant Baptism. Nor will we either party, or any of us impose upon any that hereafter may join in communion with us; but do all promise (freely and cordially, without casting reflections, etc. on the persons or practice of any) to leave every one to his or her liberty of judgment and practice herein; each of us walking conscientiously up to our light; engaging and endeavouring in the strength of Christ that our difference in judgment shall not cause breach of union or affection " (John Taylor, *History of College St., Northampton*, 1897, p. 5).

In 1775 Benjamin Beddome of Bourton-on-the-Water drew up a covenant of this type for the fellowship at Chipping Norton. Five years later, in 1780, the church in Oxford was reconstituted, Daniel Turner, of Abingdon, whose views have been more than once quoted in these pages, taking a lead in the matter. The new Covenant then adopted contained the following:

" Whereas some of us do verily believe that the sprinkling of the infant children of believing parents in the name of the Father, the Son and the Holy Spirit, is true Christian baptism; and others of us do believe that true Christian baptism is that which is administered to adults upon the profession of their repentance, faith and experience of the grace of God, by immersion in the name of the Sacred Three; yet notwithstanding this difference of sentiment, we promise and agree to receive one another into the same affection and love; and for this, among other many reasons: because we can find no warrant in the Word of God to make such difference of sentiment any bar to communion at the Lord's Table in particular, or to Church fellowship in general; and because the Lord Jesus receiving and owning them on both sides of the question, we think we ought to do so too " (E. C. Alden, *The Old Church at New Road*, 1904, pp. 14-15).

The little church at Roade, in Northamptonshire, reaffirmed a covenant of this type in 1781. At the time, however, the new life which was beginning to show itself in and through the Northampton Association of Particular Baptist Churches led to a number of churches which had been of " mixed communion " becoming stricter in their practice. The growth and expansion of Nonconformity, and the establishment of causes in the new industrial areas in the closing decades of the eighteenth century and the early decades of the nineteenth, tended to be along separated denominational lines. The Bunyan tradition lost its vigour. Most of the Baptist churches of the North of England and of Wales, and the churches in and around London formed under the inspiration of C. H. Spurgeon, opened their membership only to those baptised on profession of faith.[1] Many churches would receive at the Lord's Table only those baptised as believers, thus continuing the tradition of what are now known as Strict Baptist churches, which are strict both in their Calvinistic theology and in their practice.

Bunyan's broader conceptions were, however, never entirely forgotten. When, in 1869, with the help of the London Baptist Association, the Downs Chapel, Clapton, was erected, the constitution of the church formed to meet within it stated :

" Membership of the Church is open to all who confess faith in Christ. We desire to have the Church as open as the Kingdom of God, and its gate neither broader nor narrower than that by which men enter into Life. All who are members of Christ's body are welcome to our fellowship, irrespective of opinion on matters wherein we are all learners, and none masters or lords. We seek not uniformity but unity—the unity of faith in Christ—and trust the love of God to keep us in unity of spirit and bonds of peace. . . . The question of Baptism is left entirely to individual judgment and conscience. The immersion of believers is the only ordinance taught or practised as baptism, but we make no difference in the manner of cordiality of our reception of Christ's disciples. The rule ob-

[1] Cf. W. Y. Fullerton, *C. H. Spurgeon,* 1920, p. 291 : " Mr. Spurgeon's position was Calvinistic, accompanied by open Communion. . . . The Tabernacle . . . admitted people to the Lord's Table who were not baptised, and refused them membership unless baptised."

served is—Let every man be fully persuaded in his own mind, and do according to his own understanding of Christ's will."

In the latter part of the nineteenth century and the early decades of the twentieth a large number of Baptist churches in all parts of the country opened first the Lord's Table, and then the membership, to others than baptised believers. Certain churches in the midlands, once of the mixed communion pattern, then more strict, reverted to their earlier and broader custom. The opening of membership in so wide a fashion as that described in the Downs constitution just quoted—and not a few Baptist as well as Congregationalist churches are similarly based —has resulted in recent days in there being a considerable number of persons in fellowship, and sometimes in office as deacons, who have not been baptised at all, either as infants or as professed believers. The possibility of such a situation would hardly have occurred to any of the Reformers or to the pioneers of the seventeenth century. Indeed, it was probably hardly foreseen even in 1869, though by then what had earlier been known as " positive institutions " or " gospel ordinances " had begun to lose their authority over an increasing number of persons.

Whether such a situation is regarded as gravely disturbing or not depends largely on the view taken of the authority and purpose of baptism. If " spirit-baptism " is more important than " water-baptism," and if " water-baptism " should be administered only to those already in conscious touch with the Spirit, then those who have never submitted, or been submitted, to the rite are at least in no worse case than those who have been " baptised " as infants. But if the rite may not only symbolise but convey to the faithful the grace of God, and if a part of its meaning lies in its outward linking of men and women with the visible historic Church, then clearly much is lost by those who observe one of the gospel sacraments, but are content to ignore the other, and much is lost also by the local fellowship itself.

III

The very considerable variety of practice in regard to baptism from the beginnings of Baptist witness down to our own day is naturally reflected in differences of interpretation. Moreover, Baptist apologetic has inevitably tended to concentrate far more on questions of the subject and mode of baptism than on questions of meaning. In 1893, Silvester Horne set about writing a *Manual of Church Fellowship*, intended for use both in Congregational and Baptist churches, with the particular denominational principles set out in an appendix. Of his experiences in trying to discover Baptist teaching, he wrote thus in his diary: " I visited Dr. Clifford, but could not get from him any manual that contained a statement of their view of Baptism. I wrote to Dr. Angus, but received nothing more definite from him. My own Baptist deacons did not agree concerning it. Some thought it was an admission into the Church; some that it had nothing to do with the Church, but was simply an individual act. So I am left to try and make some principles for this degenerate denomination " (*Life*, p. 78). Horne himself may have been clear as to the purpose and meaning of infant baptism, but it is fair to point out that of recent decades among Congregationalists there have been very wide variations in thought and practice. Should the baptism of infants be confined to the children of believers? Is it more than a ceremony of child-dedication by the parents and of public recognition by the Church of its responsibility in the matter of training? Is it fairly described, in the words of an acute Anglican, as " a picturesque and dramatic method of registering the name of the infant as an honorary member of the Christian society " ?[1] If not, what more is there to be said? These

---

[1] N. P. Williams, *Ideas of the Fall and Original Sin*, 1929, p. 552: " The argument *a praxi ecclesiæ* is the only, but also a sufficient ground for affirming the legitimacy and laudability of Paedo-baptism: and . . . those who do not trust the instincts of the historic Church to the extent which this argument requires should in logic either

questions have been agitating, and still agitate, Congregationalism, and no authoritative answer has been given to them.[1]

The differences of view regarding believers' baptism shown by Silvester Horne's Baptist deacons might be matched in almost every generation from the time of Smyth to our own. A number of illustrations of it have already been given. There have always been some ready to treat baptism as a rite of initiation, the divinely ordained means of entry into the visible church, whilst others have stressed its individual significance. The strict Calvinist, John Gill, may be quoted from the eighteenth century, as a particularly explicit exponent of the latter view. Baptism, he wrote, " is not a church ordinance ".

" I mean it is not an ordinance administered in the church, but out of it, and in order to admission into it, and communion with it; it is preparatory to it, and a qualification for it; it does not make a person a member of a church, or admit him into a visible church; persons must first be baptised, and then added to the church . . .; a church has nothing to do with the baptism of any, but to be satisfied they are baptised before they are admitted into Communion with it. Admission to baptism lies solely in the breast of the administrator, who is the only judge of qualifications for it, and has the sole power of receiving to it, and of rejecting from it " (*Body of Practical Divinity*, 1770, III, p. 311).

Gill believed in baptism as a positive ordinance in-

abandon the custom altogether or interpret it as a picturesque and dramatic method of registering the name of the infant as an honorary member of the Christian society."

[1] Cf. D. W. Langridge, *Congregational Quarterly*, October, 1941, p. 313 : " Baptism has dwindled to little more than a quaint and picturesque survival; a dedication, a welcome and an intercession on behalf of the precious little newcomer "; and for an attempt to re-state and re-establish Calvin's teaching among Congregationalists and others see N. Micklem, " The Sacraments," in *Christian Worship: Studies in its History and Meaning*, 1936, J. S. Whale in *The Ministry and the Sacraments*, 1937, and the same writer's *Christian Doctrine*, 1941, especially ch. vii.

tended to last until the end of the world. Its " ends and uses " he describes as six-fold : (1) to represent the sufferings, burial and resurrection of Christ, (2) for the remission of sins—" not that that is the procuring or meritorious cause of it, which only is the blood of Christ; but they who submit unto it may, by means of it, be led, directed and encouraged to expect it from Christ," (3) for the washing away of sin, and cleansing from it—" a means of directing to Christ the Lamb of God," (4) for a salutary or saving use and effect " by leading the faith of the baptised to Christ as delivered for his offences, and as risen for his justification," (5) for the answer of a good conscience through submission to an ordinance of God, and (6) for an evidence of love to God by thus obeying the command of Christ (*ibid*, pp. 339f).

Another interesting and important exposition occurs in Andrew Fuller's 1802 Circular Letter for the Northampton Association. It is entitled " The Practical Uses of Christian Baptism." He closely links Christian baptism with that of John the Baptist, and, unlike Calvin, sharply distinguishes both from the rites of the old covenant. For him baptism is " a solemn and practical profession of the Christian religion." Baptism in the name of the Father, the Son and the Holy Spirit commits the individual to belief in the central Christian affirmations and beliefs. Immersion signifies the remission of sins by the death of Christ. " Sin is washed away in baptism in the same sense as Christ's flesh is eaten, and His blood drunk, in the Lord's Supper : the sign, when rightly used, leads to the thing signified." The whole ordinance suggests separation from the world, the separation both of the individual and of the Church, and entry into " a new state of being " (*Works*, 1824 edition, VIII, pp. 583f).[1]

[1] For an interesting study of the subject emphasising very much the same points as Fuller, but with all the resources of modern Biblical criticism, see H. G. Marsh, *The Origin and Significance of New Testament Baptism*, 1941. Fuller would, however, have made very vigorous reply to Mr. Marsh's six pages attempting to leave room for the baptism of infants.

Abraham Booth's verbose volumes, *Paedo-Baptism Examined* (1787), Vincent Tymms's *Evolution of Infant Baptism*, A. H. Newman's valuable *History of Anti-Pedobaptism* (1902) and many other works of less significance all focus their attention on the early centuries of Christian history and have very little to say about the meaning of the rite. It has been left to our own generation for Baptists to attempt a reasoned exposition and interpretation of their position. Dr. Wheeler Robinson's *Baptist Principles*, which first appeared in 1911 and has been many times reprinted since then, represents a notable and widely influential attempt, first, to trace the history of believers' baptism and then to defend it as " Scripturally sound, psychologically true, intellectually free, symbolically rich in meaning " (*op. cit.*, p. 73). Like Smyth, he is not afraid of the term " sacrament." In the New Testament, he argues, baptism implies a cleansing from sin, the gift of the Holy Spirit and an experiential union with Christ in His redeeming acts, deeper in meaning than words can express. The act and the experience cannot be separated; the one has a part in conditioning the other.[1] As a pendant to Dr. Robinson's work, we may note Dr. Underwood's consideration of New Testament baptism as " a dramatic representation of regeneration " (*Conversion: Christian and Non-Christian*, 1925, pp. 109f).

The Baptist Union in its 1926 reply to the Lambeth Appeal of 1920 had not a great deal to say about baptism, save that Baptists administer it to those only who make

[1] Cf. J. V. Bartlet's definition of a sacrament as " a symbol conditioning a present deeper and decisive experience of the Divine grace, already embraced by faith " (*E.R.E.*, II, 377); and the statement by F. W. Patterson, of Nova Scotia, at the Atlanta Congress: " The term ordinance, etymologically, can never express the whole truth. Baptism and the Lord's Supper are ordinances, but they do not derive their validity, even chiefly, from the fact that they are ordained. It is true that they are not sacraments if, by sacrament, we mean that which in and of itself imparts grace; but to the man of faith they are true sacraments—confessions of faith, pledges of loyalty, oaths of allegiance; and to all such they are vehicles of God's grace " (*Report*, pp. 173-4).

a personal confession of repentance and faith and that the method of immersion " guards the thought of that inner baptism of the Holy Spirit which is central in Christian experience."[1]   In 1922, however, certain Baptist leaders, conferring with Anglicans at Lambeth Palace, had accepted the view that baptism is " by the ordinance of Christ and of His apostles the outward and visible sign of admission into membership of the Church " (Bell, *Documents*, I, p. 147).   The important Committee appointed by the Baptist Union Council in 1932 on the question of possible union between Baptists, Congregationalists and Presbyterians showed, when it reported five years later, that most modern Baptists would agree in regarding baptism as in some sense " a means of grace " having the authority of Christ Himself.   The Committee was prepared to urge Baptists to reconsider sympathetically a more sacramental, i.e. Calvinistic, view of both baptism and the Lord's Supper.   But they found themselves deeply divided as to the relationship of baptism to church membership.   There have been and there remain at least three sections among Baptists : (1) those who believe in open membership and open communion after the Bunyan pattern, (2) those who would keep both membership and the Table for only those baptised as believers, and (3) those who feel that the Table should be open but that membership should be closed.   The Report of a Baptist World Alliance Commission, presented at the Atlanta Congress in 1939, shows the same divisions to be present in the main areas where there is organised Baptist witness and accepts them as at present inevitable (*Report of the Atlanta Congress*, pp. 115f).   These differences, as we have shown, are to be found throughout the four hundred years of modern Baptist history.   They cannot easily be resolved.   They have their origin in the New Testament itself.   The case for the subject of baptism being a believer is overwhelming, and this is now very generally admitted by scholars.   The exact relationship of the rite to the

[1] See Appendix B.

experience of the Spirit and to membership of the Church
is not so clear. "Our sources," says Dr. George Johnston,
in a recent study and with reference particularly to
Acts ii. 14ff, viii. 15f, ix. 17 and x. 44, " are not consistent about Baptism and the moment when the Spirit was
received." Another candid modern student has thus expressed it : " A study of the New Testament teaching on
baptism leaves us in no doubt that it is impossible to
deduce therefrom a uniform doctrine. . . . Baptism was in
its earliest form an experience symbolised by the performance of a rite and not a rite which conveyed a fixed
interpretation."[1]

[1] Johnston, *The Doctrine of the Church in the New Testament*, 1943,
p. 64. H. G. Marsh, *op. cit.*, pp. 202f. The conclusion of Marsh's
careful study is that John the Baptist, who stood in the prophetic
succession, was responsible for " an inspired interpretation of the
tebilah, in which the emphasis was shifted from a narrow racial conception to the proclamation of a spiritual Israel prepared for the
coming Kingdom wherein spiritual and moral, and not physical, considerations alone counted "; Jesus gladly submitted to the rite as
thus interpreted, and it continued to be practised generally, though
not universally, by His followers till the time when it was ready to
provide them with ε not inadequate symbol for the baptism of the
Spirit; throughout faith is regarded as essential. On the tebilah see
H. H. Rowley, " Jewish Proselyte Baptism," *Hebrew Union College
Annual*, XV, 1940.

Chapter Six

SOME MODERN ISSUES

I

OUR review has been mainly historical, though we have noted a number of important modern pronouncements which indicate the new setting of many of the old problems and certain new issues that have recently emerged. Three outstanding factors in the situation to-day are, first, the development in extent and authority of the Baptist Union; secondly, the widespread casualness in the local church in regard to what may be roundly described as " church-manship "; and, thirdly, the general religious situation in this country and, in particular, the changed relationships between different Christian bodies. Each of these points requires some notice.

As we have seen there were proposals even in the seventeenth century for a General Assembly of Baptists. It seemed to many the natural development of that association together of local churches which was regarded as an essential part of their life and witness. Various hindrances prevented anything effective being done. Differences in theology, differences in practice, the fact that many churches were composed of both Baptists and Paedo-baptists, the general situation of Dissenters, the physical difficulties of travel and communication—all presented obstacles to any general union. For a century and a half or more, it was in Associations that the local churches found and expressed their wider interests and fellowship. In the eighteenth century the Baptist Board, at first a Coffee House Society, drew together the ministers of London and neighbourhood, while the Particular Baptist

Fund began its long and generous service to ministers and churches in all parts of the country. It was not until the early years of the nineteenth century that the proposal to have some general gathering or organisation was successfully revived.

The Baptist General Union—as it was called—was established in 1813. It was thought of as a society, in an age that loved societies. The founders expressly disclaimed " all manner of superiority and superintendence over the churches; or any authority or power, to impose anything on their faith or practice; their sole intention is to be helpers together " (*Baptist Magazine*, 1813, p. 351). Each year the Union arranged one day's meetings for worship and conference, and for some time it was known as " the denominational meeting." There were no permanent officers. Its declared aims were to increase support for the Baptist Missionary Society and the growing number of Academical Institutions or Colleges for the training of ministers, to foster village preaching, to promote interest in the *Baptist Magazine*, the Particular Baptist Fund and the Widows' Fund, and to consider the establishment of a school for the children of ministers. These were all laudable objects, and they indicate lines of service which it was increasingly clear had to be undertaken on a national rather than a local scale. But the lack of effective organisation prevented anything satisfactory being done at the annual meetings and the General Union languished. In 1831-2 the Baptist Board considered how the work of the Union might be made more useful, and attempts were made to survey the denominational field. Not, however, till 1863, when the Union was reorganised and two yearly general meetings, together with quarterly committee meetings, were agreed upon, can it really be said to have come to life. By then, it should be noted, the Congregational Union, formed in 1831, was well established and had survived its first storms.[1]

The Baptist Union slowly but steadily grew in strength

1 See Albert Peel, *These Hundred Years*, 1931.

during the last three decades of the nineteenth century. It owed much to its first full-time secretary, Samuel Harris Booth. Under his guidance it survived the stresses of the Down-Grade controversy, and drew together the churches of both the General and the Particular Baptist traditions. The real architect of the Union's present position and structure was, however, John Howard Shakespeare, who was appointed secretary in 1898. In the words of T. R. Glover, he " taught all Baptists to form large ideals for their church, to conceive of it as a great society, where differences of tradition should not outweigh the fact of a common faith, and where women should have their function as well as men; to realise it in its world-wide range and significance; and to live more consciously as members one of another." The twenty-six years of Shakespeare's secretariat saw the transformation of the status and authority of the Union. The Baptist Church House was provided as a denominational headquarters in place of two or three rooms at the top of the Baptist Mission House. A large sum was spent by the Union on the building of new chapels, and this was followed by a sustained and successful attempt to organise a denominational scheme of ministerial recognition and sustentation. In passing, it may be noted that it was the Presbyterian system of ministerial appointment and support that was again and again appealed to by the promoters of the scheme. What was done was found to involve the division of the country into a number of areas for administrative purposes and the appointment to each of a minister as " General Superintendent " The rising costs of living during the 1914-18 war compelled the Union, in the carrying out of the new responsibilities it had undertaken, to raise further additional sums of money. The total invested funds of the Union when J. H. Shakespeare became secretary amounted to only £180,000, of which all but £5,000 belonged to an Annuity Fund. When Shakespeare died in 1926, the invested funds approached £750,000, and the annual income of the Union was more than four times what it had been in 1898. Nor was this all. Through membership of the United Board, the Union had become responsible for the appointment of chaplains to the fighting services; through membership of the Federal Council of the Evangelical Free Churches, it had become the official mouthpiece of all Baptists in their official and general relationships with other Christian bodies. A transformation had taken place in Baptist polity.

The past twenty years have seen the further development of the work of the Union and a continued growth in its influence and power. A central Superannuation Fund for ministers has absorbed the old Annuity Fund and increased its range and benefits. The invested funds of the Union which in 1926 amounted to £750,000 are now in the neighbourhood of £1,250,000. Fresh centralised efforts have been made to encourage church extension. Matters connected with ministerial training and recognition have received increasing attention. The Union has itself established an Order of Deaconesses and undertaken their training. As the mouthpiece of Baptists in their relations with other churches, with the Government and with public bodies, the Union has gained almost every year an increase in its prestige and authority. On every side new opportunities of service show themselves.

The development of the Union, among churches with the individualistic traditions of Baptists, has not been easy. To support its day to day work the Union has relied, first of all, on the affiliation fees of churches and Associations, and secondly, on the subscriptions of personal members who now number some 1,500, and who may sit in the annual Assembly side by side with the delegates of the churches. Theoretically, the Union remains a voluntary association of churches, Associations, colleges and individuals, without what our fathers would have called " church-power ". In practice, it has become the great centralised organ for the expression of much of our churchmanship. It has undertaken with growing efficiency and success responsibilities which formerly rested upon local churches or Associations of churches, without any serious facing by Baptists of two important questions : first, what is involved in all this for the Baptist doctrine of the church and the ministry ; and secondly, are the constitution of the Union and the way in which its Council and Committees are elected and function proper for the exercise of church life and church order ?

II

The fifty or sixty years that have witnessed this remarkable growth in a central denominational organisation have seen also a decline in the strict and responsible churchmanship of the local congregation. To some extent the two things are related. Inevitably and rightly, the local church has had to surrender or delegate certain of its powers, in order to secure the help of the whole Baptist community. The denomination as a whole is clearly entitled, indeed compelled, to satisfy itself as to the credentials and fitness of those who are to receive grants in aid, or those who are to be sponsored for public appointments. It is only right that it should satisfy itself as to the proper functioning and management of communities which are to be assisted with a building subsidy or an annual grant for the maintenance of a minister. But, as was suggested in the discussion regarding the ministry, far more is involved than efficient business arrangements.

The local companies of believers have recognised that the representatives of the churches acting together must undertake certain lines of service and they have, whether consciously or unconsciously, gone far to shift the centre of real authority in church matters. " The churches appearing " at a general council or assembly, said the General Baptists in 1678, " make but one church." Increasingly of recent years there has been talk of " the

Baptist Church,"[1] by which is meant all the Baptist churches conceived as a unit for certain ecclesiastical purposes. Whilst some of this talk has no doubt been careless and ill-considered, yet it does indicate the fact that the conception of the Church has been widened from that of its purely local expression. A local church may at any moment, should it seem right, leave the fellowship of the Baptist Union. It continues to play a very large and essential part in the management of its own affairs, and, in particular, in the calling of a pastor. All church members continue, at least in theory, to share in the government of the church, which in that sense is democratic, and not from above, either by a hierarchy or by a synod. Nevertheless, it has been recognised that the sovereign authority of Christ may be seen and expressed within the ordered life of the whole Baptist community as well as in the local company of believers, and the latter voluntarily accepts certain limitations of and restrictions upon its authority as the price of wider fellowship and more effective service.

The duties which the Baptist pioneers of the seventeenth century laid upon those who formed themselves into Christian churches—the choice of church officers, their adequate support, the preaching of the Gospel in the world and the gathering of new companies of believers into a church-state—are now undertaken to an increasing extent by the churches in co-operation with one another. The evidence given in the preceding pages suggests that many of the early Baptist leaders would have been quite ready for this. What they would have asked was that in acting together the true marks and forms of the Church were not lost. It is, however, more important to note that the wider conception of the Church is true to the New Testament. The word ἐκκλησία has always a universal and unitary as well as a local implication. It is right that Free Churchmen should stress the significance of the frequent appearance

[1] Note the official acceptance of the designation in connection with the work of the War Damage Commission. Dr. Dakin, *op. cit.*, pp. 8, 45 and 47, denies that such language is permissible.

6

of the word in the plural and attached to a particular community of believers in a city, or even in a house. It is also important to insist that in a true sense " the whole mystery of the Church is present in each local part", and that Christ Himself may be in its midst. It is, however, obtuse to ignore the fact that in the New Testament ἐκκλησία is also applied to groups covering a very wide geographical area (e.g. Acts ix. 31, xx. 28). Further, the great passages in the Pauline correspondence which use the word in the singular of the one Church (e.g. 1 Corinthians xii. 28, Colossians i. 18, 24, Ephesians *passim*, 1 Timothy iii. 5, 15), together with Matthew xvi. 18 and phrases like " the Body of Christ ", " a holy nation ", " a peculiar people ", etc., which refer to believers corporately, have all application to the Church visible, for the later distinction between the Church visible and the Church invisible would not have occurred to the Christians of the first century. K. L. Schmidt is followed by many scholars who have no brief for Roman or High Anglican theories of the Church, in the view that the universal and unitary significance of ἐκκλησία is primary and fundamental. " It was one Church in many manifestations; " said P. T. Forsyth, nearly thirty years ago, " it was not many churches in one convention " (*The Church and the Sacraments*, 1917, p. 62 and Chapters II and III *passim*). Many of our modern developments —within the Baptist denomination, and also in the wider ecumenical movement—are attempts, blundering perhaps, but sincere, to express in better fashion this New Testament conception of unity and to get away from the narrowness and poverty of an exaggerated and degenerate independency.

The Church in this wider sense is, however, made up of, or expresses its life through, many local churches. A disturbing factor in the modern situation is the light way in which the obligations of local church membership are now often regarded. Our fathers would surely have questioned whether a community of people could rightly be described as a church if they had not some kind of regular pastoral oversight, and if the sacraments, and in particular the Lord's Supper, were not regularly observed among them. It is instructive to note how hesitant they often were to admit companies of believers to separate existence as " churches ". In the closing years of the eighteenth century, from College Street Church, Northampton, under the leadership of the two Rylands, regular worship was started in forty or fifty surrounding villages. Only with considerable reluctance, and with a very clearly expressed sense of the solemnity of the step which was being taken, were separate " churches " formed in the villages. Those at College Street first sought clear evidence that a proper church-state could be maintained, that is, that duly qualified church officers were available, a pastor as well as deacons, and that the sacraments would be regularly and fitly observed by all the members, and church discipline properly maintained.[1] We are now prepared to allow the name " churches " to groups of men and women, sometimes extremely small in number, who have no regularly functioning church-meeting, no proper diaconate, no pastor, and among whom the Lord's Supper is only rarely observed. In much larger communities the church has come to be regarded as a kind of voluntary association or society, good in its way, but with its forms not a necessary or essential part of the Christian life. Many even of those who like to have their name on a church roll think so lightly of it that they do not feel it necessarily involves regular attendance at Christian worship. They are not gravely troubled if they fail to be present at the Lord's Table or at the Church-Meeting. It has even become possible for deacons to be lax in these matters.

The widespread opening of membership has resulted in communities of the most mixed ecclesiastical origins and with no strong traditions of their own. Theory and practice in regard to church, ministry and sacraments have in

[1] See, e.g. E. A. Payne, *Bugbrooke Baptist Church*, 1930, pp. 7-14, and Taylor, *The History of College Street, Northampton*, 1897,

consequence become vague and casual. There may to-day be many associated with a so-called Baptist church, some even among its deacons and leaders, who are content to remain without the sacrament of baptism. On the other hand, where membership has remained closed to all but baptised believers, the church roll has often little real relationship to the effective life and witness of the fellow-ship. The most devoted workers as well as the most generous givers may be unable to share in what we are still sometimes told is the really characteristic mark of our type of churchmanship—namely, the selection by the members of their pastor. All kinds of shifts and com-promises are sometimes indulged in to meet this situation.[1] Further, many who have been baptised on profession of their faith, and who believe that this is clearly the New Testament manner of observing the rite, feel no strong obligation to be in membership with a Baptist church if, on other grounds, such as nearness to their home, or size, or social attractiveness, or general quality of preaching and worship, they are drawn to one of another tradition. It is not very easy to estimate which is the larger number —those who have been Baptists but are now in fellowship with other churches, or those who are associated with Baptist churches but have no convictions regarding what is supposed to be their distinctive witness.

III

We are here brought face to face with the general reli-gious situation in this country. The matters to which attention has been called are not peculiar to Baptists. They affect in one way or another all the branches of the Church, and, as was indicated in our first chapter, they are increasingly the concern of all. There is a general

[1] That this is no new problem may be seen from a discussion of it in J. D. Humphreys, *Correspondence and Diary of Philip Doddridge,* 1829, Vol. I, p. 313.

lament that churchmanship is not taken seriously. There is general perplexity in regard to the nature and meaning of the Church. We cannot isolate our problem, or treat it in abstraction from the life of our times.

Baptists are but one of the Free Church groups in this country. For more than three hundred years they have shared the fortunes of so-called Protestant Dissenters, those rejecting the national religious settlement—first arranged in the sixteenth century and re-established in 1662—on the ground that they could accept neither uniformity of worship in terms of the Book of Common Prayer, nor episcopacy as the divinely appointed method of church government. Many, but not all, would add as a further ground of dissent their objection to any nationally-established or state-form of religion. The Free Church tradition has been a long and notable one, and it has made rich contribution to English life.[1] Its history may be traced from the first protests in the sixteenth century, through the bitter and involved struggles of the seventeenth, to the limited recognition secured in 1689. Next came a sharing in a vast uprush of spiritual power, and an eager evangelism throughout newly industrialised England. Before the Evangelical Revival had entirely spent itself probably half the church-goers of this country were to be found in Nonconformist places of worship. It was impossible any longer to deny to Free Churchmen full civil rights. Throughout the Victorian era they showed increasing strength and confidence, and at the beginning of the twentieth century their outlook might be not unfairly taken as " representative of the temper of the English people."[2]

From 1893 when the National Free Church Council was formed, or even earlier, the different Free Churches drew very close together. The things that divided them seemed of minor importance. There was co-operation in practical

[1] See E. A. Payne, *The Free Church Tradition in the Life of England,* 1944.

[2] Cf. D. W. Brogan, *The English People,* 1943, p. 121.

affairs and mutual borrowing on an extensive scale. Hymns, forms of worship, leadership and scholarship were common to all. A strong anti-ecclesiastical temper was to be found throughout the Free Churches, the product partly of the individualism of the age and partly of conscious reaction from the Oxford Movement. There was far greater interest in the practical application of Christianity than in the visible church either local or in its wider expressions. The natural consequences of these things are to be seen in our present perplexities regarding churchmanship. Though the dreams that some have had of a United Free Church have so far failed to be translated into fact, it may well be questioned whether any attempt at a revived segregation of the different Free Church traditions is not now as certain to fail as would be any attempt to return to a pre-Darwinian world-view.

Recent decades have seen increasing hesitancy and loss of confidence on the part of Free Churchmen. Professor Brogan regards " the decline of Nonconformity " as "one of the greatest changes in the English religious and social landscape." It cannot, of course, be considered out of relation to the waning power of organised religion generally, which has been characteristic of the present century. There has been a disintegration of the intellectual, moral and spiritual sanctions which formerly held men and women to the traditional forms of the Christian religion. Not only churchmanship but the faith itself has been challenged. The discoveries of science and the theories based thereon, changed economic conditions and, not least, the shattering effects of two world wars have combined to shake the foundations of all the churches. The Free Churches, based as they have been upon the voluntary principle, have inevitably suffered heavily. There have been many who have felt, with Professor Brogan, " the comparative irrelevance of the peculiarly Nonconformist (as apart from Christian) view of the contemporary world and its problems." We may be quite unprepared to agree to this as a final verdict on our witness, and yet admit how widespread is the acceptance of it at the present time.

For a proper appraisal of the present situation, two further points must be noted.   The modern missionary movement has laid the foundations of Christian communities throughout Asia and Africa and in other parts of the world, and there has been a deepening desire to enter into and express Christian fellowship with these " younger " groups, whatever the pattern of their churchmanship. And, further, the Anglican Church, over against which the Free Churches developed their life, has itself profoundly changed.   The Lambeth Appeal of 1920 is but one illustration of a new outlook and temper, specially notable because it came from the whole episcopal bench. Of recent years Anglicanism has given a more consistently spiritual lead than ever before in its history.   Christian truth and charity are therefore widely felt to demand a much less rigid separation between Christians than characterised the religious history of this and other countries from the sixteenth to the nineteenth centuries.   The dispassionate reading of Christian history makes it clear that God has had His servants in all branches of the Church. However strongly the individual or the community may hold to certain principles or practices, these things ought not, so it is increasingly felt, to prevent the clear outward expression of common Christian discipleship.

IV

It is because of this situation that those of many different ecclesiastical traditions are feeling compelled to re-examine the doctrine of the Church.   And, of recent days, there is the added incentive that in many lands, east and west, it is the Church which has been the indestructible centre of spiritual resistance to tyranny.   The scholars turn again to the study of the New Testament and of Church History.[1]   The denominational leaders

[1] See Appendix C.

look once more at the origins and witness of their own communities. The ministers, of whatever church, examine their credentials and authority. Every thoughtful believer is moved to question his own relationship to the Body of Christ and to the channels through which the Holy Spirit has operated and still operates. The widespread spiritual drought has caused many to ask whether among the old wells which could be re-opened that of a more serious churchmanship is not, perchance, one holding at least some of the water of life.

It is a hopeful sign that a new, though wistful, seriousness has come over all Christians in regard to these matters. What is important is that thinking and prayer about the Church and its ministry and sacraments should be both honest and informed. No superficial generalisations will meet our need, no bare repetition of ancient formulæ, no beating of a denominational drum without reference to the notes sounded by other regiments of the Church Militant. " It is simply disastrous," as Dr. Shakespeare reminded us a quarter of a century ago, " when men, wrapped in grave-clothes of dead controversies, utter battle-cries which have lost all their power " (*The Churches at the Cross-Roads*, p. 31). Archaism, as Professor Toynbee has pointed out, is a futile thing. One cannot remount the stream of life.

Nevertheless the past, rightly understood, has much to say to us. Father A. G. Hebert, in a recent book on *The Form of the Church*, remarks: " Probably the greatest of all obstacles in the way of a true reunion is that to a very large extent the original and authentic Free Church traditions have ceased to exist; the loss of the old-fashioned forms goes hand in hand with a loss of the old Protestant spirit " (p. 121). One does not need to accept Father Hebert's particular application of this, much less the main contentions of his book regarding episcopacy, to realise that there is truth in his words. Elsewhere he remarks that " many Anglican Catholics would bear witness that they have far more living contact and mental sympathy with the neo-Protestant school in the Congregationalist[1] and other Free Churches, than with some fellow Anglicans " (p. 100). This will come as no surprise to those who consider the seriousness with which the early Reformers and the Separatists busied themselves with the true nature of the Church and the forms through which its life should be expressed. Nor will it disturb those who regard " Baptist convictions as a particular form of the consciousness of the Catholic Church " and remember that " catholicity is measured by depth of conviction, not by breadth of opinion " (H. Wheeler Robinson, *The Life and Faith of the Baptists*, 1927, pp. ix-x).

We have sought in these chapters to set out some of the evidence which must be the special concern of Baptists as they consider their own witness. They, as much as any, need to recover a more serious churchmanship. It is needed in the local fellowship, at public worship, at the Lord's Table and in the church meeting. It is needed also in the councils of the denomination as a whole, and, particularly, in the adaptation of the Baptist Union organisation and machinery to the high responsibilities now placed in its hands. But above all Baptists require a renewed baptism with the spirit of John Smyth, the spirit of the Gainsborough covenant. They possess a birthright of freedom which makes possible change and experimentation. It should make them courageous, adaptable and resilient. They should be able to meet the challenge of the modern world with less difficulty than those for whom traditional practice has great and even sacred authority. In these pages we have seen how deep, wide and strong was the churchmanship of the fathers, and at how many points it may help us in our modern difficulties. But it is the assurance that God has yet more light and truth to break forth out of His Word that should be of most value to us.

Nos decet respondere natalibus nostris. " It behoves

---

[1] Father Hebert's book is in the nature of a comment on and reply to Mr. D. T. Jenkins's *The Nature of Catholicity.*

us to be worthy of our birth." The words of Cyprian may be applied to our rich historical tradition, but they have an even more pointed reference. The bishop of Carthage was exhorting his friends to be worthy not of their natural birth and inheritance but of their baptism.

THE PARTICULAR BAPTIST CONFESSION
OF 1677

CHAP. XXVI.
Of the Church.

1. The Catholick or universal Church, which (with respect to internal work of the Spirit, and truth of grace) may be called invisible, consists of the whole[1] number of the Elect, that have been, are, or shall be gathered into one, under Christ the head thereof; and is the spouse, the body, the fulness of him that filleth all in all.

2. All persons throughout the world, professing the faith of the Gospel, and obedience unto God by Christ, according unto it; not destroying their own profession by any Errors everting the foundation, or unholyness of conversation,[2] are and may be called visible Saints;[3] and of such ought all particular Congregations to be constituted.

3. The purest Churches under heaven are subject[4] to mixture, and error; and som have so degenerated as to become[5] no Churches of Christ, but Synagogues of Satan; nevertheless Christ always hath had, and ever shall have a[6] Kingdome, in this world, to the end therof, of such as believe in him, and make profession of his Name.

[1] Heb. 12. 23. Col. 1. 18. Eph. 1. 10, 22, 23, & ch. 5. 23, 27, 32.

[2] 1 Cor. 1. 2. Act. 11. 26.
[3] Rom. 1. 7. Eph. 1. 20, 21, 22.
[4] 1 Cor. 15. Rev. 2 & ch. 3.
[5] Rev. 18. 2. 2 Thes. 2. 11, 12.

[6] Mat. 16. 18. Ps. 72. 17 & Ps. 102. 28. Rev. 12. 17.

4. The Lord Jesus Christ is the Head of the Church, in whom by the appointment of the Father,[7] all power for the calling, institution, order, or Government of the Church, is invested in a supream & soveraigne manner, neither can the Pope of *Rome* in any sense be head [page] thereof, but is[8] that Antichrist, that Man of sin, and Son of perdition, that exalteth himself in the Church against Christ, and all that is called God; whom the Lord shall destroy with the brightness of his coming.

5. In the execution of this power wherewith he is so intrusted, the Lord Jesus calleth out of the World unto himself, through the Ministry of his word, by his Spirit,[9] those that are given unto him by his Father; that they may walk before him in all the[11] ways of obedience, which he prescribeth to them in his Word. Those thus called he commandeth to walk together in particular societies, or[12] Churches, for their mutual edification; and the due performance of that publick worship, which he requireth of them in the World. [page]

6. The Members of these Churches are[13] Saints by calling, visibly manifesting and evidencing (in and by their profession and walking) their obedience unto that call of Christ; and do willingly consent to walk together according to the appointment of Christ, giving up themselves, to the Lord & one to another by the will

[7] Col. 1. 18. Mat. 28. 18, 19, 20. Eph. 4. 11, 12.

[8] 2 Thes. 2. 3-9.

[9] Joh. 10. 16. chap. 12. 32.

[11] Matt. 28. 20.

[12] Mat. 18. 15-20.

[13] Rom. 1. 9. 1 Cor. 1. 2.

of God,[14] in professed subjection
to the Ordinances of the Gospel.

7. To each of these Churches
thus gathered, according to his
mind, declared in his word, he
hath given all that[15] power and
authority, which is any way needfull, for their carrying on that order in worship, and discipline,
which he hath instituted for them
to observe; with commands, and
rules for the due and right exert-
ing, and executing of that power.

8. A particular Church gather-
ed, and compleatly Organized, according to the
mind of Christ, consists of Officers, and Members;
And the Officers appointed by
Christ to be chosen and set apart by
the Church (so called and gathered) for the peculiar Administration of Ordinances, and Execution
of Power, or Duty, which he
intrusts them with, or calls them
to, to be continued to the end of
the World, are[16] Bishops or Elders and
Deacons.

9. The way appointed by
Christ for the Calling of any person, fitted, and gifted by the
Holy *Spirit*, unto the Office of
Bishop, or Elder, in a Church, is,
that he be chosen thereunto by the
common[17] suffrage of the Church
it self; and Solemnly set apart by
Fasting and Prayer, with imposition of hands of the[18] Eldership of
the Church, if there be any before [page]
Constituted therein; And of a
Deacon[19] that he be chosen by
the like suffrage, and set apart by

[14] Act. 2.
41, 42.
ch. 5. 13,
14. 2 Cor.
9. 13.

[15] Mat. 18.
17, 18.
1 Cor. 5.
4, 5, with
5. 13.

[16] Act. 20.
17, with
v. 28.
Phil. 1. 1.

[17] Act. 14.
23. See
the origi-
nal.
[18] 1 Tim.
4. 14.

[19] Act. 6. 3,
5, 6,

Prayer, and the like Imposition
of hands.

10. The work of Pastors being constantly to attend the Service of *Christ*, in his Churches,
in the Ministry of the Word, and
Prayer,[20] with watching for
their Souls, as they that must give
an account to him; it is incumbent on the Churches to whom
they Minister, not only to give
them all due respect,[21] but also
to communicate to them of all
their good things according to
their ability, so as they may have
a comfortable supply, without
being themselves[24] entangled in
Secular Affairs; and may also be
capable of exercising[25] Hospita-
lity towards others; and this is required by the[26] Law of Nature,
and by the Express order of our [page]
Lord Jesus, who hath ordained
that they that preach the Gospel,
should live of the Gospel.

11. Although it be incumbent
on the Bishops or Pastors of the
Churches to be instant in Preaching the Word, by way of Office;
yet the work of Preaching the
Word, is not so peculiarly confined to them; but that others also[1]
gifted, and fitted by the Holy *Spirit* for it, and approved, and
called by the *Church*, may and
ought to perform it.

12. As all Believers are bound
to joyn themselves to particular
Churches, when and where they
have opportunity so to do; So all
that are admitted unto the privi-
ledges of a *Church*, are also[2]

[20] Act. 6.
4.
Heb. 13.
17.

[21] 1 Tim.
5. 17, 18.
Gal. 6.
6. 7.

[24] 2 Tim.
2. 4.

[25] 1 Tim.
3. 2.

[26] 1 Cor.
9.
6-14.

[1] Act. 11.
19, 20, 21.
1 Pet. 4.
10, 11.

[2] 1 Thess.
5. 14.
2 Thes. 3.
6, 14, 15.

under the Censures and Government thereof, according to the
Rule of *Christ*. [page]

13. No Church-members upon
any offence taken by them, having performed their Duty required
of them towards the person they
are offended at, ought to disturb
any *Church* order, or absent themselves from the Assemblies of the
Church, or Administration of any
Ordinances, upon the account of
such offence at any of their fellow-
members; but to wait upon *Christ*,[3]
in the further proceeding of the
Church.

14. As each *Church*, and all the
Members of it, are bound to[4]
pray continually, for the good
and prosperity of all the *Churches* of
Christ, in all places; and upon
all occasions to further it (every
one within the bounds of their
places, and callings, in the Exercise of their Gifts and Graces) so
the *Churches* (when planted by
the providence of God so as they
may injoy opportunity and advantage for it) ought to hold [page][5]
communion amongst them-
selves for their peace, increase of
love, and mutual edification.

15. In cases of difficulties or
differences, either in point of Doctrine, or Administration; wherein either the Churches in general
are concerned, or any one Church
in their peace, union, and edification; or any member, or members,
of any Church are injured, in or
by any proceedings in censures not
agreeable to truth, and order; it

[3] Mat. 18.
15, 16, 17.
Eph. 4. 2,
3.

[4] Eph. 6.
18. Ps.
122. 6.

[5] Rom.
16. 1, 2.
3 Joh. 8,
9, 10.

is according to the mind of Christ, that many Churches holding communion together, do by their messengers meet to consider,[6] and give their advice in, or about that matter in difference, to be reported to all the Churches concerned; howbeit these messengers assembled, are not entrusted with any Church-power properly so called; or with any jurisdiction over the Churches themselves, to exercise any censures either over any [page] Churches, or Persons: or[7] to impose their determination on the Churches, or Officers.

[6] Act. 15. 2, 4, 6. & 22, 23, 25.

[7] 2 Cor. 1. 24. 1 Joh. 4. 1.

CHAP. XXVII.

On the Communion of Saints.

1. All *Saints* that are united to Jesus Christ their *Head,* by his Spirit, and Faith; although they are not made thereby one person with him, have[1] fellowship in his Graces, sufferings, death, resurrection, and glory; and being united to one another in love, they[2] have communion in each others gifts, and graces; and obliged to the performance of such duties, publick and private, in an orderly way,[3] as do conduce to their mutual good, both in the inward and outward man. [page]

2. *Saints* by profession are bound to maintain an holy fel-

[1] 1 Joh. 1. 3. Joh. 1. 16. Phil. 3. 10. Rom. 6. 5, 6.

[2] Eph. 4. 15, 16. 1 Cor. 12. 7. 1 Cor. 3. 21, 22, 23.

[3] 1 Thes. 5. 11, 14. Rom. 1. 12. 1 Joh. 2. 17, 18. Gal. 6. 10.

lowship and communion in the worship of God, and in performing such other spiritual services,[4] as tend to their mutual edification; as also in relieving each other in[5] outward things according to their several abilities, and necessities; which communion, according to the rule of the Gospel, though especially to be exercised by them, in the relations wherein they stand, whether in[6] families, or[7] Churches;

yet as God offereth opportunity is to be extended to all the houshold of faith, even all those who in every place call upon the name of the Lord Jesus; nevertheless their communion one with another as *Saints,* doth not take away or[8] infringe the title or propriety, which each man hath in his goods and possessions. [page]

[4] Heb. 10. 24, 25 with ch. 3. 12, 13.
[5] Act. 12. 29, 30.

[6] Eph. 6. 4.
[7] 1 Cor. 12. 14. -27.

[8] Act. 5. 4. Eph. 4. 28.

CHAP. XXVIII.

Of Baptism and the Lords Supper.

1. BAptism and the Lords Supper are ordinances of positive, and soveraign institution; appointed by the Lord Jesus the only Law-giver, to be continued in his Church[1] to the end of the world.

2. These holy appointments are to be administered by those only, who are qualified and thereunto called according[2] to the commission of Christ. [page]

[1] Mat. 28. 19, 20. 1 Cor. 11. 26.

[2] Mat. 28. 19. 1 Cor. 4. 1.

7

CHAP. XXIX.

Of Baptism.

1. BAptism is an Ordinance of the New Testament, ordained by Jesus Christ, to be unto the party Baptized, a sign of his fellowship with him, in his death,[3] and resurrection; of his being engrafted into him; of[4] remission of sins; and of his[5] giving up unto God through Jesus Christ, to live and walk in newness of Life.

2. Those who do actually profess[6] repentance towards *God,* faith in, and obedience, to our Lord Jesus, are the only proper subjects of this ordinance. [page]

3. The outward element to be used in this ordinance[7] is water, wherein the party is to be baptized, in the name of the Father, and of the Son, and of the Holy Spirit.

4. Immersion, or dipping of the person[8] in water, is necessary to the due administration of this ordinance.

CHAP. XXX.

Of the Lords Supper.

1. THE Supper of the Lord Jesus, was instituted by him, the same night wherein he was betrayed, to be observed in his Churches unto the end of the [page] world, for the perpetual remembrance, and shewing forth the sacrifice in his death[1]

[3] Rom. 6. 3, 4, 5. Col. 2. 12. Gal. 3. 27.
[4] Mar. 1. 4. Act. 26. 16.
[5] Rom. 6. 2, 4.

[6] Mar. 16. 16. Act. 8. 36, 37.

[7] Mat. 28. 19, 20, with Act. 8. 38.

[8] Mat. 3. 16. Joh. 3. 23.

[1] 1 Cor. 11. 23, 24, 25, 26.

confirmation of the faith of believers in all the benefits thereof,
their spiritual nourishment, and
growth in him, their further in-
gagement in, and to, all duties
which they owe unto him;[2]
and to be a bond and pledge of
their communion with him, and
with each other.

[2] 1 Cor. 10. 16, 17, 21.

2. In this ordinance Christ is
not offered up to his Father, nor
any real sacrifice made at all, for
remission of sin of the quick or
dead; but only a memorial of that[3]
one offering up of himself, by
himself, upon the crosse, once for
all; and a spiritual oblation of all[4]
possible praise unto God for
the same; so that the Popish sacrifice of the Mass (as they call it)
is most abominable, injurious to
Christs own only sacrifice, the [page]
alone propitiation for all the sins
of the Elect.

[3] Heb. 9. 25, 26, 28.

[4] 1 Cor. 11. 24. Mat. 26. 26, 27.

3. The Lord Jesus hath in this
Ordinance, appointed his Ministers
to Pray, and bless the Elements of
Bread and Wine, and thereby to
set them apart from a common to
an holy use, and to take and break
the Bread; to take the Cup,[5]
and (they communicating also
themselves) to give both to the
Communicants.

[5] 1 Cor. 11. 23, 24, 25, 26, etc.

4. The denial of the Cup to
the people, worshiping the Elements, the lifting them up, or carrying them about for adoration,
and reserving them for any pre-
tended religious use,[6] are all
contrary to the nature of this Or-

[6] Mat. 26. 26, 27, 28. Mat. 15. 9. Exod. 20. 4, 5.

dinance, and to the institution of Christ.

5. The outward Elements in this Ordinance, duely set apart to [page] the uses ordained by Christ, have such relation to him crucified, as that truely, although in terms used figuratively, they are sometimes called by the name of the things they represent, to wit[7] body and Blood of Christ; albeit in substance, and nature, they still remain truly, and only[8] Bread, and Wine, as they were before.

[7] 1 Cor. 11. 27.

[8] 1 Cor. 11. 26 & 5. 28.

6. That doctrine which maintains a change of the substance of Bread and Wine, into the substance of Christs body and blood (commonly called Transubtantiation) by consecration of a Priest, or by any other way, is repugnant not to Scripture[9] alone, but even to common sense and reason; overthroweth the[11] nature of the ordinance, and hath been and is the cause of manifold superstitions, yea, of gross Idolatries. [page]

[9] Act. 3. 21. Luk. 24. 6 & 5. 39.

[11] 1 Cor. 11. 24, 25.

7. Worthy receivers, outwardly partaking of the visible Elements in this Ordinance, do then also inwardly by faith, really and indeed, yet not carnally, and corporally, but spiritually receive, and feed upon Christ crucified[12] & all the benefits of his death: the Body and Blood of *Christ*, being then not corporally, or carnally, but spiritually present to the faith of Believers, in that Ordinance, as the Elements themselves are to their outward senses.

[12] 1 Cor. 10. 16. ch. 11. 23. 26.

8. All ignorant and ungodly persons, as they are unfit to enjoy communion[13] with *Christ;* so are they unworthy of the Lords Table; and cannot without great sin against him, while they remain such, partake of these holy mysteries,[14] or be admitted thereunto: yea whosoever shall receive unworthily are guilty of the Body and Blood of the Lord, eating and drinking judgment to themselves. [page]

[13] 2 Cor. 6. 14, 15.

[14] 1 Cor. 11. 29. Mat. 7. 6.

THE BAPTIST REPLY TO THE LAMBETH APPEAL, ADOPTED BY THE ANNUAL ASSEMBLY, MAY 4, 1926

We, the representatives of Churches in membership with the Baptist Union of Great Britain and Ireland, gathered in Annual Assembly, greet in the name of our Lord Jesus Christ all Christian people, and at this time especially those within the Anglican Church.

The ' Appeal to All Christian People,' issued by the Lambeth Conference of 1920, and transmitted to us by the Archbishop of Canterbury, has stirred deeply our minds and hearts. We received it with the respect and sympathy due to a message from brethren in Christ representing a great historic communion and moved by a spirit of brotherly love towards their fellow Christians; and we have sought to give it the prayerful consideration which it manifestly deserves.

Our reply has been postponed in order that the Federal Council of the Free Churches of England might report upon conversations held with representative Anglican Bishops for the purpose of elucidating the Appeal and the Resolutions that, in the Report of the Lambeth Conference, accompanied it. These conversations having been suspended, and certain documents having been issued by the Joint Conference of Bishops and members of the Federal Council, we are now able to present our reply.

We recognize fully and gladly the courtesy and lofty purpose of those who made the Appeal. These qualities are manifest not only in the document itself but also in the attitude of their representatives throughout the discussion of the high matters which they brought before us. We associate ourselves with our Anglican brethren in longing and prayer for a larger unity among all who follow and serve our Lord and Saviour Jesus Christ. While we cannot recall without thankfulness and pride the loyalty to truth which constrained our spiritual ancestors to form the Churches of our faith and order, we sorrow sincerely for whatever has been unworthy in the relations of Christian communities to one another; and we express our repentance for any bitter or unjust word or deed through which we may have obscured the testimony of the Gospel or hindered the advance of the Kingdom of God.

We believe in the Catholic Church as the holy society of believers in our Lord Jesus Christ, which He founded, of which He is the only Head, and in which He dwells by His Spirit, so that though made up of many communions, organized in various modes, and scattered throughout the world, it is yet one in Him.

We believe that this holy society is truly to be found wherever companies of believers unite as Churches on the ground of a confession of personal faith. Every local community thus constituted is regarded by us as both enabled and responsible for self-government through His indwelling Spirit who supplies wisdom, love, and power, and who, as we believe, leads these communities to associate freely in wider organizations for fellowship and the propagation of the Gospel.

We reverence and obey the Lord Jesus Christ, our God and Saviour, as the sole and absolute authority in all matters pertaining to faith and practice, as revealed in the Scriptures, and we hold that each Church has liberty to interpret and administer His laws. We do not judge the conscience of those who take another view, but we believe that this principle of the freedom of the individual Church under Christ has the sanction of Scripture and the justification of history, and therefore we cannot abandon it without being false to our trust. Moreover, it is plain to us that the headship and sole authority of our Lord in His Church excludes any such relations with the State as may impair its liberty.

This view of the Church determines our attitude towards the special issues raised by the Lambeth Appeal.

The Scriptures, in and through which the Spirit of God speaks, possess for us supreme and unique authority. While we recognize the historic value of ancient creeds, we cannot give them a place of authority comparable with that of the Scriptures.

Christian Baptism and the Communion of the Lord's Supper are duly received by us not only as rites instituted and hallowed by our Lord Himself but as means of grace to all who receive them in faith.

Because we hold the Church to be a community of Christian believers, the ordinance of baptism is administered among us to those only who make a personal confession of repentance and faith. We baptise by immersion in water in accordance with the mode of baptism received by our Lord and practised by His earliest followers as recorded in the New Testament, and because this symbolic representation guards the thought of that inner baptism of the Holy Spirit which is central in Christian experience. In our judgement the baptism of infants incapable of offering a personal confession of faith subverts the conception of the Church as the fellowship of believers. We recognize that those concerning whom Jesus said ' Of such is the kingdom of heaven ' belong to God, and believe that no rite is needed to bring them into relation with Him. But many of our Churches hold services at which infants are presented, the duties, privileges, and responsibilities of parents emphasized, and the prayers of the Church offered for children and parents.

The Lord's Supper is observed regularly and devoutly by our Churches. Its value for us depends upon both the presence of our Lord and the faith with which we receive the bread and wine that show forth His redemptive sacrifice; but not upon the official position of a celebrant or upon any change in the elements due to words of consecration. It seems to us contrary to the simplicity that is in Christ that the full effect of the Lord's Supper as a means of grace should be held to depend on episcopal ordination.

In general, the place given to Sacraments by the Lambeth Appeal would, it appears, exclude from the universal Church of our Lord bodies of devoted Christians with whom we enjoy fellowship, and to this exclusion we cannot essent.

Our doctrine of the Church determines our conception of the ministry. We hold firmly the priesthood of all believers, and therefore have no separated order of priests. The ministry is for us a gift of the Spirit to the Church, and is an office involving both the inward call of God and the commission of the Church. We can discover no ground for believing that such commission can be given only through an episcopate, and we hold that the individual Church is competent to confer it. For us there is no more exalted office than a ministry charged with preaching the Word of God and with the care of souls. Those called to devote their whole lives to such tasks are held in special honour. Yet any full description of the ministerial functions exercised among us must also take account of other believers who, at the call of the Church, may preside at the observance of the Lord's Supper or fulfil any other duties which the Church assigns to them.

Our ministry is one of those which our brethren of the Anglican Church cordially recognize in their Appeal as having been manifestly blessed and owned by the Holy Spirit as effective means of grace.' Since God has used it in building up Baptist Churches throughout the world which now comprise more than eleven million communicants, we cannot in any way deny its validity and sufficiency.

The deepening sense of friendship and unity between the various parts of the one Church of Christ gladdens us. We thank God that many ancient misunderstandings are passing away, that in our own country hostility and bitterness are giving place to charity and co-operation, and that the Lambeth Appeal by its language and spirit has drawn the Churches nearer to one another.

It will be gathered from this reply that union of such a kind as the Bishops have contemplated is not possible for us. We would say this not only with that frankness which we believe is the highest courtesy among Christian brethren, but with the assurance of our regret that the way in which they would have us go with them is not open.

Further progress in the direction of Christian unity can be secured, we are convinced, only by unreserved mutual recognition. We gladly acknowledge the reality of the ministry of our Anglican brethren, whose representative Bishops have similarly acknowledged the reality of our ministry. This mutual recognition is significant and full of hope.

We believe that the time has come when the Churches of Christ should unite their forces to meet the need of the world. We therefore are prepared to join the Church of England in exploring the possibility of a federation of equal and autonomous Churches in which the several parts of the Church of Christ would co-operate in bringing before men the will and the claims of our Lord.

We assure our brethren of our earnest prayer that the blessing of God may rest upon the Churches of the Anglican Communion, and that He may continue to impart abundantly to its members the riches of His grace.

Finally, we would reaffirm our belief in the real spiritual unity of all who are loyal to Christ and His truth, and our eagerness to welcome every means by which, in common action for the spread of His message and the helping and healing of men, that unity may be displayed to the world.

Grace be with all them that love our Lord Jesus Christ in sincerity.

Appendix C

SOME MODERN BOOKS ON THE NATURE
OF THE CHURCH

Baptist thinking on the matters dealt with in these pages must take into careful account the results of the modern study of the New Testament and of the life of the primitive Church. It may be useful, therefore, to call attention to some of the more important books available in English. Bishop Lightfoot's *Dissertation on the Christian Ministry*, first published in 1868 as part of his commentary on *Philippians*, is " a standard classic " on its subject. Most modern treatment starts from its contention that what was originally a two-fold ministry (episcopoi—presbyters and deacons) became only later a three-fold ministry of bishops, presbyters and deacons. In 1881 Hatch published his *Organisation of the Early Christian Churches*, which sought to prove the Gentile origin of the term " bishop " as distinct from the Jewish term " presbyter "; the book excited considerable controversy, and its theory was adopted and developed by Harnack. At about the same time the text of the *Didache* or *Teaching of the Twelve Apostles* was discovered and seemed to give clear evidence of the prophetic character of the earliest Christian ministry. The date and significance of the *Didache* have continued, however, down to the present day matters of keen discussion. In 1888 Gore attempted a " High Church " reply to Hatch and Harnack. His book, *The Church and the Ministry*, has had a very large circulation and has exerted a considerable influence on Anglican thought; in 1919, and again in 1936, it was revised and brought up-to-date by C. H. Turner. Gore argued that Christ instituted a visible society with a three-fold order of ministry and that " the apostolic succession must be reckoned as a permanent and essential element of Christianity." F. J. A. Hort's *The Christian Ecclesia* appeared in 1897; it is a sober and objective review of the New Testament evidence and has become a standard work. More recent scholars such as C. H. Dodd and R. Newton Flew confess their continued indebtedness to Hort. Also in 1897 there was published R. C. Moberly's *Ministerial Priesthood*, another " High Church " criticism of Lightfoot's thesis, which still has influence in certain circles. T. M. Lindsay's *The Church and Ministry in the Early Centuries*, 1902, is an interesting and competent survey of the whole field by an eminent Presbyterian scholar; it may still be recommended as one of the best books on the subject. C. H. Turner in "The Organisation of the Church," *Cambridge Medieval History*, Vol. I, 1911, and in *Studies in Early Church History*, 1912, and *Catholic and Apostolic*, 1931, maintained the general standpoint of Gore, as did the contributors to *Essays on the Early History of the Church and Ministry*, edited by H. B. Swete, 1918, and B. J. Kidd in his *History of the Church to 461*, 1921. On the other side we may note Gwatkin's *Early Church History*, 1909, which acknowledged its dependence on Lightfoot and Hort, various writings of J. Vernon Bartlet, including his 1924 Birkbeck Lectures, *Church-Life and Church-Order during the first Four Centuries*, 1943, and P. T. Forsyth's *The Church and the Sacraments*, 1917. In 1929 the Anglican, B. H. Streeter, published *The Primitive Church*, which contends in candid, lively and provocative fashion for " a far greater diversity and variegation in Primitive Christianity than is commonly recognised." His views called forth various "High Church" protests, including *Episcopacy Ancient and Modern*, edited by Claude Jenkins and K. D. Mackenzie, 1930, but Streeter re-asserted his main contentions in *The Cambridge Ancient History*, Vol. XI, 1936. More recent contributions from the "High Church" standpoint include A. M. Ramsey, *The Gospel and the Catholic Church*, 1936, important for its attempt to relate the nature and order of the Church to the death and resurrection of Jesus, L. S. Thornton, *The Common Life in the Body of Christ*, 1942, and A. G. Hebert, *The Form of the Church*, 1944. From the "Free Church" standpoint R. Newton Flew's *Jesus and His Church*, 1938, is an important contribution; it is an elaborate and detailed argument, and has valuable references to the work of recent continental scholars such as Karl Holl, K. L. Schmidt and G. Gloege. Side by side with Flew's work may be set the recent study by a Scottish Presbyterian, George Johnston, *The Doctrine of the Church in the New Testament*, 1943, and, as a stimulating addition, D. T. Jenkins's *The Nature of Catholicity*, 1942. The composite volume which represents the report of the Theological Commission appointed by the Continuation Committee of the

Faith and Order Movement, *The Ministry and the Sacraments,* edited by R. Dunkerley and A. C. Headlam, 1937, has in it much important material regarding the views of the different ecclesiastical traditions. T. S. Eliot's *The Idea of a Christian Society,* 1939, raises a number of important contemporary issues. It is clear that the debate of the last seventy-five years must be regarded as still inconclusive. It is equally clear, however, that the basic Free Church contention that Faith comes before Order, the Gospel before the Church, has not been invalidated.

INDEX

Anabaptists, 15, 18, 20, 60f.
Angus, Joseph, 12, 46, 70
Anglican Church, 9, 19, 24, 45, 61, 70, 74, 82, 87, 102
Atlanta Congress (1939), 14, 65n, 73n, 74

Baptism, 8, 13, 22, 25, 30, 37, 41, 54, 60f, 97f, 103
Baptist Associations, 12, 27, 29f, 76, 79
Baptist Board, 77
Baptist Catechism (1752), 49, 59, 62n.
Baptist Confessions, 12, 20f, 35f, 46, 47, 50, 52f, 61, 65
Baptist Magazine, 38, 77
Baptist Missionary Society, 45f, 77
Baptist Polity Commission, 9, 14, 42
Baptist Register, 12, 31, 38, 40
Baptist Union, 29f, 31, 46f, 59, 73, 76f, 102f.
Baptist Union Council, 11, 13, 30, 33f, 74
Baptist World Alliance, 14, 74
Bartlet, J. Vernon, 73n, 107
Beddome, Benjamin, 49, 58, 59, 62n, 67
"Bishops," 24, 36f, 42, 93
Booth, Abraham, 54, 55, 73
Booth, Samuel Harris, 78
Brogan, D. W., 85, 86
Brown, Dr. Charles, 47
Bunyan, John, 53f, 65f, 68

Calvin, 50, 53, 62, 65, 72
Calvinism, 14f, 18, 20, 41, 51f, 55, 68, 71
Carey, William, 39f, 44, 45f.
Chipping Norton, 44, 67
Church Discipline, 23, 26, 29, 37, 89
Clapton, Downs Chapel, 68f.
Clifford, John, 17, 70
Collins, Hercules, 40, 41
Communion Hymns, 57f.

Communion Service, *see* Lord's Supper
Cyprian, 89f.

Dakin, Dr. Arthur, 12, 34, 47, 51, 81n.
Deacons, 35f, 84, 93
Deaconesses' Order, 79
Doddridge, Philip, 38n, 84n.

Eastern Association, 30f.
Edinburgh Conference (1910), 7; (1937), 12

Fairbairn, A. M., 10
Flew, Dr. R. Newton, 10, 106, 107
Forsyth, P. T., 26n, 82, 107
Fuller, Andrew, 38n, 39, 45, 46, 72

Gainsborough Covenant, 16f.
General Baptists, 15, 21f, 35f, 53, 64, 80
General Superintendents, 37, 78
Gill, John, 12, 40, 42f, 56, 71

Hall, Robert, Senior, 39
Hall, Robert, Junior, 54, 56f, 58
Harnack, 10, 106
Hebert, Fr. A. G., 26n, 88, 107
Helwys, Thomas, 16, 22, 36, 61, 63
Horne, Silvester, 70
Hymns for Communion, 57f.
Independency, 25, 27f, 37
Institutes (1559), 50, 62, 65

Jenkins, D. T., 27n, 89n, 107
Johnston, Dr. George, 75, 107

Kent & Sussex Association, 31
Kiffin, William, 54, 66
Kinghorn, Joseph, 54, 56

Lambeth Appeal (1920), 12, 59, 73, 87, 102f.
Lausanne Conference (1927), 12, 13, 33f, 49, 59

SCRIPTURE REFERENCES.

Made and Printed in Great Britain by
The Kingsgate Press, London, W.C.1

THE BAPTIST TRADITION

An Arno Press Collection

Asplund, John, The Universal Register of the Baptist Denomination in North America. 1794

Bacote, Samuel William, Who's Who Among the Colored Baptists of the United States. 1913

Baker, J.C., Baptist History of the North Pacific Coast. 1912

Baker, Robert, A. Relations between Northern and Southern Baptists. 1954

Baptist Ecclesiology. 1980

British Baptists. 1980

Burkitt, Lemuel and Jesse Read, A Concise History of the Kehukee Baptist Association from its Original Rise to the Present Time. 1850

Colonial Baptists. 1980

Colonial Baptists and Southern Revivals. 1980

Dagg, John Leadley, Manual of Theology. 1858

Dawson, Joseph M., Baptists and the American Republic. 1956

Freeman, Edward A., The Epoch of Negro Baptists and the Foreign Mission Board. 1953

Gaustad, Edwin S., Baptist Piety. 1980

Gaustad, Edwin S., ed., Baptists: The Bible, Church Order and the Churches. 1980

Guild, Reuben A., Early History of Brown University, including the Life, Times, and Correspondence of President Manning, 1756-1791. 1897

Howe, Claude L., Jr., The Theology of William Newton Clarke (Doctoral Dissertation, New Orleans Baptist Theological Seminary, 1959). 1980

Jeter, Jeremiah Bell, Recollections of a Long Life. 1891

Jordan, Lewis G., Up the Ladder in Foreign Missions. 1901

Knight, Richard, History of the General or Six Principle Baptists in Europe and America. 1827

Lambert, Byron C., **The Rise of the Anti-Mission Baptists** (Doctoral Dissertation, University of Chicago, 1957). 1980

Lewis, James K, **Religious Life of Fugitive Slaves and Rise of the Coloured Baptist Churches, 1820-1865, in what is now Ontario** (Bachelor of Divinity Thesis, McMaster Divinity College, 1965). 1980

McBeth, H. Leon, **English Baptist Literature on Religious Liberty to 1689** (Doctoral Dissertation, Southwestern Baptist Theological Seminary, 1961). 1980

Macintosh, Douglas C., **Theology as an Empirical Science.** 1919

McKibbens, Thomas R., Jr., and Kenneth L. Smith, **The Life and Works of Morgan Edwards.** 1980

Morris, Elias Camp, **Sermons, Addresses and Reminiscences and Important Correspondence, with a Picture Gallery of Eminent Ministers and Scholars.** 1901

Olson, Adolf, **A Centenary History as Related to the Baptist General Conference of America.** 1952

Pitman, Walter G., **The Baptists and Public Affairs in the Province of Canada, 1840-1867** (M.A. Thesis, University of Toronto, 1957). 1980

Powell, Adam Clayton, Sr., **Against the Tide.** 1938

Purefoy, George W., **A History of the Sandy Creek Baptist Association, from Its Organization in A.D. 1758, to A.D. 1858.** 1859

Seventh Day Baptist General Conference, **Seventh Day Baptists in Europe and America.** Two volumes. 1910

Shurden, Walter B., **Associationalism Among Baptists in America, 1707-1814** (Doctoral Dissertation, New Orleans Baptist Theological Seminary, 1967). 1980

Smith, Elias, **The Life, Conversion, Preaching, Travels, and Sufferings of Elias Smith.** 1816

Stealey, Sydnor L., ed., **A Baptist Treasury.** 1958

Stiansen, P., **History of the Norwegian Baptists in America.** 1939

Taylor, John, **A History of Ten Baptist Churches.** 1827

Tull, James E., **A History of Southern Baptist Landmarkism in the Light of Historical Baptist Ecclesiology** (Doctoral Dissertation, Columbia University, 1960). 1980

Valentine, Foy D., **A Historical Study of Southern Baptists and Race Relations 1917-1947** (Doctoral Dissertation, Southwestern Baptist Tehological Seminary, 1949). 1980

Wayland, Francis, **Notes on the Principles and Practices of Baptist Churches.** 1857

Whitsitt, William H., **A Question in Baptist History.** 1896

Wood, Nathan E., **History of the First Baptist Church of Boston (1665-1899).** 1899